Ego 1

40 days and 40 Nights on the Camino de Santiago

By

Paul McGranaghan

"A journey is an hallucination".

- Flann O'Brien, *The Third Policeman*

Contents

Twilight of the Idols

"Joseph Stalin, do you bring me joy?"

His crafty, feline eyes meet mine. No, I think. Joseph Stalin does not bring me joy. I place the biography in a hessian bag. I lift another book from the shelf. *"Gabriele D'Annunzio*, do you bring me joy?" Gabriele does not even meet my gaze. Goodbye, Gabriele. I put him in the bag on top of Stalin. I can fit between twenty to twenty-five books in each bag before I have to start on a new one. I've filled eight bags already, and by the time I'm finished I will have gotten rid of almost every book I own.

"Nicolo Machiavelli, does your *Prince* bring me joy? Vasily Grossman, does your *Life and Fate* bring me joy? Kieran Allen, does your *Corporate Takeover of Ireland* bring me joy?" No is the answer to these questions, and the bags continue to fill up. Burgess, Marx, Ballard, Kafka: do you bring me joy?

No, no, no, no they don't.

The next day the local library service will receive a donation of hundreds of books, most of them in pristine condition. Some of them have never been read. *"Fidel Castro*, do you bring me joy?" Some are more like sculptures than books; their meaning makes me keep them. Squat blocks of paper and ink, sitting where vanity might otherwise have placed a bust of a fabled writer: "Montaigne, do you bring me joy? Seneca, do you bring me joy?" There are old text books. *"Essentials of Neuroscience and Behaviour*, did you bring me joy?" Not Joy, no. They join the others.

Some things I can't donate: a dictionary battered to onion skin rags held together by parcel tape; books with bits underlined that would only set strangers' minds wondering. And there are old magazines: *Red and Black Revolution*, that I must have bought from an anarchist at some protest a long time ago ("protesting, did you bring me joy?"); an Italian music magazine from the days when I had an Italian girlfriend ("did you bring me joy?"), and Irish language newspapers yellowed with age. There are calendars dating back to when I was a teenager. One is entitled *Tolkien Centenary 1892-1992*. In another I see in my teenaged handwriting: '24th August 1991 – Communism falls in the USSR'. There is a bag of newspapers from 12th September 2001. All the things I cannot give to the library go into the recycling bin. The bins are emptied on Monday. It's Wednesday and the recycling bin is already full.

Then there is the stuff I burn. Before asking each book if it brings me joy, I fan through its pages. Sometimes a receipt from years ago flutters to the ground, sometimes I dislodge a bus ticket that I had been using as a bookmark. I also find old cinema tickets, old theatre tickets; I find old boarding passes to

Italian airports, to airports in England, to Dublin, to Spain, and as I fan through the countless pages dried leaves flutter to the ground: Leaves between leaves.

Between the pages of *The Portable Nietzsche* I find a photograph of myself taken about ten years ago. On the back of it there are greetings from colleagues saying that they are sorry I'm not going to the party. What party? I don't remember what I did instead. ("Staying away from the party, did you bring me joy?"). One of the names on the photograph jumps out at me because I had seen her on an Irish-language channel. She was in an ad for a chat show, wearing a hijab now and lowering her eyelids as if to say "well, as a matter of fact...". So that's what happened to her. I remember wondering how she could ever have changed her life like that, now here I am disposing of my precious library and binning the paper-trail of my existence.

All these tickets, flyers, boarding passes, pictures, and slips of paper representing arrivals and departures, meetings and greetings, first hellos and final goodbyes, all of them go into the fire. They are part of that library too: the products of a wandering mind. I get rid of my diaries too, all but the one I have just returned with. I burn them and with them an interminable number of official letters from banks, utility companies, employers, the student loan company, Mensa, various opticians, dentists, and a bundle of promotional postcards depicting street art that I must have collected over years of downing coffee in trendy Dublin watering holes. All these mementos of my life are going up in smoke.

When I have filled the bags with books, and the recycle bin with paper, and when the hearth is filled with black ash rippling red, I look at what has survived this exorcism and ask it "do you really bring me joy?"

It's Day Fifty-Two of the Camino.

*

There is one newspaper article I keep. It is from the local paper, *The Strabane Chronicle*, Thursday November 26th 2015. Almost a year ago to the day. Page seventeen: *"From Strabane Glen to the 'bone church".*

I remember the day the reporter called to interview me for the article, a rainy early evening on Macken Street. I spoke to him, sheltering from the rain in the porch of the gym. He wanted to talk to me about a story I'd written about a trip to the Czech Republic, one shortlisted by *The Irish Times* as part of a travel writing competition. This is the story:

Kutna Hora

The skulls of hundreds of people lined the walls. They rose in pyramids. They grinned above the lintel and formed part of a chandelier. They had even been fashioned into a coat of arms. Whoever these bones had belonged to had long since been forgotten. I doubt if they would have recognized themselves.

I'd waited all morning, listening to the first four notes of Smetana's *Vysehrad* repeating over and over again until my train was announced. I had no idea why I wanted to see a room full of human remains. It was unusual, I suppose, and it seemed to possess an honest charm that Prague lacked.

Now, there I was: confronted with stacks of empty skulls, empty eyes, empty mouths. What had they thought about, or seen? Who had they kissed?

Who had they been?

In the guide they were the bones of the Sedlec ossuary. Nothing more.

By accounts, the bones had been disinterred to make room for their descendants, now also dearly departed. I'd seen this before, near Bari where the bones of the victims of an Ottoman siege were heaped in glass tanks in the walls of a church.

They'd been displayed, but not like this. These skulls and cross-bones had been fashioned into necklaces to adorn the walls of what my guidebook called the 'bone church'. Piles of them stood like tetrahedrons of cannonballs. Others, maybe strangers when their owners were alive, were fixed together as ornaments. The only colours were grey and butter yellow from the candles. Some stacks of skulls had passages through them and, looking in, my gaze was met by so many unblinking sockets.

These skulls did not bring Kutna Hora its fame. That had been achieved by the people these skulls had belonged to. Kutna Hora was a silver town and, in its heyday, the *de facto* Czech capital. The basilica of Saint Barbara had been paid for with it. It doesn't have domes, but tented roofs and it overlooked a valley filling with autumn leaves when I stood there wondering where I could go to eat.

Life is short compared to the length of death, yet there is always time for a good meal. There is much to be said for a tavern by a bone church. The food, delicious in itself, assumes a greater savour when served after an eccentric reminder that the teeth biting into the food could one day grin down from a windowsill and that the tongue that tastes it and asks for more dark ale will one day not exist.

Stuffed to the gills, waddling like a heavily pregnant woman on the cusp of childbirth, I left the inn that had attracted me with its promise of 'Alchemical Cuisine'. I hadn't actually tried 'Master O'Kelly's Enochian Compound' (spiced chicken, to the lay-man), but the ossuary had worked its magic.

I thought of those dead and heard them whisper: 'Enjoy it while you can'.

*

I read through the newspaper article: *"He's also a former prize-winner for travel writing with the BBC for an article he penned on Strabane Glen"*. That's true, I remind myself. That happened, and this was the story:

Ashes

This is the overhang from which, fleeing mitred Redcoats, Hamilton leapt; or rather, from which leapt Hamilton's horse, with Hamilton spurring it on. Strabane Glen is narrow, but not so narrow that a highwayman can vault it on horseback. In the course of his fall, legend transformed him from a *tórai* into a *dullahan*: From a highwayman into a headless horseman. Passing beneath Hamilton's Leap I feel as though I'm being watched.

It's mid-winter. Last night it was -20°C after a day and a night of heavy snow. This morning I awoke into a marble silence. The beluga hills, swan-curved and silent under a dove-down sky, are as smooth as porcelain and as cool as milk. The glen is buried deep within them, and buried within the glen is a unique wildwood.

By the time I get there the sky has chilled blue, there is ice in my beard, and ice rimes my coat. The trees and bushes are winter antlers of albite feldspar, calcite, and quartz. The cold draws all the moisture out of the air. Deep, freeze-dried snow scatters underfoot. My steps sound like wing-beats.

Around me trees fountain like frozen geysers of blue and white. My footprints pay out like an astronaut's umbilicus. Ringing in the ice, under snow-covered briars, the sound of trickling water underpins the silence. Its low murmur whispers disembodied music; distant anvils under the earth.

The houndstooth stream runs and chimes against varnished pebbles. For ten thousand years it has carved out the glen. Glaciers once towered above the Sperrin Mountains to the east; waterfalls thundering from their cyan cliffs. Their meltwater created the stream. Working, wearing, filing the faultline with a ten thousand year long draw of a rasp, the stream has carried away the ages to the sea. The chasm walls show stone swept smooth as potter's clay. Having brushed away millennia of schist the stream exposed the ancient igneous rock and, in doing so, set the foundations for an island of ash trees below the surface of the earth.

Ash trees were considered wholesome talismans by the Celts. They would pass a sick child through a split ash. The split was then bound in the belief that the child would heal in tandem with the tree. Travellers' staves were made from ash. When Vikings came they brought their own ash-lore: *Yggdrasil*, the Tree of Life, was an ash. The first man, *Askr*, was carved and smoothed from ash. Its strength lent it to combat. Ash is named after the Saxon assegai: *Æsc*.

Today these ash trees are protected by law. No such protection was given to the neighbouring ancient oak-wood and it was reduced to rafters and whiskey barrels. No law saved the blackthorns torn up for the bypass. Recently, Rio Tinto Zinc sought to extract gold from the Sperrins by grinding ore with cyanide. Farmers yoked to those thin, stony highlands surrendered custody of the landscape in exchange for the price of a freer life. But an assay revealed no treasure worth having so the Gorgon looked away, the farmers remained shackled to the seasons and the soil, and the pine-tanned rivers were spared the poison. As was the glen. So far.

Protected by a signature and a stamp, charmed by disinterest and good luck, the glen has turned feral; the old bridges rot. Fallen trees and their broken limbs set hurdles and barricade the path. Frozen ivy tresses cascade like fistfuls of chainmail. Trees list like the masts of shipwrecks limescaled with ivy coral. And everywhere, everywhere, white flames of snow cover everything. It drops from boughs in aerosols of hissing frost.

Split trunks reveal time rippling out through the wood just as it ripples through the countless leaves of mica in the cliffs. Life slept through these inconceivable ages until it awoke to this hidden world of crystal and shade. I see the tallest ash trees spanning histories indexed in rock. I see in them the Tree of Life, *Yggdrasil*, still growing, still living. Still.

Millennia above, where the trees touch the skin of the modern world, time races by. Down here, this lost woodland is seasoned with folklore. I remember tales of woodsmen lured away by the secret music, sly and knowing melodies drawing them underground. I imagine walking out of the glen to find that a century has elapsed in the outside world; my town altered, its people replaced, their attitudes incomprehensible: and I, dusted with frost, not aged by a day.

A snow-bound path rising between clotted firs spills onto a hill road of slush the colour and texture of fudge. To either side white fields tile the hillsides. There is my town. Coal smoke tarries over its rooftops, ice paves the river, and the first stars glitter in the cobalt sky.

*

Kutna Hora, did you bring me joy? *Ashes*, did you bring me joy?

Yes. Yes, you brought me joy. Why did I stop writing? I used to write things like this:

The Noble Rot

Trickling, the bloodstone necklace of a centipede; amber fingers strumming the sides of its meandering body as it weaves, gliding after its prey into the bowels of the compost heap. Its golden antennae savour air as pungent as oyster pulp. Picture its jaws: spring-loaded sickles aching for release.

The compost heap hulks in a mighty chest at the bottom of my garden. Its wood has bleached grey from sun and rain. Algae stain it. Into it fall the off-cuts and peel of vegetables, grass, fruit cores, eggshells, coffee grounds, leaves and uprooted weeds. I open the lid of the chest and there they are: silver slug trails; lace woven from spun sugar. They trace a filigree as delicate as Damask over the umber cud of the compost. On warm days the chest fructifies like a rumen digesting the ripe curds of rotting plants. Deep in its core the compost ferments and reduces to a soot as creamy as graphite and as black as mole velvet.

A host of sprites, millions seen and unseen, visible and invisible, make this their home. I watch their cryptic rituals, their hunting sorties, their errands and evasions. The compost heap is dusted with a motile peppering of minute flies whose ciphers are broadcast in a rarefied language of semaphore and brinkmanship, of pheromones and mime. Their vital quests for mates and immortality, played out amongst the charnel of last season's crop, are no less urgent or as serious as the high dramas of greater creatures. Through them plough the lead scutes of woodlice, their gills breathing the damp atmosphere released from corrupted stems and withered roots. They graze like trilobites on a primal seabed, drinking in the foetid sap from wet and blackened leaves; from brown, cloying thatch.

Clinging to the lid and walls of the chest, coiled within the whorl of their shells; snails, still as eddies. Stone-grey shells, each a dreaming ziggurat. By them, apricot yellow and glistening like raw plum-flesh, the slick muscle of creeping slugs. They drive their dim horns into the savoury meat of the compost, their tongues rasping, the gross blowholes on their backs brimming with stale breath.

High above my home, on the swell of the valley, the dairy farm winters out on a diet of sour silage. In the milk mid-winter mornings the byre is swept out with a chain dragged across the icy concrete floor. The muck and straw is gathered and added to the manure heap. Piled up to the white sky, it steams like rank ox-flanks in the silver sunrise. At its heart, febrile bacteria drive the temperature as high as 70°C. Snowflakes melt as soon as they touch it and an ochre broth stains the barnyard from the manure heap to the gutter. The manure marinades until the days begin to lengthen, stretching in the warm sunlight like basking hares. Then it is churned into the earth where it cradles new growth in a heady, aromatic womb.

On the farm and in my garden, through the ale and ichor of the bilge and busted mire lives are lived out, unrecorded and unremarked upon. And here they will end. Here they will conclude a journey that began with the first germs of life in the first seas. Chance brought them here, just as chance brought me here to see them.

I open the lid of the chest and there they are: onion bulbs, melting; their bruises wrapped in fungal gauze. Such familiar forms. Over time they disfigure. They warp and collapse into slime. And the millions whose universe this is face just the same fate.

As do we all, I reflect, before opening the casement hatch at the base of the chest and digging out a spadeful of fresh soil the colour of anthracite. I plough this into my vegetable patch. Everything that had reached up to the sun has collapsed into ruin. Yet now, at its conclusion, it coaxes the seeds I've set in the furrows, and bears life out of death.

*

Writing, did you bring me joy?

Yes, yes you brought me joy. I pick up the travel diary that has lain in my rucksack since my return. I open it and I begin following my ghost across Spain from Saint Jean to Santiago de Compostella.

Part One: Rise

At 6am I wake up seconds before my alarm begins to sound. For the first time in months I spring out of bed. I flick on the lights and strip everything off my bed. I stuff my bedclothes into bin-bags. I shower and brush my teeth and then my toothbrush, the toothpaste, the towel and shampoo go into another bin bag. I dress in under a minute. I pull open the curtains; black glass reflects the bare room. Everything is gone. I am gone.

I lace up my old walking boots, heave my rucksack onto my back, and jam a hat on my head. I take a photo of the empty flat. I've spent three years of my life cooped up in here and now it's over. I close the door for the final time and put the keys in an envelope. I leave this on the table in the hall, under junk mail for the landlord. Then I close the front door behind me and sling the bin-bags into the bin, and with them go the shoes I wore to work, their laces tied together like a bolas. I walk down the garden path and past the spreading chestnut tree. I cannot remember my final step away.

The AirCoach is pulling into the stop as I approach. I tell myself 'don't run' but I do for the last few meters to meet it before it pulls away. The driver nods me on board. All the way through the gathering light I say goodbye to all those familiar Dublin places: the shops, the newsagents, the street corners, the parks and thoroughfares which framed my life. In Terminal One I sit upstairs with a coffee, trying and failing to convince myself of the self-help notion that airports are magical places filled with anticipation.

On the way through security I set off the metal detector and they swab my hands to check for chemicals and find nothing. Then I'm beyond security, where people are free to take to the air. I go to my gate. I wait. I note the people with rucksacks, their hiking poles telescoped into short batons. I am not wearing outdoor gear. I have the cotton trousers and shirt I wore yesterday on my last day of work. I have a rust-red jacket and my hat is a fedora. My hiking boots are about ten years old and have been from the Arctic Circle to the Sahara desert, from the Atlantic Ocean to the border of Byelorussia. They walked through the chambers in the heart of Auschwitz, across the sands of a bull-ring in Andalucía, and they hung over my shoulder as I climbed Cruach Phádraig barefoot. They look like plain, battered leather boots. I have checked in my rucksack. I doubt I look like I'm intent on hiking the length of Spain.

Getting to Spain means going first to Saint Jean, and getting to Saint Jean means getting to Bayonne, and getting to Bayonne means getting to Biarritz. That's where my plane is going. From the window above the wing I see the atmosphere of our planet coating the world as a membrane coats a cell. Iceberg clouds sail by. They have been conjured up from the surface of the oceans by the sun. There is blue solar radiation and white ephemeral ranges of surf. They look like the eruptions of breakers dashed against the coast. The air is boiling, and the sky rises to navy darkness: the sea turned upside down.

The RyanAir flight is quicker than expected, and the plane to Spain arrives in the rain. "Diddly-diddly diddly-doo" sings the Scottish captain, "RyanAir wishes you a safe onward journey". There is a round of applause and someone shouts "Up the Dubs!"

There is a bus waiting outside the airport going to Bayonne, and if I want to take it I will need to spend a whole euro. The AirCoach in Dublin had been nine times the price and I double-take before tapping a one euro coin down on the driver's console. Biarritz is drowned in grey cloud and slow, interminable rain. I look out the window, my back turned to the other passengers, and watch the tidy houses of Biarritz give way to older, overgrown houses on the approach to Bayonne. This is the Basque Country and there are *pelota* courts with vertical lines painted on their walls, and stencils of *pelota* players on the bus shelters. Street signs are in French and Euskara.

At Bayonne station I buy my ticket, speaking in French and being answered in English, and I find the platform my train is to arrive at. I'd rather wait in a cafe and on the way there I pass four armed soldiers in combat fatigues. France is at war with its demons. I haven't seen anything like this since I was a child in Northern Ireland.

*

Across the road from the station there is a cafe outside which are plaster statues of The Blues Brothers sitting on a bench. For a second, but only a second, I'm tempted to sit between them in my fedora. It's raining, anyway. I order a coffee and sit outside at a table that is a big barrel. They have these in Irish theme pubs and I wonder if they were ever used or are just made for display, cranked out by some set-design factory in a Chinese industrial estate.

There are Irish people in the cafe. I hear someone say they're from Gaobh Dobhair. Some of the others order in English and the waiter starts to tell them that everything on the menu is no longer available, citing the late season, which could either mean falling temperatures, falling numbers of visitors, or both.

Visitors? Or Pilgrims? Or Tourists? Which one am I?

I have promised myself to do this as a pilgrim; I'll stay in the most basic places, carry only what I need, and eat simple food, because that is what I think a pilgrim does. But I'm sitting at a French pavement cafe, wearing a fedora and sipping an espresso. What is a pilgrim anyway?

I wander up and down the street to stretch my legs, but have little time to see what there might be to see. Bayonne reminds me of Waterford. I stop there for a moment, contemplating the water of this river I cannot name, and I wonder what I would have been doing otherwise. It's Saturday, and I picture an aimless circuit of Dublin: Morehampton Road, towards Baggott Street, stop off in a cafe, contact friends who don't reply, on towards Stephen's Green, down Dawson Street, browse the bookshops, probably buy something, and on through Trinity, and then along Pearse Street and under the railway bridge and over the Rosie Hackett bridge to O'Connell Street, to browse the bookshops, and on up to Parnell Street to browse the bookshops; If there's nothing on at Cineworld, there is all that to walk back. What a difference a day makes.

I think of when I decided to come here, when I decided to quit working and living in Dublin. This was during the summer and I was speaking with a colleague who was "going to do The Camino". I'd only the vaguest of ideas what The Camino entailed. I'd seen the film, *The Way*, and I'd heard about it as much as anyone had, but I'd never considered doing it for the same reason I'd never considered bungee jumping or hang-gliding, although I had paid my dues to Life Experiences by having gone sky-diving.

About four years prior to this I'd spent the worst month of my life in Lugo teaching toddlers with puppets, the recovery from which took a lot of red meat and whiskey, but which had also placed me on one of Camino routes: The Northern-Primitive Route had passed by my front door. I'd given the pilgrims scarce attention, and ignored the scallop shell motif on the bollard at my street corner. But I took a day trip by bus to nearby Santiago de Compostella, the destination for these pilgrims, to escape my puppet hell more so than to see why they were going there. I'd stood on the steps of the cathedral, looking out over the square as pilgrims greeted one another. I couldn't understand why these hikers were so happy at arriving in front of the cathedral. I strolled around it and in one plaza saw a busker in blackface playing blues on a guitar with a toy cigar in a pair of giant red lips clamped to his mouth. And that had been my experience of the Camino.

Casting my mind back further, perhaps those ramblers on the Cantabrian coast were pilgrims, as were those hikers who'd arrived late in a hostel in Llanes (I think) and snored with such stentorian vigour that I spent that night sleeping on a couch in the lobby. But that was during a driving holiday, when I was living in Jerez de la Frontera and had gone north for Easter Week to escape the religious madness.

*

So I stand in Bayonne, watching the water make its way to the sea without any effort. My thoughts do not peer into the future. I'm sick of making plans. I think only of the train to Saint Jean, and the moment by moment decisions that will become a feature of the Camino. I know I like to travel and I know I wanted to leave Dublin, but what I don't know is why I am here and what will happen.

I had no doubt when I decided to leave my job: time really is short compared to the length of death, and once gone it will not come back. You can spend money, waste it, you can give it away; yet there is always the possibility of getting it back again, by fair means or foul. But time is a one way system; it radiates from you like body heat, taking with it your youth, your ambition, your stamina, your courage, and for some it will take with it your mind, your memories, and your dignity as it goes. The time of your life is all you have, and it is not paused when you are at work, or stuck in a queue, or sitting in front of the TV, or hungover, or listless, or at a loose end. Without speeding up or slowing down, it goes, goes, goes.

So, if not now, when? I've saved enough and have no debts, not even a credit card. What's the alternative?

I'm not drawn to the Camino by notions of 'sorting my life out' or 'finding myself'. I mocked the half-baked books for infantile adults that filled up the bookshops of the city. There were countless books on self-therapy, colouring in books for adults, strange diets revolving around certain plants or imagined, cultish takes on tribal lifestyles. Dublin was not so much a secular society as one that believed in anything if it came with nice packaging. In terms of quack theories and nonsense diets, yuppie secularism trumps any number of religious sects.

Christianity in Dublin was a religion critical of irrelevant matters or smitten by right-on jingoism. It did not nourish, and it did not give: This religion just seemed to be staffed by elderly ewes, whose sad and defeated murmurs were drowned out by the cacophony of a mall-minded country where male impersonators shrieked about craft ale as their girlfriends farted into pints and laughed about it afterwards.

*

I let the river carry these idle thoughts away with it, and I turn back to the station. There are few others there, all carrying rucksacks and hiking poles. I am sitting on a bench at the platform when there comes the sound of party-blowers from the station entrance and a group of people in shorts and t-shirts come out onto the platforms. Sticking from their back pockets are Irish tricolours together with another flag: navy and azure chequers with three burning castles: "Up the Dubs!"

They group themselves at the end of the platform and begin making a racket on the party-blowers, which are large whelk-shells into which the hooter of a party-blower had been fixed. They have these things hanging around their necks on strings and after a short countdown of one-two-three, start blowing into them. They are so loud that they smother the sound of the announcements and the station master has to come out on two occasions to tell them to knock it off. But they are unfazed, and laugh at being chastised in French.

When the train arrives, it arrives at another platform and the station master shoos us across the lines to where it waits: a single carriage that seems to have been built especially as a shuttle service. The journey follows a river and is long enough to fall asleep on, which happens soon after the landscape changes from the town to the farms to the first cliffs and peaks of the mountains. I see three griffon vultures circling the thermals and when I awake the hills are forested, the train is slowing, and Saint Jean wanders past the window and halts.

I walk up from the station, past a large sign displaying a map of the town around which many pilgrims have gathered in silence. I walk along such normal, suburban streets that I feel that this isn't some well-worn and ancient pilgrim path at all, but a wrong turning into some housing development in a rural sleeper town; but then I see city walls, and when I pass under an arch I find myself on cobbled streets. Steep cobbled streets, and I have to bend forward to hike my rucksack up to the pilgrim centre. Here I leave my rucksack inside the door and wait my turn.

The woman at the desk smiles as she rushes through a huge list of *albergues* (pilgrim hostels), from here to Santiago, and a map of the route displayed by altitude. The route is divided into stages, and she draws a red dot at the very start to show where I am, and also how far I'll have to go. Day one is a steep parabola. She draws another red dot on the other side of this. This second red dot represents Roncesvalles, my first destination within Spain. She asks for my Pilgrim Passport, the *Credencial*, and I fish it out of a small holster I'd bought at an airport ages ago. The holster is designed to keep a hidden supply of money under your clothes so as to foil thieves. I have my *Credencial* in it.

The *Credencial* is a booklet in which I will have to collect stamps, like passport stamps, as I continue along the Camino. It serves to prove that I am a pilgrim and that I have travelled the Camino. Should I make it to Santiago de Compostella, presenting this booklet to the authorities will result in me being awarded a *Compostella* – a certificate of achievement that I'll be able to hang on my wall to be marvelled at by dinner guests.

The pilgrim office issues *Credenciales* of their own, but I bought mine from the pilgrim office in St. James's church in the rebel Liberties, Dublin, some weeks before. The Irish *Credencial* is small and sleek, with a varnished green cover depicting the Celtic cross and the sea-shell, whereas the *Credencial* issued by the pilgrim office in Saint Jean is a long concertina of tough card. The woman sets the stamper above the first blank space in my *Credencial* and does nothing. I take the hint and press down on it. I feel like I am turning the key in the ignition during my first driving lesson. The stamp, the *sello*, is made: a wobbly, blurred image where Saint James – *Santiago* – appears to have a skull for a face. The woman dates it the first of October 2016 and draws a snail on it in red biro.

"Bon Chemin", says she.

"Merci", says I.

Outside I overhear two of the Dubs saying that the woman had been rude to them. They are sitting on the steps of a hostel near the pilgrim office. "To think you come all this way", says one, "only to be treated like that".

*

The street runs down to the river, passing one hostel after another with signs on their doors saying that there is no room at the inn. I get the impression, and I cannot say why, that everyone here is somehow friends with everyone else, that everyone here is a seasoned pilgrim with good reasons for being here. In short, I feel like I am back on the streets of Dublin, an immiscible soul being carried along through a place I've no reason to be in.

I cross the river and find my way to a hostel that is open, that has space for me, and I go in where, in an old hall around which spirals a hefty wooden staircase, the receptionist – the *hospitalero* – gives me a little spiel about 'finding your way' and 'loving yourself' and 'not being proud' before charging me €18 and advising me not to lace my boots at the very top so as to avoid shin splints.

This is more than I expected to pay for a hostel bed, but in addition to this, I buy a flask for water and a pair of bungees to hang washing on my bag to air-dry. They will also keep my tote bag attached to the outside of my rucksack. The tote bag is filled with things I think I'll need in an emergency such as yellow plastic trousers that could fit on the back-end of a pantomime elephant, a poncho, a torch that used to be the front light of a bicycle, and a notebook and biro. This tote bag cannot fit in the rucksack even if I wanted it to owing to the rucksack being full to the brim with things I think I'll need including a spare hat, tracksuit bottoms, evening trousers, a wooden box containing a bottle of ink and dip-pens, several boxes of painkillers and band-aids, a bottle of hand sterilising gel, a tablet for booking a flight home at the end, and a device like an electric razor for sanding off the calluses from feet.

After buying the water bottle, and the bungees, I go for a meal in a place by the river where, *in lieu* of tea and oranges that come all the way from China, I have a pizza and beer. The waiter is a scrawny, new-born creature who points at empty tables and says "you sit there" when asked if there is a table. When no table is available he walks up to someone nearing the end of their meal and asks "you finished? OK?" He performs this witty butler act without a hint of job satisfaction and I later remark in my notebook that he was "an ignorant little shit – a real bad-mannered asshole who's going to get a thump one of these days".

I sit out on the patio, under a tent-roof, as the rain patters down. The people next to me are Australians who are also welcomed by the ignorant little shit and I tell them not to take it personally as he is a real bad-mannered asshole with everyone. The Australians are bikers, a couple driving though Spain and France and nearing the end of their odyssey. We get to talking about Cangas de Onis and the *Reconquista*, because they visited Covadonga, before talking about people we know and experiences in *sharia* countries. They are curious to know why I am doing the Camino and I tell them I finished my job yesterday and handed back the keys to my flat. They ignore the fact that this isn't a reason to do the Camino, but say it was a good thing to do anyway. I say goodbye to them before going for a walk. It's getting dark at 8pm.

Saint Jean is Basque and their symbols and language are everywhere. I go into the church. I haven't been in a church for a long time. I stopped going when I was in my early teens, walking to church on a Sunday morning only to sit in the graveyard and read James Bond thrillers. In Ireland, the Catholic Church was rejected with the society it was associated with. Irish people might say that Catholicism fell out of favour because of the child abuse scandals, but the truth was that it was the product of a provincial world of boring farmer's sons who were drafted into the clergy to spend their inexperienced lives doling out communion and reciting psalms as though they had been sentenced to a lifetime's community service.

This Basque church has great stone bowls of ashes in which candles are fixed and burning. The missal is in Euskara as are the Stations of the Cross and other notices. I compare this with Ireland and see the amount of psychological metamorphosis that needs to happen for the Irish to actually be Irish and not just tourists in the rubble of their own history. I think it was Seamus Heaney who described those Irish who speak English as having ears that have swallowed the rapist's tongue; but I've been known to be wrong.

Well maybe. I'm no expert, and I'm tired.

Tomorrow I begin the Camino. Today I walk the battlements of Saint Jean, looking out at the mountains I will begin to climb tomorrow, and listening to the beech mast falling. It sounds like rain dripping off leaves after a shower. I find myself at a portal through the city walls: Saint James's Gate, and make a point of walking through it, believing this to be an official starting line for the Camino, oblivious to the fact that as I do this there are pilgrims walking towards Santiago from Lisbon, Vienna, Le

Puy, and Budapest. There are even pilgrims travelling along the north coast by boat, having been rowing all the way from Dublin.

Back in the hostel I meet the first pilgrim of the Camino. Jesus is Spanish. He tells me that a lot of Spaniards start here as the route into Spain is important in Spanish history. It's where the Basques limited Spanish expansion and the way by which Napoleon's forces invaded the Iberian Peninsula. Another pilgrim hands out fun sized Twixes to everyone, and as I go to sleep, I hear laughter muffled by my ear-plugs. It sounds like a duck quacking.

DAY ONE

I'm in France. Or am I? I'm in the Basque country, in Saint Jean and it's pitch black outside. I'm woken, not by my alarm, but by the other pilgrims moving around. Sleeping bags are zipped up and rolled up and tied up, flip-flops smack off heels as people bustle to and from the bathrooms, there are mumbled voices but no whispers, and then the lights come on. I'm using a sleeping sheet rather than a sleeping bag, and it packs into a pouch that I clip to the outside of my rucksack. My towel is still damp despite having been hung up on my ersatz washing line: one of the bungees stretched between two bunk beds. I fix it to the outside of the rucksack. I get dressed and go down to the dining room.

Across the long table is a scattering of off-cuts of that dry, almost stale, bread they eat in continental countries. From Spain to Poland, it's the same polystyrene foam coated in bark. The vending machine coffee is too weak to defend itself, but its breakfast with whatever bread is left plus jam. There are other pilgrims there, some of them with bicycles.

I wander into the garden. The darkness is fading to magpie blue and birds are beginning to sing. I stay a while and listen to them, then walk to the end of the garden. It's the inability to break the ice with strangers that has kept me outdoors. I go in and say a few hellos to the remaining pilgrims who are chatting in English; but they introduce themselves as being German, and American, and Danish. I eat and tidy up a little, not out of a sense of pilgrim obligation, but to compensate for having said so little. Just to prove that my silence is harmless, that I'm not being hostile.

I say goodbye to some who are leaving and they reply with "Buen Camino". And they go, following in the footsteps of the thousands upon thousands who have walked through this town to Santiago, century after century. I go upstairs and swing my rucksack up onto my back. I have no walking poles, considering them to be ridiculous and faddish, and then I walk down the wooden stairs and along the corridor to the street.

It's daybreak, pale and grey, and my plan is to go to the church and hear the mass before setting off. This, I think, is more in keeping with the tradition of the Camino. It's a pilgrimage, after all. And as I stand there wondering what to do with the time before the church opens I hear steps behind me and another pilgrim emerges from the hostel. She is one of the Danes, American-Danish as she explains, and suddenly we're off, up the long straight street to the Spanish Gate, westwards and upwards, away from France towards Spain, across the mountains of the Basque country.

Now, what is a plan? What is chance, and what is fate? If my plan to 'do the Camino' is simply to turn up, start walking, and end up in Santiago, then my daily plans are next to non-existent. Yet at the first instance of having a plan, it doesn't happen. There is no mass, and my fanciful idea to retrace my steps up to Saint James's Gate, just in order to have my first hiking day actually start at what I think is the 'official starting point', doesn't happen either.

Instead I walk up through the Spanish Gate in the company of a total stranger and, as soon as we are out of Saint Jean, we decide that the wrong way is the right way and detour off the designated route just as it begins.

Now here's food for thought: Everything that happened up to this point had to happen for this moment to exist. Change the past and you change the present, *Terminator* fans. And all that is to come has this moment as its starting point. The past creates the present; the present creates the future. And so, all events in what we think of as the past, present, and future, are suspended in one great causal nexus – with each event necessitating its forebears and determining the existence of its descendents. So what might look like a mistake is no mistake, but the inevitable outcome of all that has preceded it, and the source of all that follows.

On we go. My new-found friend is travelling Europe because she has a European visa. She has it because her grandparents are Danish, but while she's here, she says, she might as well walk the Camino and see Spain. She volunteers an insider's view on the forthcoming US elections; having favoured Bernie Sanders she feels lumbered with Hilary Clinton, a person she has no time for, but since the opposition has the gold-plated figurehead of Donald Trump as a battering ram, she has stuck with the Democrats. But talk runs dry as the gradient of the path picks up, breathing becomes a conscious effort, and the lack of other pilgrims begins to prey on our minds.

Mile after mile, the green meadows of the low mountain slopes ring to the sounds of cow-bells. Bells, cattle, plots of vegetables, tomatoes, and gourds; but no people. An approaching car slows and the grinning driver assures us that we are on the road to Saint Michel before driving off. We thank him but neither of us raises the question as to where Saint Michel is and as soon as we get to fork in the road I pull out my guidebook and we check the map.

There, in the lower left-hand corner of the first map is the hamlet of Saint Michel, and leading away from it is a line of purple dots representing an earlier Camino route that joins the main route – the *Camino Francés* – half way up the hill before us. We turn the map until it orients to the real world before us. That way, we decide, and begin the hike up a slope with such a punishing gradient it could be scaled with ropes.

We stop talking. Our breath is laboured. We stop to remove layers, which in my case means a trendy jacket and a fedora, and rolling up my sleeves. We push on, each step levering our body weight a fraction closer to the top of the mountain. We are about an hour into the Camino de Santiago and already we are gasping for breath. Then, as though seeing a ship from the beach of a desert island, we see the bright orange and yellow figures of pilgrims in hiker gear walking on a path high before us. Buoyed by this we go on and when we set foot on the Camino Francés the sense of relief causes us to laugh. But my legs ache and each rise in the road causes me to slow, which in turn puts distance between the Danish-American and myself. We pass a group of Londoners who tell us that they need a rest. One of them steps on a slug which bursts with an audible pop. One of them tells no-one in particular that they can't wait to get back to civilization.

We keep going, and now there are small groups of pilgrims standing by the side of the road looking out over the countryside. The sun is now well clear of the horizon and mist is forming In a band up ahead. The road curves, but the Camino does not; it continues on along a track guided by stone walls and embankments of bracken and brambles. I meet the Danish-American who is doing squats to prevent cramping. The path sometimes becomes gravelly and crumbles underfoot, and it winds up hairpin bends, along which those who came on bike have to get off and push, but the views become grand and aquiline before the track rejoins the road and dissolves into the mist.

The road ahead is little more than a watermark and my breath begins to smoke as though on an icy day. I pass by a guest house with people taking a break over coffee on the front patio. I can't imagine stopping for a break, not when there is so far left to go and so much distance left to conquer. Alone, I walk on, higher and higher, and I am musing on how far up the mountain I must have climbed since leaving Saint Jean when a tidy, unprepossessing building appears around a corner. This is the hostel at Orisson, and it is to be my bed for the night. It has taken me two hours to get here. I order a coffee and go and sit on the viewing terrace, where I look at a blank wall of mist and begin to feel the chill. As I go in for a second coffee, I see the Danish-American talking with Jesus from the hostel. He is telling her that she shouldn't walk with her laces untied as it is bad for her feet. She tells him that she only untied them when she was relaxing during her break. But she is tying up her boots and when I ask her if she's off, she says yes.

She walks up into the mist as I get another coffee and sit at a table outside the door where the mist is condensing on the varnish. I do not see her again.

*

Should I stay or should I go?

Two hours seems too short a day. At home I had no issue with cycling from my home in Strabane to Lough Neagh and back, or around Inishowen, after having cycled to it first; I'd enjoy cycling to Boa Island, or hop on the bike and pedal off to catch the Ferry to Toraigh Island where they all spoke Irish and gannets dive-bombed shoals of fish far from its cliffs. I liked to cycle to Glenveigh and hike, or cycle to Mount Errigal, climb it, climb back down, and cycle home. Long distances under my own steam were the norm. Two hours feels like a day wasted. What am I going to do in Orisson?

When I had got my *Credencial* in Saint James's in Dublin, I was advised to book ahead and reserve a room in Orisson. The first day is strenuous, they said, and it will make things easier. And so, with Google Translate standing in for years misspent in French classes, I'd made a reservation.

Still: 10am and I've arrived. What now?

I wander indoors and tell the *hospitalero* that I've a reservation but was wondering about moving on. What would he advise? He says he can't advise, but that whatever I choose it will be the right decision. So I get another coffee and sit outside, the cloud thickening on the mountain all around. And it feels as though that is an excuse rather than a reason – the cloud hides the view. I decide to stay and the *hospitalero* agrees that I have made the best decision. "Today is cloudy", he says, "but tomorrow you will thank the French boy when you will have the best views".

I am shown to the dorm. There are three bunks and I'm the first there. I try to sort out my rucksack. The trek up to Orisson has shown me just how heavy it is, and although I know I only need very little, something prevents me from jettisoning a lot of what I have. But I make a start with the jacket and three blank notebooks. I also leave a Camino guide, as I've brought two with me and prefer the one with the maps and its eccentric daily reflections. I add the notebooks and the guide to a small polyglot library in the corner of the room. I fold up the jacket with every intention of forgetting it.

I repack the bag, but feel that I have made very little difference, then decide to walk a little way up the mountain. The cloud has lifted slightly. I don't take my bag, just my new water flask that I fill from a push-button tap – a *fuente* – outside the hostel. There is a place just ahead, Pic d'Orisson, which will do as a destination. I'm the only one on the road as I begin the ascent.

But I'm not the only one at Pic d'Orisson. There is a shepherd in a black beret looking out over a slope upon with sheep are grazing. A sheepdog sits like a sphinx on the grass. Pic d'Orisson is a crag of rock upon which stands a statue of the Virgin. All around the feet of this statue are personal items and photos left as offerings, including a child's artificial leg. This is the same as at a holy well near my home, Saint Brid's Well, a pool ringed by trees in which are hung all manner of trinkets including children's dolls and action figures, holy medals and weathered photos, and strings of rosaries in all colours and made from all materials. Looking at this I am reminded of how Catholicism has preserved so much of Europe's animist and polytheistic past, with the Virgin being just one of a number of figures who serve as tutelary deities over springs, crossing places, high passes, and bridges. I have heard people say that this is a bad thing, but I don't think it is. I don't think these charms work, but I am a European, and these symbols are part of my inheritance as much as they are a window into the past.

The sheepdog watches over the sheep. The Virgin watches over the road. High above, a griffon vulture watches over us all. On the higher slopes, cows and horses graze; their bells sound like a spoon being stirred in an empty pot, which just serves to remind me that these animals are destined for the dinner table. There is also a cross by the roadside and at its feet is a tin box with a sign telling me to 'Open the Box'.

Yes, sir. I will.

The box is full of little notes left by pilgrims. They are blessings for the path ahead. Beside the path there are also cairns, some with trinkets added to them, some with names written on their constituent stones. I walk back to the hostel, feeling a dim but present nip in my left hip with each step.

*

It's dinner time in Orisson. I've washed in a shower operated by a single token, to conserve mountain water, and changed into my evening clothes which are little different to my hiking clothes. Those clothes, which were soaked through with sweat on the steep hike to Orisson, are in a washing machine together with a few items of other pilgrims' gear. These other pilgrims are the Dubs. They arrived earlier to the sound of their whelk-shell party-blowers and I meet them in person just outside the door of the dormitory. They are from Ballyfermot, graced with the idiosyncratic accent of south-west Dublin, and have no problem offering advice on what to pack: "A spare teacher" informs one, picking at the sleeve of his t-shirt, "and a hah for when is cold", pointing to his beanie hat, "spare shorts, y'know", pointing to his Bermudas... One set of spare clothes – anything else you can get on the way. I think of my full rucksack and full tote bag. The group are here at the behest of Ron and Maeve, husband and wife, who walked part of the Camino before and are back with their friends. They say they are having their bags sent ahead each day and will finish in Pamplona.

Ron has a photo album on his phone and he swipes though visions of their past and my possible future. They were here during the summer. They tell me that they walked to the wine fountain at Iratxe and filled their water bottles with the free wine; this after telling me that they needed five litres of water a day in the heat. There were photos of them brandishing flasks of wine, drinking it on haystacks, and then sunburnt after having just woken up on a haystack. Like most Irish people, the sun tends to burn rather than bronze. Their happy red faces beam out of the photo like two joyous radishes.

At dinner the sole topic of discussion is why we are all here and what our destinations are. Not everyone is going to Santiago; some are going further – to Finisterre. Others, like the Dubs, are walking only part of the way. At the end of the meal the French begin to sing a pilgrim hymn – *Ultreia* – which no-one but them seems to know, but I get the feeling that we are supposed to. They falter as they realise they are on their own, but pick up a little and trill for a while before the awkward silence. The feeling is of a national anthem to which nobody knows the words, an experience all too familiar to the Irish in the room. When the French stop singing, the Germans sing, then the Spanish, and when it is the turn of the Irish the Dubs sing 'Molly Malone' and thump the table. I don't sing, and feel so aware of this it's embarrassing. But the dinner is good natured and filling and it ends with small groups, bonded by common language, huddling over wine.

Outside the dormitory I put the clothes in the dryer, but they emerge warm and damp and so I hang everything up without a thought as to how the morning dew will just make them cold and wet. The dorm is now full. Three women from the same family are there: a mother, her daughter, and the mother's sister-in-law. They tell me that they are making a point of walking only a small part of the Camino, and chose this part because they think it is the prettiest. Another woman, from Belfast, says she is going to go to Santiago and then Finisterre if she feels like it. The last bunk is occupied by a Danish pilgrim, who survived an accident and now has to test her eyes every day with portable optician's charts. She demonstrates this procedure for us, and we look at her looking at the charts.

Darkness falls. Outside the refuge, there is the sound of talking in different languages and singing in German. This mingles with the thin, pulsing of crickets and the distant hoots of whelk-shell party-blowers.

DAY TWO

The *hospitalero* was right. The cloud has gone; the sky is clear, and a sunrise of the richest ochre, chilli red, amber, cinnamon, and citrus yellow burns across the eastern mountains. The night sky seems to race away from it.

Coffee in a bowl and toast with jam; it doesn't quite hit the spot, so I eat the fruit I bought from the bar, which was supposed to be for later. So this is my daily routine: roll up the sleep-sheet and clip it to my rucksack, throw the rucksack up on my shoulders, walk, arrive at a hostel, unroll the sleep-sheet, shower, leave the towel drying and get a bite to eat, sleep, repeat. The thought of this does not fill me with a sense of monotony. Rather, it seems so simple, such a plain way to live each day, that I look forward to it. The pleasure is not in what I am doing, but in what I am not doing. I'm not at work.

I'm not at work!

Free at last! Free at last! Thank God Almighty, I'm free at last!

*

It's Monday, and I contrast it with the Monday before it, when it was just another manic Monday. I do appreciate earning money; but the routine corner-cutting and spiv culture of the managerial rank failed to inspire devotion me. I had one of those jobs that needs a 'self-motivated individual'. You have to be self-motivated for jobs like that, because the work won't motivate you. But it's history now: There are no niggling emails, no *plámás* of clients or agents, no idiotic reports about nothing in particular written in pseudo-academic English, no wasting of time on people who just don't care. Prior to leaving I met with my friend Agnieszka who was job hunting and we fell to ridiculing the inane job descriptions that were paraded by recruitment agencies. After all, if you ask a child to name ten jobs they will give you ten important and interesting jobs, ten jobs we couldn't do without. They will say things like Farmer, Teacher, Shop-Keeper, Baker. They won't say: Expert Empowerment Associate, Marketplace Commentary Advocate, Public Quality Implementer, or Monthly Creativity Agent. Which is never to say that the people who hold such bogus jobs are as stupid or fraudulent as the jobs themselves. People are capable of so much and jobs like that force them to do so little.

*

On the road up from Orisson everyone is in high spirits. People greet each other with 'Bon Chemin' or 'Buen Camino' and there is constant enthusiasm for the landscape. The sunlight falls on lakes of mist from which rise islands of fields and forests. I walk at my usual city speed and the sunlight casts my shadow onto a neighbouring hillside. I watch my shadow walking along like a character in Indonesian shadow-theatre. I pass by the tin box by the cross at Pic d'Orisson and I leave a message: *Beannachtaí gach lá ar an mbóthar go Santiago.*

Onwards and upwards – Ultreia – and the nip that worried my hip the evening before returns but this time it is much more acute. The thought crosses my mind that the sudden steep hike yesterday morning may have been short, but it was a sharp shock nonetheless and I might have injured myself. I wince going up the steeper inclines, but the scenery asks me to stop and I pause in the silence to watch the vultures and kites, and to watch sunbeams pass across the forests. Higher I go and then I receive my third stamp in my *Credencial*, from a man selling eggs and fruit from what his sign tells me is the last place to get a French stamp. It might as well say it is the last place in France, and he the last man in France because I see not another soul between leaving his pop-up shop and the Spanish border, which is a cattle-grid.

Soon after this the rocky incline makes its presence felt in my hip and the ache turns into a series of biting, stinging jabs with every step. The summit appears as protruding epiphyses of rock on a narrow dry gully, and once through it the path falls away in a cascade of rubble. It races downwards and I pace between the stones, descending step by step until I walk into a spell-binding beech forest. The path mellows. The slopes of the mountain are carpeted with copper beech leaves. All around me the trees pause, biding time until the days begin to lengthen again and they can resume their silent growth. Everything here seems to be waiting, as it has waited before, and a single leaf suspended on a thread of gossamer serves only to accentuate the calm.

And then it is gone. I walk out of the forest, past some small utility buildings and there is the great monastery of Roncesvalles [Spanish], or Roncevaux [French], or Orreaga [Basque]. I call in at the tourist office but am told to go straight to the monastery to register my arrival. I do so and discover that I am the second person to arrive and the office is not yet open. I sit outside in the yard and white cats come and lie on the bench beside me. As I eat a slice of Basque cake that I bought in Orisson the cats actually stretch out their paws for some. When I give them a tiny piece they throw it straight down the hatch.

Pilgrims keep arriving, including the Dubs who arrive one by one and sit out at the table eating jellies. When it is time to book in, I also buy a scallop shell on a red string. It has the cross of Saint James painted on it. I see these shells tied to rucksacks but I don't want to risk breaking it when I set my rucksack down against a wall. I decide to wear it around my neck. I buy it because Ron showed me a picture of him drinking the free wine at Iratxe from such a shell, and I feel that it's keeping with tradition to do likewise. Oh, yes.

*

Roncesvalles is a big, clean, modern hostel and in high season it must be a machine. I set my rucksack down by the locker in the dormitory and look again at how much stuff I have brought with me. There is a drop-box for unwanted items. I leave my spare t-shirt's spare t-shirt, a pair of biker braces, and the track-suit bottoms. I drop the box of toothpicks into a bin. I repack my bag and still feel that it's full. I shower and change, and bring my clothes to the laundrette where a *hospitalera* says she will take care of it. She is Basque. Some of the other *hospitaleros* are Danes. I hear them telling other pilgrims that they volunteer for a fortnight each year.

My hip is still bothering me as I walk up and down the stairs, but I see others hobbling, or wincing as they walk as though walking on hot coals. One Japanese pilgrim went over on his ankle and the sprain looks as though he has a golf ball buried under his skin. I leave the hostel and spend a while at a nearby cafe sipping a beer and watching the activity around the hostel. At one point a man with a donkey shows up, the donkey laden with all his baggage. At the sight of this I feel sorry for the donkey and feel that my own rucksack is not actually all that bad. It also reminds me of how Saint Francis of Assisi had called his body 'Brother Donkey'.

Back in the hostel, I meet Ron and the Dubs who are sunbathing outside the monastery. Maeve has a headache and so I give her some of the painkillers I brought with me. They are strong, leftover from when I was in hospital for an operation. The full strength ones are gone, which is just as well. When I had the operation I was so drugged I left the hospital and went sunbathing in the hospital flower beds as I waited for my taxi. We go on a tour of the monastery and learn that during the winter the snow fills the courtyard and spills in through the cloister doors, filling them to the lintels. There are also the chains won from the Moors that appear on the flag of Navarra.

The meal is the Pilgrim Meal: three courses with all the wine and strange, insipid continental bread you can take. It is at a nearby restaurant, and the waitress is short-tempered asking baffled pilgrims "¿lomo o pescado?" They have no idea and she becomes glaring and rude. I find myself translating for them: "pork or fish?" It can't be easy serving so many people day after day when they don't know two words of your language. At my table are pilgrims from Germany, Norway, America, and Bosnia – the minority Croat population. As we get to the end of the meal the Dubs begin to get up. "Come on" they tell us, "it's time for mass".

Well, there's a novelty. I haven't been to mass in about twenty years.

A lot of the pilgrims don't go, but continue chatting over dessert, and I wonder just how much of a pilgrimage this really is. Were it not for the Dubs I'd sit and chat over dessert too.

I go, and I take communion for the first time since I was an undergraduate, and I offer the sign of peace with strangers who do not share my language. I see others doing the same. At the end we are asked by the priests to approach the altar and he gives us a blessing in all the languages we represent, including Japanese and Korean. After the service I look in the crypt and see a giant iconic cross, a small replica of which had hung in my childhood bedroom. Back at the hostel I wind up in a group photo with the Dubs and a few others. The dormitory hums with low voices and the rustling of rucksacks and sleeping bags.

The lights go off at 10pm sharp.

DAY THREE

So now I am in Spain and this is the Camino. And there is nothing else in my life now but for the Camino. I brought my phone with me to be used for sending a single text to my father once a week so that my parents know I'm still alive, and as an alarm clock. But both functions are irrelevant. I have decided to send postcards at every stop-over and the alarm is redundant when you are awoken by pilgrims getting ready from 6am onward.

This is how my day in Roncesvalles starts. I've packed my rucksack, rolled up my sleep-sheet, and am walking away from the monastery-hostel when my alarm goes off. It's a pleasant enough as alarms go, a Welsh folk song being played on a harp, which has the paradoxical effect of lulling the listener to sleep, and I think about letting it run on as I stroll under the stars on the way to the cafe for breakfast. But one can have enough of a good thing and I have to stop, open the bag and dig through its compacted contents until I find the phone and switch it off.

This is the last time I'll touch that phone today. It's part of a strategy of avoiding the world beyond the Camino, which is a world I have grown sick of. If newspapers are like trawlers' nets that haul up all the cruelties of the world, then the internet is a dredger. So much nonsense getting into your head is like too much slurry leaking into a stream; sooner rather than later the stream is a sewer.

So there will be no internet, and if I hear about what's happening in the world I'll hear about it from another pilgrim. In this respect I'll be like one of the dead from *Cré na Cille*, who find out news from the outside world when a new corpse is consigned to the graveyard to gossip beside those who have gone before them.

*

Having switched off my alarm and with my rucksack back on my shoulders I walk to where the pilgrim meal had been the previous evening. The sky is clear and starry and I pause to watch the blinking lights of an aircraft moving through Orion. I follow the outline of the Starry Plough, from handle to lip and beyond in a straight line to where the pole star glows. That is north, and turning I face west: Almost eight-hundred kilometres in that direction Santiago is waking up and getting ready to welcome pilgrims who had passed through Roncesvalles weeks ago.

Breakfast is quick, coffee and bread, and eaten alone surrounded by people I do not know. I leave the restaurant, cross the road, and begin walking. It's still dark and the path runs through a forest. I slow down, seeing the bobbing willow-the-wisps of pilgrims' torches far ahead of me in the gloom. Passing cars send strobing lights through the trees, and my ears are alert to rustling in the undergrowth as hidden animals scurry away. The light of the day begins to clear the sky above the canopy, and when I emerge from the forest dawn has broken.

I am on the outskirts of Burgete, where a notice tells me that the forest I have just walked through was once home to a coven of witches. They met their end in the town, executed in public. It is a grim tale, and I am reminded of the fate of poor Bridget Cleary, a Tipperary woman who was murdered by her husband Michael who believed her to be a changeling – that is to say, a demonic body-double, his real wife having been switched for this changeling by the fairy folk. He killed her and burnt her body, or set her alight while she was still alive, hence the newspapers of the day carrying news that Bridget had been burnt as a witch. Having killed her, Michael went up into the Tipperary hills to wait for the fairy hunt, when he was convinced that he'd see his real wife in their company dashing off across the countryside on a demon horse. That's where the police found him. He spent fifteen years in Portlaoise prison before emigrating to Montreal by way of Liverpool. This happened in 1895, and did much to convince the British that the Irish were savage heathens, if they didn't think that anyway.

This morning Burgete looks ethereal; a peaceful phantom town drifting into being from a bed of mist. Behind it are black mountains and a pink sky. Burgete was once home to Ernest Hemmingway who enjoyed the local trout fishing. There is a hotel here with a piano whose ivories he is reputed to have tinkled in his youth prior to carving his initials into it. Ernest enjoyed the Basque county, and set *The Sun Also Rises* here. I walk through the tidy streets and out into farmland, having the most basic of conversations with the French pilgrim who had been on the bunk opposite me yesterday. He says that Pamplona will be his destination, but that he has already walked across France. Despite my ambition to walk across Spain, his achievement strikes me as nigh on super-human. He is a friendly fellow, and I feel a slight pang of guilt as I had written him off as a nutter owing to him slathering his entire body in Deep Heat, like in *Withnail & I*. But perhaps long distance hiking can do that to you.

Now the sun has also risen and the mist on the fields is golden. I have swapped the fedora for my other hat, a wide-brimmed white cowboy hat. I walk past fields of cattle and pause beside some photographers to watch a griffon vulture circle and come to land in a meadow. The mist condenses on spider webs and they look like lace doilies pegged out between the spikes of barbed wire fences. The path rises, running up past foaming hedgerows of rowan, rosehips, sloes, and elderberries. The aroma of blackberries mingles with the briar-leather smell of the cigar being smoked by the pilgrim up ahead. Sunlight catches round red leaves and makes them glow.

There are some moments when the path is strenuous, but not many; my sore hip eases a little, but not much. At one point I actually goad myself up a steep embankment, as though goading a farm animal – "go on, get up!" The same people pass me, then I pass them when they are resting, then they pass me again. I meet the three women from my dorm in Orisson, all from the same family, and they give me ointment to kill the pain in my hip. Later I pass them as they are admiring cattle in a meadow and I never meet them again.

I stop at a cafe in Espinal and have just sat down when the Danish pilgrim with the eye-chats appears with another Irish pilgrim. The Dane is Lena, the Irish pilgrim is June. We are then joined by Jim, a tall American who aims to walk to Santiago, then Finisterre, then Portugal before going home. Eric from Norway, together with his professional's camera that "weighs quite a bit", a couple of kilos, joins us and we sit and chat, the conversation turning to tales of Brexit and Trump and how crazy it all is. Jim says that if Trump wins he will be on the first rocket to Mars.

Well, we could sit and lament the *Resistible Rise of Arturo Ui* at home. I don't want to talk about it here. I move on. The path is now sharp.

It tunnels up through oceanic forests, rich and verdant, of strong greens and browns, and where the sunlight pierces the canopy and strikes the ground it is brilliant and scalding. Some leaves are responding to the shortening days: their leaves are yellowing, reddening, tanning, and liver-spotted. But the sun is still hot and the forest chimes with life, and I proceed in fits and starts as I stop to marvel, to appreciate, to love all that I see and hear.

Beyond the forest I stop for coffee at a little place with a dying lawn studded with plaster animals, wooden anteaters, and a fountain for drinking water that is a hosepipe with a tap. I get to speak Spanish without being answered in English. It feels like a compliment.

Beyond the cafe the path is concrete with a crazy-paving pattern moulded into it. It is hard underfoot, an unpleasant feeling after the forest path, and I wonder if my old boots will hold up on the journey ahead. The path begins to break up into huge lumps of uncomfortable gravel; then it is gone, replaced by scree of fist-sized rocks on a bed of dust. The air smells of pine before the beech trees suddenly vanish and dry conifers are there catching the sun above a rocky floor where lizards slip off the path into cover. One didn't slip so fast in the past and had to learn the hard way: it has no tail. The path seems only to ascend and the world is spread out below me through every gap in the trees.

Then the path plummets. There is a cataract of sharp ridges, like vertebral columns, and sometimes I have to tilt backwards to avoid falling forwards. This continues, twisting, turning, and then it's all gone. I have arrived before the Bridge of Rabies.

It is the Bridge of Rabies because it was once thought that leading your dog back and forth across the bridge three times would cure it of rabies, although it would be quite an endurance test to walk with a rabid animal over such a narrow space. Having crossed it, I am in Zubiri. I make my way to the Municipal, the large, council-run hostel, and am the first in my dorm. I take a cold shower and hand wash my sweat-sodden clothing, before getting changed. I cross back over the Bridge of Rabies and walk down to the river. The water level is low, unlike when Martin Sheen was washed away by it in *The Way*, and I take off my boots and socks and dip my feet in the water. The sun is fire, the water is ice; I make some notes in my journal, but stop to watch the water flowing past and muse about its origins high in the mountains, and its destination down by the sea. Jim, the American stops by; he says he has a relative in the hotel trade in Pamplona and is offering people cheap deals on fancy hotel rooms as a consequence. I thank him, but I want to do the Camino in the most basic way, and that means no luxury. Jim isn't staying in Zubiri, and he goes.

Two Italians sit nearby and begin chatting in loud voices. I don't want to risk sun-burning my feet. Or is it that the Italians are annoying me? Or are they providing me with an excuse to go? I leave and sit in a cool side-street, at a table where I have a beer and watch pilgrims arrive. By doing so, I have crossed the Bridge of Rabies three times.

When I return to the dorm there are two other pilgrims, a French-speaking man and his Oriental wife. She is complaining; he is consoling. I go through my rucksack, disposing of a wooden box, the electric gizmo for sanding feet, a pencil case, and another t-shirt I'd forgotten I'd packed. I find a lot of sweets that I'd taken from a huge bag in the dining room in Saint Jean. I put them by the table just inside the door with a note: *Para Todos*. Then I go for a walk.

Zubiri feels like a sleeper town for some bigger place. There are tidy streets and a closed tourist office with no windows and a metal door that looks so unappealing I don't go in, vowing to get a postcard at the next place. Which will be Pamplona. Pamplona; so that it the bigger place. I have an expensive sandwich in the *polidesportivo* as a cycling team lounge and drink beer. I wander back along the one long street that seems to be the town and someone shouts at me from a bar. It's the Dubs.

They invite me to join them for beer and pizza, for which they will accept no money, but tell me to pay it on. They have strange tales to tell, including how one of them had his heart stopped by paramedics during a resuscitation effort. He had died and been returned to life on three separate occasions. Having eaten nothing all day bar the expensive sandwich, which was just hard bread and dry cured ham, and with the waiter plying the table with free shots of *Patxaran*, the local brandy, together with all the beer and good cheer, I wind up showing off my tattoos, kissing one of the Dublin girls, and going to sleep in the Municipal with Korean graffiti on my arms.

DAY FOUR

I wake up at 6am with a clear head despite the previous night. I get my act together and set out under the stars. I plan a silent voyage beneath the vastnesses of deep space, but this ambition is soon thwarted. Just outside town a magnite mine is in full swing; diggers, heavy machinery, and bright arc lights roar and blaze. The excavations in this place are so profound that they pierce the water table. The water is pumped up to the surface and supplies the town. This is the water that I've filled my flask with.

The dark path is cleared for a few meters ahead of me by my headlamp, but there comes a point when the sun becomes stronger and I can see the road ahead curving up the slopes of the hills. Three Italian women are chatting and walking up ahead, and beyond them another group whose distant conversation sounds Korean.

But I walk alone, and this morning my own company is worse than any other company I could have. Innocuous things from the past, miniscule errors, minor miscalculations, and petty concerns that seem to have fossilized in my memory now spend the early morning gnawing me from the inside out. Even the camaraderie of the previous night now feels like an embarrassing disgrace.

Everything begins to annoy me: the winding, dipping, white gravel path, other pilgrims, a one-minute wrong-turning in the hamlet of Esquiroz, the fact that Basque is widely spoken but I don't even know how to say 'hello' in it – and I keep seeing signs reading 'This Isn't Spain!' – and lots of slogans in Basque that I cannot understand, and the pain in my leg which has returned and keeps snipping at my hip with each step.

If the gibbering of my simian mind forces my pace, the pain in my hip forces me to slow down. Slower, and then calmer as I wander along by a deep, clear river, watching a trout drifting downstream and my morbid self-reproach is lifting when Eoin arrives. He is also from Northern Ireland and is hiking whilst off work for a week and of whom I have a dim memory from the night before. He is in high spirits, laughing about the previous evening, and we chat all the way to the next cafe where we meet another pilgrim, Dot from Bavaria, who had started early owing to insomnia.

Eoin walks on. Then I walk on. And as soon as I'm in my own company again, the heckling thoughts return and they thicken and harden as the countryside gives way to the urban world. The long, white gravel path that I have dogged since Zubiri vanishes, and great concrete canyons spring up around me.

In the suburbs of Pamplona the wooden fences that were used for running bulls are still up and the air is still stinking from the smell of the animals. The pain in my leg is now so bad that each step is painful. I keep having to rest, and at one point I'm sitting on a bench by an ornate *fuente* shaped like a fish when an old man stops to speak to me and tells me he'd met his wife on the Camino. Eoin, who had somehow fallen behind me, passes me by and reminds me that the group from last night have arranged to meet at a quarter to seven outside Pamplona cathedral. I'd forgotten. It had been my idea.

Halting and starting, stalling and smarting, I continue. At the Magdalena Bridge I see Jim again, who is jotting something in a diary. I remove my rucksack before sitting on the edge of the bridge, remarking that it would be a fine thing if I toppled backwards off the bridge with it strapped to my back. It would indeed be quite the lark. What Jim and I discuss is now lost to history, but I leave to check in at a nearby hostel. The stamp for this hostel is in the adjacent church, and I have stamped my *Credencial* before realising the place won't be admitting pilgrims for another four hours. So I move on.

Again, there are no such things as mistakes, but were this hostel open the rest of this story would be different.

*

I reach the old city of Pamplona. For the past few days I have inhabited a world where people exchange cheerful greetings, talk with strangers, and are happy to see one another. Now, no-one smiles and waves when they see you, let alone introduces themselves. The city is rude, indifferent, lacking in curiosity about the humanity that courses through its streets. This is also the Camino.

I cross a bridge and arrive before the old walls of Pamplona's old town. Entry is via the French Gate, complete with drawbridge. I make my way to the hostel, a converted church, directed there by an Italian pilgrim who had slept in the bunk below me in Roncesvalles – that day's Pilgrim Number One. I book in and meet a Canadian mother and daughter, the Koreans from the night before – and to whom I display my Korean graffiti, and a couple from the Canaries whom I'd seen a few times earlier and who'd asked after my health on the way here.

Earlier in the day I'd seen them in the church where I stamped my *Credencial*. They had bothered me. Why? Later they had stood right beside me on a hill path, chatting to another pilgrim, as I was trying to take five minutes and connect with the day. That had annoyed me too. Why? This had been just after I passed a man selling oranges from a shoebox in the forest. I bought nothing from him. Why?

Sitting now on my bunk in Pamplona, listening to them talk with the Canadians, I realise that everyone is nice. And being in the mood I'm in I think: You think everyone is bad and then you get to know them and you realise they're good – because you think you're good until you get to know yourself and realise you're bad. I should be thinking this in a black polo-neck, holding a skull and staring up at the spotlight.

So much for that.

I shower and write up a few notes in my journal as I wait for the washing machine to finish. There are no chairs and I write standing up. I might as well. This town is linked to Ernest Hemingway and he wrote standing up.

*

The machine doesn't wring out my clothes and so I leave them hanging in the courtyard, positioned to catch the last rays of the sun that make it over the rooftops. In the event I abandon the towel, buying a new one from the Camino Shop. This new towel is made from some type of space-aged velour, very light, and which folds up to the size of my fist. I also dump my *Credencial* holster, which has begun falling to pieces. I buy a new one from the same shop. It's blue with a yellow arrow and serves as a foretaste of the souvenir industry that is fed by pilgrims. The yellow arrow – *la flecha amarilla* – is a symbol painted along the entirety of the Camino so as to stop pilgrims losing their way. The yellow arrow also graces a cloth wristband I buy while I'm in there. An impulse buy. Along with an Irish tricolour I buy to tie onto my bag, despite having no real affinity for it. I've always thought a better Irish flag would be a golden harp on a blue background. All people of sound mind agree.

At a quarter to seven I arrive at the cathedral and meet the Dubs. I have a millisecond of embarrassment saying hello again to the girl I kissed, but we are soon in an Italian restaurant and in our cups. Everyone who was in Zubiri, and Jim who was not, convene and I find that rather than disdain for me, which I'm sure everyone would have, they tell me that I was funny the night before. Lena says she hadn't laughed so much in a long time. Tears, she tells me, had run down her face. For some reason I feel grateful to them all, as though they have forgiven me for something.

We get together for a group photo. This is the last evening this group will be together. The Dubs are going to Bilbao tomorrow. I've only known them a few days and I'm sad to say goodbye to them.

DAY FIVE

Cafe Iruña is empty. I sit at a corner table and look at the ornate pillars and gleaming tiles. So, this is where Hemingway came for his hot chocolate. It's a quarter to nine and people are busy criss-crossing the square outside.

I sit and dwell on the thoughts that had swilled around my head yesterday. I feel that they robbed me of my day as they had discoloured the experience of walking the Camino. I regret them too because they had made me refuse myself the experience of going off the track up to a church run by nuns where Joseph, not Mary, cradled the infant Jesus, and you could ring the bell for world peace, or whatever secret prayer you might be carrying.

I think that I am inhabited by a disapproving attitude, a version of me that makes me feel guilty about enjoying myself, or having fun, or just being who I am. I am guilty about being myself, which might be no different for feeling guilty for being at all. I wonder why, and I wonder what can be done about this. I might have the hint of a problem, but no solutions present themselves.

Another thought comes to mind. All my other 'holidays' have been solitary. I went to places and saw things, but didn't interact a lot. Small conversations here are there are memorable because they are rare. On this trip, the human factor seems paramount. For a very long time, for as far back as I can remember, I have willed myself to believe that people don't matter, or that they are bad news, or that they are unlikeable. There: another problem hinted at, but again no solution is evident.

I feel guilty for being myself, and I feel that people are not on my side. I can only wonder why.

*

I go for a stroll around the city. In a shop window there is a girl's pink schoolbag with the motto – in English – "Be Free, Be You", and I fancy the notion that this is the Camino speaking to me. I make my way up to the battlements at Rincon Caballo Blanco and just sit there, which I would once have called 'doing nothing', but it's impossible to do nothing.

The Dubs are due to leave at noon, but I don't want to say goodbye (which is an abbreviation of 'God be with you') to them, so I ask at their hostel if I can leave a message, and I can, so I do. Then I hike out of town, following pilgrims up ahead, being followed by pilgrims far behind. I'm following pilgrims who have already arrived in Santiago; I am being followed by pilgrims who are just setting out from Saint Jean.

The sprawling busy city peters out and the sunburnt fields take over beyond the university. I cross a motorway flyover, pausing to watch the traffic racing below the dawdling pilgrims: the fast modern road and the slow ancient path. Same planet, different worlds. Ahead of me, on the crest of a hill, is a castle as described by a child. It is a block with battlements and a squared turret from which flies a flag with a cross on it. I am about to enter Cizur Menor.

After a steep hike, I walk into the town and am greeted by a fast-talking man who understands my pidgin Spanish as much as I understand his speedy Castillano. We understand enough though, nodding and smiling, and we wish each other well. I wander through town and find myself in a little park across from an ancient covered well. Trees shade the benches and I sit down. My leg has been hurting almost since I began. It could be injured, an injury I could have caused during my first hour of the Camino when I'd not gone to the mass, but hiked the wrong way towards Saint Michel and then up that fiendish gradient. I remind myself that this isn't a race, that I have given up a job and an apartment to do this, and that it would be damn fine thing if I had to go back limping after a week, scrounging around for my job back like the village idiot. *Please, Sir, I want some more...*

This awful vision plays on my mind as I sit on the shady bench sipping water and giving my legs a rest when I hear the sounds of tapping coming down the empty road. It's June and Lena, both decked out in hiking gear and clattering forwards with the aid of their hiking poles. They smile and wave and stop beside me. June begins doing yoga. They are wearing whelk-shell party blowers around their necks.

"They gave them to us", says Lena, "so that if we get lost we can find one another".

"We're to look out for one another", adds June. She had taught them laughing yoga in Orisson and she has a picture on her phone to prove it. It's a ring of faces, arranged like petals on a flower, each one grinning.

June and Lena move on, their hiking poles clacking off the pavement as they turn a corner. I stay a while longer watching he sunlight in the leaves above my head. When I leave Cizur Menor, I am following two butterflies dog-fighting above a hot, white, dusty farm track when I hear voices; it's Jim and Eric, the Norwegian photographer. We form a very loose group, as we arrive in Zizur Maior one after the other and make a bee-line to the cafe. June and Lena are already there, sitting at a table outside, their boots off, wiggling their toes. We have coffee and cake, and we have our photo taken by a waiter who asks us to say "chess!" as he holds the camera at arm's length and winces as he looks at the image on the screen.

We walk on, but everyone walks at their own pace, and at the ruins of what we pronounce as 'Gwendolyn Castle' we split up. Eric vanishes up the road and Jim stays behind. June, Lena, and I walk on, strung out along the road. I stop for a rest by a graveyard, looking back upon Pamplona and beyond it the mountains. I feel as though I have just crossed a continent.

I walk into Zirikiki where I sit next to an old man and strain to understand that that there are two hostels in town and both are good. I am tempted to walk a little way uphill to the first hostel I see, but I've had enough of uphill for today and so I venture on to the next hostel, where I find June and Lena, and where Jim passes us by. Friendly, tall, bookish, with a twitching nose, he is continuing on his mission to reach Portugal. I never see him again. It's a curious feature of the Camino that friendships that last mere days feel developed and lacking in rancour when final goodbyes are said.

Jim goes. Sandy arrives. She is also American, in her late sixties, and travelling alone. She joins Lena and I in a conversation about James Joyce's *Ulysses* and the 'Wandering Rocks' chapter, a conversation brought on by my saying that the Dublin class system was so hermetic that I'd never have met the Dubs had we all been in Dublin. Sandy is also staying here.

The conversation drifts onto how much unnecessary stuff we have brought with us. Sandy says that she had the same problem but got rid of a lot of stuff thanks to a pilgrim she had befriended. This pilgrim got her to lay out her kit on the bed and say "I am bringing you because I am worried about..." In this way she turned each thing into something attached to worry, and then the friend asked her if the worries were justified. Most of them weren't, and so Sandy continued with a much reduced load. June agrees with the spirit of this. She has read in a book, she says, a system whereby you hold each object and ask it if it gives you joy. If there is no joy, out it goes.

We four have dinner, the pilgrim meal, and after we take to reading or writing under a poem that is painted on the wall. It is in Spanish and I translate it for the others. June is pleased with it as it is an Irish poem, the one that begins:

Go n-éirí an bóthar leat

Which is translated as:

May the road rise to meet you

Or:

Buen Camino

At a neighbouring table, two Austrian pilgrims finish up and give us their wine. Relaxed, I go for a stroll at twilight. Earlier, Pamplona had been a thin sheet of concrete far in the distance, and I could reflect on how far I'd come. The mountains pushed up into the sky behind the city. This is what I have done. I remember being struck by the vast and epic nature of my achievement; but now Pamplona is lit up and it looks closer, almost to the foot of this hill.

Allotments reek from mounds of horse manure heaped there. The smell fills the air as I stand by the crash barrier at a bend in the road and photograph the crescent moon. It hangs over the hills to the west, where the future will be played out.

DAY SIX

Coffee for breakfast. I've been having coffee for breakfast for months now, but this isn't vending machine coffee from a newsagent's on the way into work; this is a coffee taken outside the hostel while watching the sunlight change the walls of the church from grey to yellow. The thought of this change in circumstances adds a great deal of satisfaction to a squat glass of milky coffee.

The road from Zirikiki drifts upwards, passing a dried well at which a pilgrim was tempted by the devil, according to local legend. The thirsty traveller kept the faith, though, and was rewarded with an apparition of Santiago himself who gave him a drink of water from a scallop shell. Today there is no ghostly saint to reward pilgrims with water. There may be no pilgrims either, as everyone on the path seems to be on some sort of high-energy sports trek.

There is refreshment though, for spirit and body, once the summit of the hill is reached. This is the *Alto de Perdón*, Forgiveness Peak, across which a procession of metal pilgrims are frozen in motion. A brief poem announces that this is the place where the way of the stars crosses that of the wind. There is a mobile cafe up here, *La Konxa*, The Shell, and I collect a stamp in my *Credencial* – a scallop, and a field of red stars.

Stopping here allows the Koreans to catch up. They want a selfie taken with me, which they do using some fancy Bluetooth apparatus. I may never see them again either, but they promise to write on my arm if I do. Then off they go, springing down the other side of the hill, travelling faster than I think is necessary to get to where they are going to.

La Konxa serves food that is made on the spot. It is fresh and filling and is good to eat looking back over the expanse of land that I have crossed. Lena arrives, telling me that "June is on her way". She and Sandy arrive together and take photos of the vista before buying something.

We eat together, greeting passersby, and when we decide to move on Sandy stays behind because she likes the view. We come down to the village of Uterga where we stop for another coffee, operating on the theory that the Camino should not be seen as long hikes between hostels but short strolls between cafes. This idea comes as a response to easing the pain in my leg, and it transforms the journey from some sort of endurance test into a rolling break time with a shifting cast.

At Uterga, we are sitting at a cafe when a bus party pulls up and disgorges a throng of Chinese tourists. They are decked out in trendy hiking gear, and are being guided by a man who claps his hands and asks rhetorical questions such as "everybody ready?" One of them isn't sure if he is ready and asks the guide if his bag his high enough. "Sure", says the guide, "you look great".

We watch them go. Lena begins to describe a book she has read in which the life of a woman is divided into three stages: The one to whom gifts are given; The one who gives gifts to others; and The one who has everything taken from her. These stages are meant to correspond with youth, middle age, and old age. The young woman receives attention, praise, actual gifts, and then children. The middle aged woman gives to her children. She gives them life in her womb, her breast milk, she cooks for them, gives them attention, time, patience, thought. Then the woman is old, her looks are taken from her, as is her fertility, her necessity as a provider, and she is left feeling without purpose.

I find this synopsis of a life to be rather harsh, and console myself with tales of dynamic elders who perform mighty feats well into their twilight years. Just look at Jacques Costeau. We are joined at our table by Barnabas and Pierre, the former American and the latter French. Barnabas tells me he has 'some Irish blood', and I am caught between asking him where he keeps it and reminding myself that nobody likes a smartarse. He is soft-spoken and I wonder, but don't ask, if despite his *Crocodile Dundee* hat he might belong to a religious order. Pierre is carrying a guitar with him. It must have been him in the hostel in Pamplona fingering his way up and down the scales and making me wonder, in my pain-angry mood, if he knew any other tunes. Both of them have that same pilgrim attitude of not having any real reason for being here. It's Pierre's fail-safe that, should he run out of money, he will pay his way by busking.

Hello. Goodbye. The kaleidoscope of meetings and farewells continues as June, Lena, and I sally forth and decide at the next town to detour to visit an esoteric church. This is the church of Our Lady of Eunete and is a strange octagonal construction, reputed to have been built by the Knights Templar. It is arrived at via agricultural access roads that run through fields of red peppers. Many of these have fallen free of their vines and lie parched and withering on the ground. There is one man in the far distance picking the peppers. I wonder if he also picks the peppers that have fallen to shrivel on the dry earth. Does he pick the pickled peppers? And if so, in what quantities? By the handful? By the armful? Or just a peck. Does he pick a peck of pickled peppers? I watch him at work and wonder what his name could be.

The roadside verges are dotted with hundreds of tiny white snails, and I cannot fathom why they are there in such numbers in the direct heat of the sun. Nor can I figure out why there are so many flies around Eunete. Nor why the group of Italians who are there when we arrive won't keep their voices down. Between the Italians and the flies I forgive the flies for not knowing any better, but I feel the sudden need to get away from the place as interesting as it is. I walk on alone to the village of Óbanos.

*

I walk into Óbanos, pushing myself up a slope so steep is was probably designed to repel invaders, and look for a hostel. Mission accomplished, I call in but there is no-one at the desk and so I sit across the street, on a bench outside the pensioners' social club and wait for someone to turn up. In time a man appears, carrying a box and vanishing inside. He can't be a pilgrim, and I go in. He appears from a side door in the foyer and greets me. We begin a conversation in Spanish, and he tells me that he had walked the Camino a long time ago. When he had finished it, he felt compelled to spend the rest of his life on the Camino and so went looking for a job. It took him a year and a half of searching before he found this job. He is lucky, he says, as he is from Pamplona and so didn't have to move far away from home. He had been a teacher. So had I, I tell him.

What do you do now?

This, I say. I walk the Camino. I was a teacher once, but then I was in administration until the day I flew to Biarritz.

The Camino will change you, he says. It will change your life.

June and Lena appear at the door. My conversation with the *hospitalero* struggles to continue. We want to talk, but his duty to the others means it has to stop, and I am left wondering about his experience on the Camino and what it did to him.

I roll out my sleep-sheet on my bunk, hand wash some clothes and leave them to drip on the line in the shady garden. There is a massive fig tree and the sound of children playing floats over the high wall. Leaving my washing, I go for a stroll around town. It is a neat place, a tidy place, and I see pilgrims passing through it, coming in from the main route as opposed to the route from Eunate. There are notice boards recounting the tale of a murder and the act of pilgrimage as atonement, and I think about how secular the Camino feels. Despite the *hospitelero*'s promises (or warnings) that the Camino will change my life, I don't see the Camino as a life-changing experience and don't see why it should be. So far I have meet a good number of people who are here to sort out their lives, or to take time out, or to find out what they want to do with their lives. There have been people who see it as a trekking challenge: Can YOU cross Spain in a month? And there have been those who just want to party on the cheap. The Camino is a novelty. It's a luxury. It's a lark. But I have yet to meet the person who is walking the Camino to get closer to the divinity in things.

I catch myself thinking this. Why am I thinking this? Haven't I settled this once and for all? There is no God. So why am I here? Why not pack in my job and just do something else? And why am I sitting in this clean, quiet town in Navarra thinking about *the divinity in things*?

*

Later, Sandy, June, Lena, and I sit down to a pilgrim meal that is straight out of a can. The others are glued to the internet on their mobile phones, coming to life to announce some utterance of Donald Trump, and the restaurant has a camcorder film of a boar hunt with dogs playing on the television in the corner. A few locals are watching the boar turning one way then the other to confront the snapping hounds, but its obvious distress fails to move them. I change seats so my back is to the television. The speakers are piping out pop music at a disagreeable volume. Even at a whisper it would still be pop music, and I feel that listening to pop music is akin to having a clown shit in your ear.

DAY SEVEN

It seems I'm not the only one who feels that last night was a downer. After the pilgrim meal, we had gone to the pensioners' social club for cheap coffee and it was there that Lena decided that we should rise early in the morning and walk to Puente la Reina under the stars to see the sunrise at the famous bridge. June and I agree. Sandy wants to rest, and won't be joining us.

So it is: tip-toeing with all our kit out into the foyer to pack up and go. I have my miner's headlamp and I lead the way. We make a point of stopping every so often to look up at the starry night sky. We stand transfixed by countless spear-points of fossil light. We pick our way along a path that runs between allotments filled with big cabbages, meeting a golden toad on the way which clambers out of my spotlight and into the grass verge. It gleams like lacquered brass, but the magic of life is within it. We walk on and emerge from among the toads and cabbages into Puente la Reina, facing a wall of graffiti that tells us that this is a Feminist Zone.

We see a few familiar pilgrims leaving hostels as we pass through the town, and see a few more as we park ourselves in a cafe for breakfast of hot coffee and buns. We leave as night is moving ahead of us into the west and dawn is following us from the east, arriving at the bridge as the sun is blushing the air above the town. It is a pleasure just to look at it. It is at this point that pilgrims from France and those who have walked through north-eastern Spain – Aragón, Cataluña, maybe Valencia – join together to continue their journey westwards. The bridge has a tower under which we pass in order to cross. There used to be another tower, housing a statue of the Virgin, but it was demolished during a war.

The reason for this demolition was that the statue had become the subject of a local myth. A small bird, a *txori*, had taken to dusting the statue and washing it with water collected from the river. As such, both the statue and the bird became much loved by the locals, the arrival of the bird each year being greeted with a fanfare. During a war between the Carlist monarchists and the parliamentarians in Madrid, the town was captured and an effort was made to demoralise the locals by shelling the bridge. It didn't work and when the Carlists retook the city, the captain responsible for the shelling was executed. Punishment, thought the locals, for waging war on the *txori* and its beloved statue. Years later, when Madrid returned in force and secured authority over the town, the tower containing the statue was demolished to show who was boss, but not before the statue was escorted in a procession to its new home in a nearby church.

This morning we watch the river fill with the dawn colours of tangerine, sherbet, and flamingo pink. When we move on it is by island hopping from cafe to cafe, hamlet to hamlet. In one we speak with a pilgrim who began walking from Belgium. In another we meet a pilgrim from South Africa who operated on another pilgrim's blisters by injecting the sole of the foot with anaesthetic and then draining them. We pass a number of elderly Italians who finish saying the Rosary and then burst into song, singing 'O Sole Mio' as the pure morning sun beams down on us all. At a roadside cafe we arrive just in time to see a tall, bearded man holding his palms up as though praying to the others sitting at the tables before he turns and strides away. We ask who he was and are told he has taken a vow of silence.

Well, well; Rosaries and silent monks. Perhaps there are pilgrims on the Camino after all.

*

In one town I stop to examine my right little toe, which feels sore, and see a large blister on it. I tell the other two that I'll catch up but have to bandage it, which I do and then have a coffee in a cafe. This town, Zirauki, reminds me of a Pueblo Blanco, the mountain towns of the south, in that its streets are narrow and steep and winding, although they are not white. When I get going, to my surprise the others are only a few minutes away and they tell me they were lost. Beyond this town someone has created a map of the world in plants on the side of a hill. There is a Roman bridge that we cross, as people have crossed it for two thousand years, and then a motorway flyover bridge that reminds me of the busy life I have left. In Lorca we meet Dot again. She has a bad cough and is upset because she was insulted by a pilgrim in her hostel who accused her of putting other peoples' health at risk. I feel sorry for her on both counts, but especially the latter as it feels out of place on what is supposed to be a pilgrimage.

La Casa Mágica – The Magic House: my berth for the night. It can be described as the hippy side of Catholicism; welcoming, with a meditation room (with a Buddha on the door), and a massage service. I ask about blisters, and the *hospitalero* shows me to the courtyard where I'm told to fill a basin with water, add salt and vinegar, and steep my feet in it for twenty minutes. I do this. June does this. I buy a bottle of wine and we share it. Then June goes for a massage, and I dry my feet and finish the wine with Lena.

It is as we are talking that the silent monk joins us. He asks us questions by typing them out on his phone. When I tell him I'm from Northern Ireland he tells me he was friends with Gerry Anderson, the late Derry DJ and television personality, and it never occurs to me to ask how he knew him. His questions are about our lives and range from something you would expect from someone trying out a few words in a foreign language ('do you have any brothers or sisters?') to more interesting stuff ('who is missing you?'), to the one everyone asks: Why are you doing the Camino?

His questions don't bother me one bit. If he said the words rather than wrote them I might have found them intrusive. But the novelty of this silent inquisition allows Lena and I to offer more information about our lives to him than we have to one another over the last few days walking. I ask him why he isn't speaking, and in response he mimes drawing a long line from his mouth and then falling asleep.

A long story? He nods and smiles.

He joins us, plus June, for dinner and we find that he has just become a grandfather and that he is writing a blog to his grand-daughter. Not a monk, then. He spent the night in a shepherd's hut on the mountain before Roncesvalles but was kept awake by the cattle-bells. He mimes a long-eared goat and a swinging bell on a collar much to our amusement.

*

My Spanish is better than I think – I am asked to mediate between a Norwegian couple and the *hospitalero*. The Norwegian is called Leif and he is travelling with his ex-wife with whom he gets on so well that they might as well not be divorced. He does not, however, get on with bed bugs. He has a series of bite-marks on his arm where he fell prey to the infamous bloodsuckers and is worried that they have hitched a ride in his rucksack. He is nervous that the *hospitalero* will kick them out. Never fear, their clothes, including rucksacks, are laundered to kill the bugs. In the interim they have to wear clothes discarded by bygone pilgrims; they sit down to dine in Bermuda shorts and baggy t-shirts, which should make them look a state but they blend in perfectly with the rest of us.

If I ended yesterday in a slump, I end this day on a high note. Perhaps it is the endless novelty of the people I've encountered, or the fact that I could be helpful to a person who needed help, or the fact that I was seeing differently. 'Seek and ye shall find', indeed: you will find what you are looking for. I take this to mean if you want to see people as nuisances, that's exactly what you will see. If you want to see people as interesting or fun, well, you'll see that instead. 'Seek and ye shall find': The world is the mirror of the mind. An ugly mind sees ugliness. A beautiful mind sees beauty.

Which would you rather have? Which would you rather see?

DAY EIGHT

I'm late for breakfast and arrive as Lena, June, and the silent hut-dwelling grandfather – who is Canadian and called Andy, are finishing. So, it's a light bite for me and then I go outside and linger, looking at the strings of glossy red peppers hanging from the neighbour's balcony. Whist I wait for the others, I have a brief spell in which to ponder my good fortune in being able to do something like this.

Lena and June emerge from behind the beaded curtain that keeps flies out of The Magic House. Lena has what she describes as "some crappy news" for me. She has twisted her ankle on the stairs. She will have to walk at a snail's pace. There is no hesitation; June and I agree that we will match her pace. A slow pace has helped my leg, and so this (literally) unfortunate turn will only serve to keep us from racing beyond what our bodies can endure. 'Tis an ill wind...

We leave town and enter a dry, sunbaked land with lots of vines and castles on hilltops. Not being from a wine-producing region, there is a great deal of novelty in seeing grapes on the vine, just as there was in seeing peppers sprouting in such profusion around Eunate. Seeing them is like seeing the silver-green fields of barley near my home in that there is such an overload of life right in front of my eyes. On the way we pass the Norwegians who are very jolly and round, and later Lena tells me of having felt dread at their tale of bed-bugs. She fell prey to these animals in the past, whilst camping, and received over one hundred and fifty bites. I take this to mean one hundred and fifty bed-bugs, but it could have been one blood-crazed individual. She needed medical assistance to recover from the toxic shock of this and this medicine in turn had induced a brief spell of psychosis. This is such an outlandish story that I feel the need to match it with a tale of an explorer I met whilst studying Zoology. This man had been in the depths of some jungle or other and had been infested by what he called 'jiggers'. These were like fleas and one of their number burrowed under one of his toe-nails and made a house a home. She spent her days excreting eggs from under his toenail and eventually became such a pain that it was the lesser of two weevils to prise off his toe-nail with a penknife and winkle out the offending tenant. He had photos and everything. He also had a stammer, which kicked in every time he said "jeh-jeh-jeh-jig-jig-jiggers".

We arrive parasite-free in Estrella, and celebrate by visiting the church.

*

Churches seem to be a divisive topic on the Camino, which perplexes me. It is, after all, a pilgrimage and although no-one is forcing you indoors to pray, their existence is testament to humanity's efforts to describe something beyond their ken. If you disagree with that, I'll tell you that not too long before willingly walking through the doors of the church in Estrella I considered churches to be monuments to ignorance. And not only churches but mosques, synagogues, shrines, and temples. There was not one stone circle, horg, basilica, or airport prayer room that did not escape my steady trickle of high-minded scorn. And yarmulkes, turbans, niqabs, wimples, cassocks, habits, foreign beards, amulets of *Mjöllnir*, hands of Fatima, prayer beads of all descriptions, and cloaks, robes, and kaftans from all four corners of the earth were symbols of one thing: the irrational, and therefore inferior, mind of the human race.

And why not? Look at all those religious people out there who throw acid in faces, commit genocide, torture, execute, bully, abuse, persecute, defame, sow discord, rape, stab, shoot, bomb, betray, and molest. 'Twas bad enough, thought I, that their beliefs are without foundation, but that these same beliefs generate so much misery must surely mean that religion was a Bad Thing and had to go.

And in this way I came to see religion as being part of the insane world I left behind when I walked out onto the Camino over a week ago. I don't see anything divine in religion; so why do I find entering this church such a pleasure? Why do I feel calm having passed through its doors? And why do I feel such a fondness for the statue of *Santiago Pelegrino* with the scallops on the shoulders of his cloak? Perhaps it is because this church is no longer part of that crazy world; it has become a pilgrim's place now, a place into which we travellers go and find a heightened sense of our own purpose. Being here fills me with such a great sense of goodwill towards the world that I am shocked to be told to "get out of the way, will you?" by a cyclist speeding down a steep street on the way out of town.

This was in the concrete, flat-pack suburb between Estrella and Iratxe. It's a Sunday and people are out cycling. There is this yuppie dad in latex and shades, looking like an overweight child, who roars at us to get out of his way. He had to slow down as he approached us. Anger welled in me but then I saw his wife, unsmiling and sullen trundling along behind him, and then two podgy teenage boys cycling so slowly they have to waver and zigzag to prevent themselves from falling over. They are chatting, uninterested in their father's quest for glory. I wonder what it must be like for them all to be cooped up together and, not for the first time in my life, I am grateful for having been spared fatherhood.

It annoys me that he is rude but then I am passing through his world, not he through mine – but actually he is passing through my world. This too is the Camino. In fact, the Camino was here before this suburb. And pilgrims were walking here before fat dads ever took to Sunday cycling.

*

That is the Camino. So is this: Iratxe. This is the much-admired wine fountain that I had bought the shell for. The fountain is one of two taps set into a shining metal plate in the wall. One tap is for water and one for wine. We get there as a woman and her dog appear. She fills her water bottle but tells us that it is treated and therefore has a bad taste. True, I have seen *fuentes* that displayed signs saying that their water was not treated, and wonder how that can be legal; but there are no such qualms in Iratxe. As it happens, the wine tastes like treated water too, but then they are hardly likely to dispense the good stuff for free.

We fill our shells and drink, and as I do so the thought flickers across my mind that this is some sort of daft advertising gimmick that I am buying into. My misgivings are exacerbated when a bus load of tourists on a family day out show up and crowd around the taps. They do no-one any harm whatsoever, but I stand apart from them, disliking crowds, disliking tourism, disliking the aftermath of the rude cyclist.

We look into the wine museum. I see the guestbook, and always curious to the thoughts of others, I flip through it. The handwriting is invariably childish and staggering, as might have been its authors after having imbibed a bit too much in the local winery.

*

We are walking along a bone dry lane when June says that she needs to rest, but I know she is lying. She is upset. She hides it well, but neither I nor Lena are stupid and we understand if she wants to be alone for a while. There is little we can say to her except that we will be a little way ahead. Both she and Lena blow a few comedy toots on their whelk-shells to demonstrate that they will never be out of ear-shot. June goes to sit by a little white building that looks like a generator shed, and as Lena and I pass by, I see a man and a woman sitting on the other side of it.

"Buen Camino" says I.

"Buen Camino" says they.

Lena and I walk along a path that skirts the edges of vast dusty fields, following directions given by yellow arrows on bollards, some of which are topped with little cairns of rocks and dried flowers.

Ahead of us we see a castle on a high hill and we sit and ponder its nature at a cafe that has a sign forbidding entry to bare-footed patrons. And as we are pondering the castle on the mountain, June re-appears. She tells us that she has had her "first religious experience of the Camino". This religious experience involved her waiting a few moments at the little white building until we were out of ear-shot before bursting into tears.

"I wailed" she says as though recounting a funny incident. And although we were out of ear-shot, the man and woman sitting at the other side of the little white building were not. These two went around the block and "told me what I needed to hear". And what June needed to hear was that she should give all her pain and suffering to Jesus Christ. It seems that she has done this because she seems in a good mood and joins us for coffee. The woman she spoke with, she tells us, runs a hostel in the next town.

"That's the Dutch Protestant place" says Lena. "I read about it in your book".

I fish out the Camino guide, and tell the others that it is indeed in the next town, and the guide had awarded it with a heart rather than stars.

We decide to spend the night there.

*

The next town is Villamayor, just below the castle. The hostel is a converted town house facing a playground. There are already a lot of people lounging around outside it and, as we are told by the Dutch *hospitalero*, there are only three places left: a double bed and a single bed in one room. We take it.

They are Christians. Lena says that in Denmark people such as this are said to be 'a bit saved'. It is a curious feature of the Camino that I am so willing to give them a fair hearing, whereas back in the world of 'reality' I think of them as being somewhat half-baked. But are they half-baked? The hostel is cosy, a family-run business managed by a couple who are Born Again, and given the date of this second birthday they are only a few years old. They say they had some sort of vision during the night, the pair of them having the same vision, which encouraged them to move to Spain and open a hostel. It is a seasonal business, they say; it's not a government Municipal, so the lean season makes it too expensive to operate. We are here at the end of this year's run.

They are the embodiment of the Protestant work ethic. As we go upstairs to unpack, the house is filled with the sounds of food being prepared in the kitchen. They slice it, they dice it, they grind it, de-rind it, grate it, shake it, and bake it. And soon the aromas of home-cooked food are drifting up the aged wooden staircase. I have no idea of the history of this house, but surely its current incarnation must rank as a happy one.

The meal is prepared by the couple who run the place, the Dutch *hospitalero* and his family, and some American volunteers. The food is fresh, delicious, plentiful, and the long tables in the dining room are populated by people from all corners of the world: Irish, American, Canadian, Manx, Japanese, English, Australian, Dutch, and German. At the end of the meal the *hospitalero* gives everyone a little book called *Living Water* in their own language. He then chats to us.

It is his table-talk that jars me a little. Coming from Northern Ireland I am perhaps over-sensitive to the subtleties of what newscasters back home call 'inter-faith dialogue'. The *hospitalero*, working in Spain, on a pilgrim route established by Catholics as a way to walk to a Catholic shrine, refers to Catholics as people who believe in anything "a guy in a purple cloak says". This smacks of ignorance, and is a bit below the belt because I feel that it is an insult directed not at a disgraced clergy biding their time on a sinecure, but the people. But I let it pass. I've heard worse, and I understand the difference between taking offence and being insulted.

After the meal we are invited to a 'Jesus meditation'. This takes place in a renovated stable adjacent to the house. One of the Americans who is helping in the place enthuses about the barn conversion because his job back home is doing up old buildings; a job which has a proper title which slips my mind. It is a nice place, with the rough old beams and white-washed clay walls maintained. The room has soft lighting and hippy throws, as well as comfy sofas and bean-bags. There are no displays of religion here bar a print of an old painting showing some people in Renaissance clothing being startled by an angel.

The Jesus meditation involves everyone sitting in a circle, bar me who opts for the sofa, and June who lies down on the floor and falls asleep during it. Soft new-age music plays in the back ground as the Dutch owner reads out passages from the Bible at intervals. He pauses between each passage to allow us to meditate on it to the accompaniment of the music and June's gentle snoring. At the end, he dispenses mint tea and everyone stays silent, sipping their tea and dwelling on what they have just heard. Or else they're just waiting to leave at the right moment. The owner comes and sits beside me and asks me why I am on the Camino. We start to talk and I feel that his questions get increasingly intrusive, as though he is a cut-price shrink. Like a good tabloid journalist, I make my excuses and leave.

DAY NINE

Up. Breakfast. The happy-clappy Christians wish me well by happily clapping me on the back. I wander downhill, and feel torn between the desire to walk on alone and wait for the others. I don't know where this comes from. There has been no argument, no ill-humour; there has been nothing but good humour. Do I need time alone? Do I want to be away from people for a while? I can't give myself a reason for going. I can't give myself a reason for staying.

So I dawdle. I turn to see the early morning light strike the top of the mountain, making the castle glow like hot metal. Vultures ride the thermals, a cloud of them drifting in wide circles around the castle. It is the burial place of kings. A flag flutters from its battlements. Neon pink contrails are scored across the ice blue sky.

I'm still dawdling as June and Lena arrive and we walk together, then Lena and I, then June and I, then I walk alone with the others chatting up ahead. Then repeat. I tell Lena about the time my bank shut down without warning when I was in Killarney viewing an ancient Yew forest. The bank had vanished during Ireland's financial hilarity and I had to return to Dublin on whatever petrol I had left, and arrived with next to nothing in the tank. I tell her this because it was a Danish bank that had pulled the plug and the last Danish person I had spoken to before Lena was the operator at the helpless-desk who said that it was surprising that I hadn't been told, but there was nothing she could do. Prior to her, I remember a Dane in the National Museum on Kildare Street with whom I got talking to about Celtic rituals. I must have known my stuff because she asked me how long I had been working there.

Lena's sore ankle keeps the pace calm and we take time to pause every so often. Below us in the valley, a motorway is dotted with the speeding beads of distant traffic. They seem to rush through the landscape with the frenzied energy of electrons, and not for the first time I wonder at how people in such close proximity as they and I could be interpreting this landscape in such different ways. I think back to when I drove from Málaga to Santander, and my experience of Spain being one of waiting to arrive. On the Camino there is no sense that I am waiting for anything, and my destination in distant Santiago feels irrelevant at such a great remove.

The road is dusty and hot. The backs of my hands are nut brown and tingle to the touch. By the roadside there is a profusion of bright and nameless flowers, and at one point I call the others because there is a hummingbird hawk moth sipping their nectar. The harvest has been brought in and the straw from the wheat fields has been baled and stacked into massive cubes as big as buildings. So vast are they that foul pilgrims have taken to using their secluded dark sides as ersatz latrines, as I discover to my dismay whilst wandering around one to gauge its size. The human remains are rotting in the heat, festooned with ribbons of toilet paper, and I feel sorry for the farm labourers who have to confront this. If there is a pilgrim code the word Respect ought to feature highly in it.

*

There is a pop-up cafe on the way where we meet Lucy, an American pilgrim who is attempting the Camino for the fourth time. She stayed with the Dutch Christians too and I remember her at the dining table telling the *hospitalero* that "it just hasn't done it for" her. Done what? She says she is judgemental, and wants the Camino to somehow magic that away. I wonder if the Camino is about getting in touch with the sacred, the divine, the holy – or is it about self-help? I have met so many people who have brought their issues with them, hoping the Camino will make things better. I wonder what they expect to be like once this miracle occurs. Do they expect to return to the world as star-children, saints, Buddhas? Lucy, it seems, is not the only judgemental one.

Judge and you will be judged: Say what you think, and people know what you're like.

I wonder how the others judge me. They never remark on this, other than Lena telling me that before Pamplona she thought I "had a darkness".

Don't we all?

*

After a series of towns and hamlets, Los Arcos feels like a city. It has a town square with a cathedral, souvenir shops, bakeries, cafes, bars, and lots of pilgrims taking a rest in the company of lots of motorcyclists. There is a motocross rally on tomorrow and the competitors are sitting around and boozing like good bikers.

Our hostel is near the cathedral and the *hospitalera* helps us with everything from our laundry to double-checking for bed-bugs. Lena, whose blood feud with these creatures means that she checks the bunks with a torch before getting into them, finds some bed-bug corpses. The *hospitalera* shows us the council certificate to show that the place was recently fumigated, but she runs an aerosol of pesticide around the bunks anyway and gives us another room. This room is free of bed-bugs living or dead, and sleeping bags and sleep-sheets are duly unfurled. Lucy arrives and is ushered into our dorm. Hearing of the bed-bugs she sprays her mattress with lavender oil saying that it repels them. The other people in the dorm resemble the Super Mario Brothers, and the lavender oil must send them to sleep as they are soon snoring like hippos.

I go for a walk and visit the Cathedral. Few people are in the pews. The centrepiece of the retable is called 'The Black Madonna', but since the candle-soot was cleaned off her face she appears sallow and not black at all. Her features are striking: Asiatic and with the faintest trace of a smile she sits, cradling the infant, surrounded by the curling, swirling clouds of the retable. Saints are positioned in such a way that the sunlight entering the church passes from one to the other as the day progresses. Clever, clever; but it is only one minor aspect of the whole, and trying to take it all in becomes difficult to do. It strikes me.

How Himalayan it seems. How exotic. And yet this is the religion I was baptised into in a church in north-west Ireland. This cathedral is as populated with images of holy figures as a Hindu temple, and although I can understand Protestant and Muslim cries of 'idolatry!' I cannot see how this is profane, ignoble, or base. The minds that set themselves the task of making this massive devotional artwork were minds coupled to souls that sought to give form to a thing they could not fathom. All the figures on display are images of people of material poverty; men broken by life only to be raised up again, crazy-holy saints who discern the divine light in things, and women of nobility and standing, powerful beyond earthly power.

How different are these holy men from those figures adorning the walls of art galleries, figures of the rich and powerful modelled on those now reduced to dust. And how different are these holy women from those images of the servile and pliant created by men for men, the macho buying-power of the Renaissance, the ancestor of pornography.

The Black Madonna smiles. The Mother of God. If mothers nurture and care, she nurtures and cares for God.

*

Outside the church, and having failed to find an open restaurant, we convene in the plaza. We consists of myself, June and Lena, Leif and Olga - the Norwegians I helped rescue from bed-bug worries, an Australian from our hostel called Kay, Andy, and an American student, Crystal, who is travelling the Camino prior to returning to her studies. All around us are equally crowded tables of pilgrims and bikers, all yammering for beer and pizza, and more wine, and this, and that, and another one of these, and two more of those, and not a 'please' or 'thank you' among them for the one waitress who has to deal with this. It can't be fun for her, and even though it takes her over an hour to make it to our table, I remind myself again and again and again that she is busy and I am not, she is working whilst I am not; she has a lot on her plate and I do not.

DAY TEN
Breakfast is shared with a large group of Mexicans who are travelling with their own coffee. They share it with everyone. It leaves an inch of sediment in the mug. One pilgrim swings his rucksack up onto his

shoulders in a way that Australians called 'Waltzing Matilda'. Kay, who is Australian, says that it is called that because the nick-name for a sheep was a Matilda, and shepherds slung them up onto their shoulders in the same way. You learn something new every day.

I leave the hostel and I shiver in the shadowy daybreak streets. I walk out of town and up a track past fences behind which big, indifferent dogs watch a strange procession of human being pass them by. The track levels out on higher ground, a landscape of olive trees and vines, and here and there I see a *guardaviña*: a little stone igloo like the bee-hive hut of an Irish hermit, in which people used to sit and watch over the vines. There are almond trees too, and by one I meet a pilgrim from Girona who is gathering the windfallen nuts and cracking them open on the road with a rock.

"Desayuno", she beams. A free breakfast. And when she has eaten her fill, she goes on her way, which is my way, and everyone's way, leaving me to continue the good work of cracking open almonds by the side of the road. This is where Andy finds me. We begin to search among the dried grass at the base of the almond tree for more nuts. They remind me of fortune cookies and I crack them open for the others who have arrived on the scene.

It's wrong to say that I never do this at home. I remember one winter going and gathering the sloes from the blackthorn trees at the edge of town and making jam (and gin) with them. But that was the only time. I have a friend who goes foraging in the woods near her home for herbs and forest plants that she uses to make salads for her lunch. I think the very idea of going and eating what is free is an anathema to many people from Ireland; it's as though paying for it makes it edible. It's as though the more you pay, the tastier it is. It's as though free food is the food of the poor, like berries, like fish, like mushrooms – fine if you buy them, but nobody will forgive you for foraging or fishing, because only the poor forage, and in Ireland to be poor is a sin in the eyes of the Golden Calf.

We don't take the almonds from the tree. I think this tree is not part of any crop; it is standing alone by the side of the road, but I am wary of taking what is not mine. I have seen pilgrims venturing into vineyards to take grapes, as though they were planted there to provide them with a snack. It's quite a thought that about a quarter of a million pilgrims walked the *Camino Francés* the previous year. If each one of them took just one bunch of grapes, that's a quarter of a million bunches lost to a swarm of human locusts. I feel that pilgrims ought to live by a code, and Thou Shalt Not Steal should be part of that code. When farmers, rather than unscrupulous pilgrims, want to harvest the grapes they use gigantic harvesting machines. The machines are strange, the way the vehicles at an airport are strange, and while watching them I feel like I'm living in the future.

I am living in my ancestors' future.

We don't eat all the almonds either, nor do we take them with us. I make a mound of them beside the rock and leave a note inviting people to eat the Fresh Almonds From Under The Tree. An actual, paid meal lies in wait for us in San Bol. San Bol and Torres Del Río are two villages living cheek by jowl. As we walk into town we see the bikers of Los Arcos roar by in the distance. We wave and shout.

There is a greengrocer's in San Bol, on a street corner and the plastic patio tables are surrounded by pilgrims munching on sandwiches and oranges. I buy a coffee, collect a stamp, and sit outside. We take to recommending films to one another and some American pilgrims are quite taken by *Goodbye Lenin!* and *O'Horten*, which they hadn't heard of before. That's my good deed done for the day.

*

Down, down to the river and up, up again, up a path so steep it demands attention. This is Torres Del Río, and passing through the town square I am hallooed from a hotel balcony by Lucy, who has had enough for one day and is delighted to have found a large room with good views, which she won't have to share, and broadcasts this from her vantage point. She isn't the only one to stop walking in Torres Del Río: June and Lena want to go on to Viana by bus, to give Lena's sore ankle a rest. Our plans are agreed upon outside the Templar church. This acts a bookend to the Templar church in Eunate. It mirrors its design, and its esoteric structure mimics the temple in Jerusalem after which the Knights Templar took their name. Outside the church we all decide what to do. Leif tells a joke in Norwegian, which is understood by Lena and another Norwegian pilgrim who laughs O-Yo-Yo-Yo. In the event, it is Kay and I who walk on, passing a beer garden in which Leif and Olga are going for a long lunch. I wave 'cheerio' to them; 'cheerio' meaning 'goodbye forever', as I don't see them again.

*

Kay complains about the heat. She complains about how far she has to walk. She complains about how steep the hillsides are that we have to walk up. When she is talking she is complaining, and when she is not talking I feel like I'm carrying two rucksacks instead of one. And every step of the way I have to keep reminding myself not to resent this, not to consider her a nuisance, because everyone is here for a reason, and their reasons are all good whether or not I understand them. And if she detects my irritation, she says nothing about it but has the generosity of spirit to share her lunch with me: fresh grapes bought in San Bol and eaten high on a slope watching a combine harvester work the raster lines of a vineyard. Contrails high above us look like waves on a beach.

At one point we follow the path up into conifer woods where previous pilgrims have left medals, rosaries, and ribbons hanging from the trees. I've seen this before, on the Camino and elsewhere, but not in such quantities, and just beyond them are hundreds of cairns; they cover the ground by the path and caught between them are thousands of messages written on scraps of paper. Many of the messages are for or about people who have died. Earlier there was a cross with a similar cairn of photos and messages. One French message read "Why, Nelly? We Suffer".

Now there are thousands of such messages written in different alphabets, written in different languages, written by people I'll never meet for people I'll never meet. There are thousands, a cemetery of memories to people who were loved, built stone by wayside stone by people who love. It is a monument to love and death, and to the victory of memory over forgetting. The cairns cover the dry blonde grass from the path to the conifers and the sunlight glints off small tokens, personal items, the glossy varnish of photos of people who could not have known that the photo they smiled for would one day be here. I want to stay here and reflect on this. It is not a church or a temple, but it is a sacred site made sacred by the countless pilgrims who have walked through this place adding their sorrow to this small field of stones and prayers.

But Kay keeps asking me if I want to leave a message: "no? You sure? Now's your chance. Positive? Sure you don't want to leave a message?" She means well, and perhaps her voice echoes that of the people who are commemorated here, because people when they are alive can grate, they can annoy through no fault of their own. It is the dead who have been reduced to sentimentality; like domestic pets, affection for them is never spurned, fondness for them is never rejected. It is the living, with their complexities and interior arguments that baffle and vex, because we are living too and we baffle and vex ourselves.

No, I tell her. I don't want to leave a message. I cannot think of what message to leave. Even if I could I wouldn't want to be seen leaving one. Kay has no message to leave either. We continue past the cairns and arrive at a small building on the wall of which is an icon fashioned from painted tiles. This is *Nuesta Señora del Poyo*, which I translate into the incongruous 'Our Lady of the Perch'. The cairns have been laid at her feet like petals. Why? I don't know. I don't want to know. Not knowing preserves the honesty of this place, the silent lamentation of the world, the genuine grief and unplanned creation of this strange memorial. There is something natural about it, like a cloud that has reached its fill and can do nothing else but rain.

*

Leaving this place and walking up to where the track crosses a road I feel something wet slither between my toes. My blister has burst and I take off my boot at a bus stop, ignoring Kay's half-serious joke that we should continue by bus. The blister doesn't look so bad, just loose skin, and Kay gives me a dressing for it. The blister smarts to the touch, but it doesn't ache. We arrive in Viana as a helicopter thumps through the sky. Part of the walk into town is on the highway and we call out when we see a car ahead so we can step as far off the road as we can without landing in the drainage ditch. Kay has prebooked her hostel and we part at its door, making arrangements to meet up later with the others.

I meet June and Lena in the town centre where they are wandering around. We go to the Municipal and check in. The room is a series of metal frame bunks, one of which is parked in front of a plug socket, which looks like a disaster waiting to happen – as well as making the socket unusable. It looks like a prison. We set out our kit and step out into the sunlight.

We are strolling down the street when we see a cafe offering footbaths and 'Jesus Meditation'. It is run by the same group who run the Dutch Christian hostel we stayed in before. The cafe owners are an American couple, who are planning to move to Chile to work on a retreat centre. They are going there for the same reason they came here: God told them to do it.

I sit with my feet in a basin of salt water during the 'Jesus Meditation', listening to a prayer the cafe-owner has created. It is designed as a letter from a parent (i.e. God) to his child (i.e. the listener), and there is nothing too remarkable in that, and it is pleasant enough, except that 'God' signs off by calling himself 'Daddy'. I can't imagine the *Pater Noster* being called The Dear Daddy ("Dear Daddy, up in the sky, I really like your name...").

There is a German pilgrim in the cafe for this, along with an English woman, and we three. Just before it starts Andy arrives and, via a message on his phone, asks if he can join in. Of course he can, says the owner. Andy, as we have discovered, is also 'a bit saved'. He is a pastor and is walking in silence so as to listen rather than preach. He told us this, via his phone, in Los Arcos as we sat out in the plaza. He does not strike me as a religious person, my idea of a clergyman being formed by the invertebrate Irish priests who snivelled and sniffed during school assemblies, or the hooting Bible-thumping bigots that popped up on the local news every evening. Andy is neither, and neither is the couple who run the cafe. Nor were the Dutch Christians, besides the comment about 'a guy in a purple cloak' – although the cafe-owner does make the point of reminding us that Hitler remained a Catholic to his death (so did Saint Francis – what's your point?) In fact the Camino has been populated by people who take their religion seriously – from the Dubs encouraging us to attend mass in Roncesvalles to the unknown hundreds who built the cairns at Our Lady of the Perch – and none of them has been a sanctimonious bore.

*

So much for the footbath. When I remove the dressing I am confronted with the following: The burst blister has taken away a few layers of skin. I think it was caused by cramping owing to the soles of my old boots being worn, causing me to walk with poor form. The top of my toe is as red and raw as a wet kidney bean, and around it there is a foreskin of steamed, blanched skin. It does not hurt, but it looks like it should. Granted, this is not in the same league as Ranulph Fiennes having to saw off his own frostbitten finger having returned from the polar ice-cap (which he did in his garden shed with a band saw), but this is my toe, not his, and therefore cause for concern.

I bandage it, say thank you to the cafe owners, and leave, telling the others I have to go and look for new boots and we agree to meet up for dinner. My expedition is not a long one, all boots being more expensive than solid gold, and so I wander over to the restaurant. The next table is shared by a bunch of students who say that the Camino is "off the bucket-list" now. It's a daft expression, from a daft film, and I can't see the value in haring around hoovering up experiences just for the sake of them. After all, if you really were on your death bed would you really think 'did that, did that, did that' as you scroll down a list of Things To Do; or would you not rather remember that moment when you fell in love, or when it was all OK, or when you were forgiven?

We go for a few beers and meet Wayne, an Australian who says that walking the Camino gives him plenty of opportunity to think about what might have been. It's important to count your blessings, but it's even more important not to chip in like some inane Pollyanna when someone is making sense of the disappointments in their life. I ask him if he knows any good cures for blisters. Andy joins us, and takes a photo of the group. I feel tired and I go back to the Municipal. In my bunk with my ear-plugs in I do not hear Lena and June calling my name from the street. They get back to the Municipal two minutes after ten. The church bells have chimed, the *hospitalera* has closed the door behind her on the way out, entombing the pilgrims with a room-full of stinking boots, and they have been locked out.

Their cries don't wake me, but I dream that I'm hiking up a long flight of steps in double-quick time, with the others struggling to the top and calling my name all the way.

DAY ELEVEN

Morning. Lena and June tell me about being locked out when they are let in again. They had tried finding accommodation elsewhere, all in vain, before running into the two Norwegians who offered them the use of the floor of their room. Not having sleeping bags, they had declined, and eventually they had no other option but to book a room in a hotel for a cool seventy Euros. Bearing in mind a Municipal is between six and ten on the whole, this represents a steep hike in their daily budget.

We go back to their hotel room for croissants. Having spent the last two weeks in dorms and hostels, the relative opulence is staggering. The room seems to be the work of a higher species, particularly when it comes to the bathroom: it glows with light and gleams the gleam of the world of tomorrow. I compare it to the Municipal bathroom: which was sodden and damp, with view from the corridor straight into the showers, and the dreaded n-word doodled on a toilet door. Perhaps my insistence on shunning a more comfortable place to sleep is just as materialistic as accepting one.

We begin our trek out of Viana, past the ruins of a cathedral from which the path to Logroño can be seen stretching away, flat and urban; it is all motorways and feeder roads, and a circular plateau beyond which is the city. We leave Viana down narrow streets, down narrow flights of steps, along narrow pavements. Almost as soon as we begin I start to hobble. June and Lena stay with me when I need to pause and change the dressing. Why they do this, I cannot say. I wonder if they feel compelled to wait, if each is held back by the other, and I wonder why I feel that this should be the case.

The path rises and falls underfoot and as we approach Logroño the first light rain of the Camino begins to fall. We get into our ponchos and anoraks and keep going. During a dry spell, I sit and change my dressing and Lena uses the term 'meatball surgery', which she says was a euphemism for field surgery during the Vietnam War. It's a term I adopt, and I have to stop for meatball surgery a few more times.

The way has been marked by pilgrims who have fashioned arrows on the ground out of stones. At one point they have fashioned an arrow out of twigs and pine cones. We arrive into Logroño along a long straight road, and the city doesn't so much appear as gradually form around us. Murals on the underpasses are devoted to the Camino, and pilgrims have written their names or encouraging slogans on the walls. We stop at a little stall outside a house where there is a stamp which says 'Water, Figs, and Love'. This stamp was created by a lady who used to sit here and welcome pilgrims to the city. Now her daughter continues the practice, but as we arrive she is not there. We stamp our *Credenciales* ourselves and continue down the hill, past vegetable plots, and into the town. Here we remember the vital step of stopping to smell the roses and lavender before calling in at the tourist office for a map. I want to have my boots resoled and need to know the whereabouts of a shoemaker.

*

The Municipal *hospitaleros* are all French. Like all *hospitaleros* they are volunteers, having been inspired to be so by having completed the Camino many moons ago. And like a lot of volunteers, they seem wary of their own jobs and make a big deal out of registering us. We are in a large, clean dorm with some Italians I later see on the patio sharpening small pen-knives and arguing over a town map as though they were going into the jungle for a week and not the local pub for a few hours. They are not the only people in Logroño who think like this; in the local hiking shop there is a massive display of knives that wouldn't be out of place on a Klingon's mantlepiece.

I need to get out of my boots so I find the local Chinese shop and buy a pair of plastic sabots for three Euros. I take an indecent degree of pleasure from putting them on. I meet June and we go to wait for Lena in a pizzeria. When she joins us we go to a tapas bar and take a break from pilgrim meals by trying a few *pinchos*. When I think of all the banal evenings wasted in Dublin, this evening asks me not to waste my time like that again, but to spend my time is a better way.

When I am getting ready to sleep I look at the little book I got at the dinner in the Dutch Christian hostel, *Living Water*. I open it at random and read:

"Get up", Jesus told him, "pick up your bedroll and walk!"

Not bad advice for a pilgrim.

DAY TWELVE

I get up. I pick up my bedroll and walk, all the way to the cafe in the town square. This is a rest day. We stay in Logroño today. There are two reasons for this. Primarily, it is Lena's last day on the Camino. She has had two free weeks before having to return to Copenhagen. Second to this, a break is necessary. I've heard that Logroño boasts one of the most dedicated foot hospitals in Europe owing in part to the swarms of crippled pilgrims arriving with gammy pigeon-feet, shin-splints, and tortured joints. It's a testament to the wisdom of Lena and June that we have got so far with only a blister and a sore ankle between us, and the sore ankle was caused by an accident on a stair-case rather than the wear and tear of life on the road. Our slow pace has also allowed the pain in my hip to disappear.

Others are not so lucky. We meet Crystal again, the American student, and she has tendinitis, as does another pilgrim, Stefan. They are sitting side by side in the cafe with bags of ice on their ankles. My toe looks ugly and it is hurting, so I make it a priority to go and stock up on bandages. I have also made the decision to get new boots, and opt to send my old boots home rather than dump them. I have half a mind to have them resoled, but I know that they will find their way into the shed or kitchen press and stay there – mementoes of all the places I took them to. They are replaced with a pair of brand new boots that I wear off and on throughout the day to break them in. As I wait for the shoe shop to open I buy enough bandages and sticking plasters to reupholster Tutankhamen. I return to the cafe having posted my old boots, and the group of us sit and drink coffee and watch the rain outside falling on the awnings of the pavement tables which are scattered with chestnut burrs from the horse chestnuts in the square.

Then it's time to go back to the Municipal. We think we might not be allowed to stay two nights in a row, but the high season is long gone and there is plenty of room at the inn. We move in again after our five hours in the cafe. I think the barista is glad to see the back of us, but he's done all right out of our tenancy. Our bunks and bags sorted out, we make our way to Decathlon, the big sports retail outlet in the retail park on the edge of town. This is Lena's idea as she wants to buy some gifts for her kids. I have no real interest in buying anything, and feel as though it will be just more stuff to carry anyway. I wander the aisles looking at the shotguns and cartridges; the fishing hooks and rock-climbing gear, before buying a tin cup that might come in handy one day and then sit outside to wait for the others. Several empires rise and fall before they emerge. Back in the city centre I visit the cathedral, having spent all morning looking at it, and sit in a pew where I let my mind wander.

As in Los Arcos, the retable is a feast for the eyes and I allow myself to dissolve ever so slightly into the cool, gilded, gloomy splendour of the place. There is no service in progress and there are only a few people wandering around admiring the statues. There are even a few people praying, but that is not only what churches are for. They are for nothing in particular except as havens from the sound of cash registers and speeding traffic; they are oases of sanity.

There is an element of this day that does not feel like a pilgrimage, or at least my concept of a pilgrimage. It feels more like a strange sort of holiday today, but perhaps that has a lot to do with it being a rest day in the company of others and there is not so much time for introspection. This can be a good thing. It well be that The Way is not a silent path taken whilst mulling over one's life, but encounters with others. I try to remain mindful of this, reflecting on how at Decathlon the thought had crossed my mind that the non-pilgrim shoppers were part of a world that had lost its way. But they weren't; no more so than I was. The aisles of Decathlon are also the Camino.

In the evening we go out to a vegan restaurant. The waitress tells us, smiling and speaking in a calm-confident voice, that the place has been open for only a few months. The food is delicious, especially in a country where vegetables seem to be there to tart up the meat. The fact that so much consideration has gone into the food to ensure no animal was harmed in its manufacture is in keeping with the spirit of a pilgrimage. I pay for the meal: a gift to the other two whose patience needs at least some reward.

Part Two: Wilderness

DAY THIRTEEN

Lena gives her ear-rings to June, and to me she gives her Swiss army knife. I have been borrowing it ever since Viana to cut up bandages for my toe. We have our breakfast in the cafe we squatted in yesterday, but neither she nor we have another day to spend in Logroño. We exchange hugs outside the cafe in front of the cathedral. We exchange email addresses too, we three. Then June and I walk west along the road, and Lena turns east, She is to fly Berlin, where she will spend a few days before going back to Copenhagen.

"It's better than going straight home. It will allow me to adjust".

*

Lena goes. We go. We walk up past the statue of two clean-living pilgrims and out along the path we took when going to Decathlon. Today we keep going, scouring the streets for yellow arrows to guide us away, away, away and then Logroño peels away to either side of us and we walk out into a nature reserve. I am no longer limping, having been rested and with my feet housed in new boots, but I know the dangers of walking too far in new footwear so we agree to stop often. The nature reserve is the perfect place to stop and we are walking to the cafe by the lake when we see a red squirrel. We stop. The squirrel gets closer and closer.

The red squirrel is *Sciuris vulgaris*. *Sciuris* means 'shadow-tail' and *vulgaris* means common. But they are not common in Ireland. The squirrel runs away up a tree as soon as we move, and scales it on the opposite side so we only see it again when it is making its way through the high branches. We go on to the cafe and sit down for another breakfast, and are joined by Myrtle, a grandmother from Australia. Myrtle walks with a walking stick, not hiking poles, but a walking stick and carries her rucksack, which is small and light.

She only carries what she needs every day, she says. I tell Myrtle what Sandy told me about how she had dispensed with a huge amount of stuff by laying everything on her bed and saying to each thing: "I'm carrying you because I'm worried that..." And with each thing she realised that she was just carrying around all these worries, these little gods of worry, worry-fetishes, and so she donated or dumped the majority of them.

Myrtle agrees, and says "the Camino will provide", which I take to mean there is always a shop nearby, or someone to help you out. Myrtle leaves before we do, but we don't see her ahead of us on the path as it follows the lake and rises up into the hills. We pause and look back over the lake, over Logroño, and back to the distant ridge of *Alto de Perdón*. The hills are covered in vineyards and there are compost heaps of vine pulp left over from the harvest. They suffuse the air with the scent of balsamic vinegar.

The path reaches the crest of the hill, overlooking the highway. There is a wire fence running alongside it and through the warp and weave of the metal netting pilgrims have worked twigs in the shape of the cross. There are hundreds of them, made of straw, made of wood, made from thistle stems, rose stems, decorated with dried flowers, with rosehips, with desiccated blackberries, with ribbons, with hair-bands; variations on a theme, as their makers are variations on a theme, as am I, and I use Lena's knife to cut two short stems from a rambling rose and add another cross to the fence. As with the cairns at Our Lady of the Perch I there is something genuine and honest about this; but like the cairns at Our Lady of the Perch, I can't help but notice that this unguarded honesty is expressed in this secret, hidden place; it is as though such a true expression can only be made in wordless silence, away from the ridicule of the world we have made for ourselves.

The path leaves the crest of the hill with its fence of crosses and spends an uncomfortable time on the hard shoulder of the highway. We walk one behind the other and call out when we see a car racing towards us. It is a grim thing to bear in mind that many pilgrims forget that the modern world is superimposed upon the ancient Camino and those who inhabit the world are experiencing something different from those who inhabit the Camino, and thus many pilgrims are killed on the roads. Such a death horrifies me. Not only is it a brutish death, but we are so used to hearing about it that it has become part of the quotidian existence of our lives. Such deaths have been accepted now as though we are accepting the existence of predators that kill people and cannot be stopped. I walk, cagey and paranoid to the sound of traffic, and we cross to where a yellow arrow beckons us having made more sure than certain that for as long as we are crossing we are not sharing the road with a motorist with a half-bored interest in making the present just go away.

Back on track. An earthen path runs through vineyards all the way up to where Navarette rests like a crown on a hill. As we walk into town we see Myrtle having a beer outside a bar. "I keep a brisk pace" she says, and raises her glass. We are the first to arrive in the hostel. The *hospitalera* is French, and works here two weeks in every year before going to Jerusalem to pick olives on the Mount of Olives.

She tells us that she spent eight years living on a boat, sailing around from country to country. "It makes for a more interesting life" she says.

I take care of our laundry, and leave it hanging to dry on a clothes horse by an open window. Then I go for a walk. The streets are hot and bright and silent but for the chatter of housemartins. I visit the church. Again, the great rushing wave of the retable soars up above me and I wonder at a world in which seemingly every town on the Camino has this at its core. At the back of the church there are two maps: one of Europe and one of the world. Pinned to these are hundreds of tiny slips of paper with names on them – these are the names of pilgrims who have come from all these different places. A little basket with blank slips is by the maps. I write our names and pin them in place. The names on the map, reads a sign, are prayed for every week at the Sunday service.

I sit in the church and think about what my friend Agnieszka told me. She met me in The Barge to drink Rebel Red and talk about the woes of job-hunting. At some point during the course of the evening she told me that she hadn't found a job; she had found God instead. It's not something you should ever have to hear in a middle-class pub. I listened to her, thinking 'oh, well – that's the end of that friendship' before finding myself asking questions, before finding myself taking an interest in her answers. We spoke long into the night as the table became crowded with empty promotional tankards and crisp packets folded into origami triangles.

She had become a Christian overnight in what she described as a "revelation", in which suddenly "everything made sense". To her, maybe, but her bright-eyed and happy monologue about how "Jesus is the best" was making its way down my ears and into my brain only to be confronted with a mind that sat there, shifting on its seat, the weak smile of a failed talent show contestant on its face.

Then she said something I could fathom. She spoke of sin not as a kind of crime, but as a kind of obstruction in the way between her and her God. Sin was like the silver backing on a mirror: with it, all that can be seen is the self; without it, it is possible to see further, to see the world, to see others. Sin had been a cliché; something naughty but fundamentally harmless – like sneaking chocolates, or having a crafty glass of sherry, or buying lingerie, or doing any number of pleasant but trivial things. I hadn't thought of it in terms of something that stops you enriching life by keeping you self-absorbed.

So I sit in the church in Navarette and think about my sins: all my Likes and Dislikes, and all my Loves and Hates, and all my Wishes and Regrets, and wondering if who I am were not just a slag-heap of experiences.

I don't know if this is praying. I don't even know what I'm doing here.

*

Dinner is the first pilgrim meal not bought off a menu. There is a kitchen in the hostel and a supermarket at the end of the street. Some of the other pilgrims have the same idea and we sit at one table and share what we have made. There is Richard from England, and Natasha from Russia. Richard is aiming for thirty kilometres a day and says he is worried about already having tendinitis. Natasha speaks in isolated verbs and nouns, but I learn that she is walking the Camino because she likes nature.

DAY FOURTEEN

We leave Navarette just as dawn is breaking and walk the gravel track by the side of the road, looking back from time to time to see the sunrise. Ahead of us there is a pilgrim with a tiny bell on her rucksack and it tinkles in the air. It is the only sound apart from our boots on the gravel. As the day grows stronger, tractors begin to power along the roads, turning off into fields to continue the grape harvest. The landscape is full of vineyards and the tractors to and fro between them. Small white vans ferry gangs of African fruit-pickers to the fields. In Logroño I saw them sitting around outside their hostel in the evening, chatting, biding time until they were collected and brought back out to harvest more grapes.

The grapes themselves are deep blue and glistening and are dumped into big metal containers towed by the tractors. Diggers raise their harvest to the sun and let it fall into the container: they look like robots performing a ritual. The path is red and runs through this landscape of men and machines, and by its edge there are cairns and graffiti left by pilgrims; the artefacts of the Camino culture.

Farmland gives way to the urban liminal. The landscape is not farmland, neither is it the city. It is man-made but uninhabited. The Camino passes through it, crossing over a tiny bridge and beneath a highway underpass. Myrtle is sitting in a park on the outskirts of Nájera with a German pilgrim, Sarah, who has sore feet. Myrtle's brisk pace and light rucksack certainly help her to stay ahead. On the path into town we fill our flasks at a *fuente* at someone's front door. Someone has a sign asking for donations for the upkeep of the *fuente*, and I oblige. Hot air balloons drift over the tree-covered hills. There is Camino poetry on the walls at the edge of town.

Break time is by the river in the clear hot sunshine. Myrtle and Sarah arrive and tell us they are going to spend the rest of the day there. Sarah is pondering whether or not to take the bus to Burgos and rest during those days she would otherwise have spent walking. Richard is there too, despite his tendonitis but he also says he will rest. In ones and twos, pilgrims arrive by the river and take a break. On the bridge there are others who pass by and I think I recognise a couple from Orisson – two German women, a couple, the last of the gang.

Nájera contains the church of Santa María de Real which contains the tombs of Spanish kings and queens. At the back of the church there is a statue of the Virgin Mary, representing a vision that a king had having followed a hawk into the cave around which the church has been built. Visions? Hallucinations? Lies? Delusions? Does it matter? I look over these tombs of people who commanded others, who were feared and respected, and wonder what they would make of the excesses of power in our modern age. For all modernity's protestations of rationalism and democracy, it has fashioned a world of epic cruelty. Our technology has not made us better than these kings and queens with their falcons and visions; it has only made us more effective. We can cure better, and harm better. Millions of us can live in a comfort these kings and queens could never have imagined, but at a cost of millions of us living in a squalor that would also have been beyond their reckoning.

And if I don't like that, well – what am I doing about it? The world assumes its character from the people who live in it, just as a block of iron is what it is because it is composed of iron atoms. For the world to change, its people must change. For it to become better, its people must become better. Iron cannot be ordered to become silver. Iron melted and boiled and refined and poured into a silver mould remains iron. For iron to become silver, the iron atoms have to cease to be iron atoms and start to be silver atoms.

These kings and queens were no different to us. Their world of wars and power were only limited by technology. No matter how nice we think we are, we are the world in microcosm. If we want to change the world, we have to become other people. The point is not to become refined or remoulded; the point is to become different.

*

Leaving the church, with its dead nobles and visions, the two of us emerge back onto the landscape of La Rioja with its vines and trailers heaped with glistening black grapes. Grapes that have spilled onto the ground seem such a decadent waste, and they form little stellar nebulae, glittering and shining in their own juices. We see the cross of Malpica in the distance as we begin the descent into Azofra. The restaurant in town is one of two and seems to be the place where the world and its dog turn up to play bridge, laugh at politicians on the television, and drink at the bar. The place is as full of locals as it is with pilgrims and each questions the other. Having thought that we are the last Irish pilgrims left on the Camino, we meet Danny and Liam who are boozing their way to Santiago. Liam is introduced as the one who slept in a ditch last night, having fallen into it and deciding it would do.

DAY FIFTEEN

The sun rises in strong colours of orange and pink. South American grape-pickers are filling plastic bottles from the *fuente*, taking turns with the pilgrims. The path is silent through a landscape of shadowy vines honeyed with light. This gives way to *dehesa* – a panorama of stubble and small woodlands. The air feels close and the sky is a sheet of white marble. Outside Ciruñela we sit on stone loungers at a picnic spot, tilt our heads back and watch the slow sky sliding by. All vision is this screen of rippled white and all sound is the squirting electrical chatter of small birds.

Ciruñela is a small town on which has been settled a vacant mass of British-style housing. In Ireland, these unoccupied housing estates are called 'ghost estates' and it feels strange and sad to see them here in this ancient land, as though some contagion has erupted from the earth. The only other people are playing golf behind a tree-lined fence. The ghost estate gives the impression of brand new ruins and they are as different from the ruins of a castle as a stillbirth is as different from the bones of an emperor.

Local bars, in an effort to rustle up custom have painted their own yellow arrows to detour pilgrims to their front doors. It feels like a shabby trick but, in a town that nobody wants to move to, 'the Camino provides' (yes, it works both ways). The arrows take us to a bar from which we watch a procession of tiny vintage Fiats of different colours. They come down the hill, past the bar, past the abandoned houses of old Ciruñela, away to the roundabout where they will pass the shunned houses of the ghost estate. One of the cars has a suitcase tied to its roof with a pink ribbon. I have no idea where they are going.

There is a large statue of a pilgrim on the roundabout, and who knows – perhaps during the busy season it is a different town. But today there are only the sun-bleached plastic flags of all the world's nations strung across the empty streets, and a thin trickle of pilgrims leaving the place, heading west to Santo Domingo where the cathedral hosts chickens in homage to a local myth.

It's a strange moment in anyone's life when they catch themselves thinking: 'I must go to the cathedral to see the chickens'. But go I do, and see them I do. And perhaps they see me. And if they do, they won't be looking at the first human being gawping upwards and taking their picture. This is surely one of these apparent absurdities that the clever sages enjoy scoffing at. But it is such surreal pageantry that adds to life, because this is the real world. This is what goes on in the real world. This is what it looks like. And there is more sanity in this cathedral with its chickens, than there is in a city full of Internet pod-people.

*

On the way out of town we meet a Swedish pilgrim. This is Anika who tells us that she gave a presentation on Ireland to her class at school for which she learned to play *Amhrán na bhFian* on the flute – a feat most Irish people couldn't boast of. We also meet Richard again, who has cocked a snook tendonitis and common sense to creak forward on his shoddy legs. The four of us take a break by a cross commemorating a peace treaty between two towns that had fought over the surrounding countryside. Sitting at the cross are pilgrims from Quebec, an older couple, who provide a change from the Anglophone echo-chamber by talking to one another in French.

Ahead of us is Grañón. Between us and Grañón is a fork in the road. Richard stays on the main path as June, Anika and I opt for the scenic route. The other two walk faster than me and so I get to walk alone for the first time since Pamplona. I see deer on the open fields of stubble and they run away as I watch them. This world is dried out, but it isn't hot. I see Richard limping up the hill in the distance.

I arrive in Grañón. I enter the town alone and wander the two streets, trying to find my bearings. The place seems forlorn; there are lots of abandoned buildings and it gives every indication of being a small rural town that has seen happier times. The hostel is the church. I get there and am greeted by June who has reserved a bed for me – it is a gym mat on the floor of a chapel. There are no pews, but there is an altar and retable at the far end depicting what looks like the Trial of Christ. This hostel is a *donativo*, which means there is no set price but you give what you can to help it stay in operation. If you are stony broke, you can take what you need. I'm not stony broke, so I give what I think is a reasonable fee. *Donativos* are the most basic accommodation you can get without living in a tent. The advantage they have over a tent is that you are flung in with a wealth of strangers with whom you must work with to prepare food, and set tables, and clean the dishes. It is wrong to think that they are filled with religious pilgrims, but there are none of the sports-trekkers that I met in the Municipals. There are one or two familiar faces: Kay is there, and Anika, as well as Danny and Liam, and Natasha who coos and talks Russian to the many cats that come in the door and look around the hiking gear by the gym mats in the chapel. She leaves the chapel-dorm and the cats follow her.

A woodpigeon calls outside. There is no-one else here.

*

"This is not a hostel, it is a hospital", says the *hospitalera*, "and this is the stamp". She gives each pilgrim a hug. They are being helped by a local man who says that by helping here the Camino comes to him, so he does not have to walk it, but one day he will, him and his wife.

If you're not making dinner (and I'm not) and you have made your bed (and I have) there is nothing else for it but to cross the street to the bar. This is where I get a stamp for my *Credencial*. At the bar I sit out with some of the others. Over *liquor de hierba* and a beer I talk to Richard who describes the Camino as his *Rumspringa*, because he's free from having his wife tell him what to do.

Then we all go back for the communal meal. I feel that the *hospitaleras* have been driven slightly crazy by their work and this manifests itself in things like getting the pilgrims to say Grace by thumping the table to the tune of Queen's *We Will Rock You* and barking out the words as a call-and-response in Spanish and then Italian. It is not the only musical interlude. One of the pilgrims is a songwriter, Mark, and he has written a song about the Camino. He and another pilgrim, Gene, write out the lyrics, which are then translated into Spanish by a *hospitalera*. I help make copies. I have no idea where he got the guitar from, but he starts strumming away and we all join in. I feel homesick for my comfort zone until it is over.

After the meal there follows a sort of prayer service in the choir stalls overlooking the nave of the church. We each, as part of this service, pass a candle round and when we receive it we say something about our trip. We can say it into ourselves without uttering a word. We can say it out loud in a language all or most will understand, or we can say it in our native language. So pilgrims say nothing, or speak in Spanish, English, or French; or they say something in Dutch, or Hungarian, or Swedish, or Russian.

When it comes to my turn I say something in Irish. The others understand what I'm saying even if they don't understand the words.

At the end we are asked to go around hugging our fellow pilgrims and wishing them well. From this alone it is easy to tell who is from northern Europe and who is from elsewhere. Hugs and 'Buen Caminos' are exchanged, and it really isn't so bad until Gene squeezes my biceps and says "you're a good man".

*

The *hospitaleras* said that in the summer they had ninety-one guests one night, and as it is their mission never to turn anyone away, they had brought mats outside where it was warm enough to sleep under the stars. But tonight my feet are like blocks of ice and there are snores in the room. The noise is so bad that one Hungarian pilgrim gets up and goes for a walk.

DAY SIXTEEN

I lighten my rucksack even more by leaving hard leather flip-flops I bought in *La Casa Mágica* in the Give/Take box. By now I can fit everything into my bag bar the sleep sheet, which remains pinned to the outside with a carabiner. I still have the waterproofs in the tote bag and that is always on top in case a storm springs up. My plastic sabots hang from the bungees strung across the back of the bag.

The *hospitaleras* hug us goodbye, and we are almost the last to leave: I hear Kay talking from an upstairs window. She is walking with a Brazilian pilgrim who has heard of a hostel ten kilometres away that is run by a Portuguese fraternity. They aim to stay there tonight. And so June and I leave *Grañón*, and walk out into a new landscape.

The vines are gone. There are only endless dunes of shorn *dehesa*. Stubble. There is little else. The landscape is dun and dusty. As we walk along the path we see pilgrims taking a shortcut across the fields; they look like astronauts on a dead desert planet. High on a powerline there dangles a pair of trainers. The cable is so high that getting them up there was quite a feat, and I ponder the events leading up to their appearance on the powerline. Across the barren hills there are monolithic hay ricks made from bales the size of cars. They send gargantuan shadows spilling across the earth.

There is a border marker between La Rioja and Castilla y León. It is a tall, thin sign depicting a crooked line: the route-map of the Camino. It seems an impossible ambition to walk all that way. The names of the towns are meaningless ciphers yet to assume a form and identity. That will only happen when we reach them. The first Castilian villages we pass through are quiet or still asleep: Redecilla, Castildelgado, and Viloria, the latter being the birthplace of Santo Domingo of chicken fame.

It is noon. The white sky is like the undersurface of gentle pool of water. The fields are choppy; they are sea-swells of sepia laced with gold dust. There are no vultures. There are no hawks. There are no vines. There are only haystacks and the distant dots of pilgrims on the way to distant Santiago.

In Belorado we sit outside a cafe, lounging, not saying or doing anything. I feel a pang of impatience, as though to go farthest is the goal of the day, rather than to go fullest. I have told myself often enough that this is not a race. Whether or not the Camino is a transformation or a cure, a maturation or a ripening, a metamorphosis or a disintegration, it needs time.

*

We take a wrong turning in Belorado, turn back, try again, and are on our way back out into the dry lands. There is a series of closed down hamlets; hostels that are supposed to be open are closed, either for the day or for the season, as are cafes, as are restaurants. The towns get smaller and smaller – a town with a population of sixty gives way to one of forty, and that to one of twenty. In the distance I can see the bullet holes of caves in a cliff-face and wonder if it would be possible to sleep in them for the night. But they are far and the next town is always around the next bend, and invariably shut.

Along the way we meet Gene who is as perplexed as we are by the vanished population of these lands. He walks a little way ahead of us and we meet him again sitting in the shade of a barn wall chatting to some of the others from Grañón. We say "Buen Camino" to them all and then meet him again at the next town where he is making up his mind to stay or continue with the others. His mind is made up for him by the experience of the local hostel.

'The Camino provides': You cannot expect a quarter of a million pilgrims to walk through an area as down on its luck as this without some bright spark deciding to cash in. The hostel is above a cramped cafe. The owner ignores us at first, keeping us waiting until she has finished skidding coffees along the length of the bar to sagging, silent men, and wiping down the spotless counter. Having established who the boss around here is, she plops open a big ledger and asks: "¿albergue?"

We do indeed want the hostel, but we want to see it first because we are annoyed by her. She tells us that only one can go and inspect the dorm, and it falls to June to be our pit canary. They vanish through a door leaving me to ask Gene if he has ever heard the expression 'to wreck your buzz'.

"No", he says, "but I guess she's wrecking the buzz, right?" He is right. I hope June is the bearer of bad news, and she is, which is great news: the place is a sardine can and, for good measure and without evidence to back this up, probably has bed bugs too.

"No, gracias", I say to the owner who dismisses us with a wave of her hand, as though knocking us back with her fingernails. Such behaviour is known as floccinaucinihilipilification, which is one of the longest words in the English language and is usually deployed by those wishing to amaze their friends and confound their enemies with their verbal dexterity. Here it is used the way nature intended.

*

Ultreia Et Suseia – onwards and upwards.

Literally so; the road rises towards a distant ridge. Ahead of us we see the two Quebecois whom we last saw at the cross on the *dehesa*. We stop in at a bar for a rest and a cold beer, which makes June merry, and Gene decides that since there is a bed free in the rooms above the bar he will stop here for the night. We chat a little, the beer, Gene's genteel humour, and June's new-found merriment doing powerful work to create a little haven of peace and happiness in an unfathomable world that nobody can control.

The path is the road over the ridge and down past ruins around which many sheep are grazing. We cross over a rushing, leafy stream: a moving glass skin of scales flowing over wings of bright green feathers. On a stop sign just before the town somebody has written 'Never Stop Walking', and deciding to puncture the personal trainer motivational self-help bubble, I fish out a marker and add 'until you find a cafe'.

The hostel of San Anton Abad is part of a plush hotel, with the pilgrim meal in the dining room. Chandeliers describe frozen fireworks and throw their light across lush carpets, polished tables, and vases of flowers. So much for my big ambitions to travel the Camino staying at only the humblest of hostels. But by now I have decided that asceticism is for freaks and is no different than gluttony, which is also for freaks. Whether you stuff yourself or deny yourself, your focus is on your self; and what is so enlightened about being so selfish?

I sit at a table with some pilgrims I saw in Grañón. There is Anika, Natasha, Richard, and Pearl who is a student in America, and Beatrice from New Zealand who is a mathematician. Dinner segues into general boozy chatter and the undrunk wine is ferried back to the hostel, where in a small lounge we find Danny and Liam, and we all continue to get on famously until a strange man appears and begins sweeping his arms crosswise in front of him. It is the same gesture used by people flagging aircraft on a runway. The pilgrims watch him as he performs his esoteric mime act. What does it mean?

It means the show is over, is the answer to that question. He keeps signalling for us to stop everything. It is a half past nine and we are all adults here, even Pearl who is only nineteen. But we turn in, abandoning the wine which is not allowed in the dorms. A few minutes later the silent killjoy returns and flicks off the lights. Beds are reached by flashlight.

By bed is a top bunk. June is sleeping below me. The bunk is rickety and sways every time June moves in her sleep. There is no side rail and I lie there hoping that I don't fall out during the night and bang my head off the table like the woman in *Million Dollar Baby*. The Camino could end in many ways, but that's one of the ways I want to avoid.

DAY SEVENTEEN

So much for an early night. Snoring has broken my sleep. After a shower, I decide to mop up in the bathroom to prevent anyone skidding. Doing this helps dispel some of the grumpiness caused by the lack of sleep, yet I make my way down to the breakfast room still feeling groggy and with my stomach groaning like a haunted accordion.

The breakfast room is striped black and white with Georgian chairs and a buffet. There is also a woman who stands by the door with her hands clasped behind her back, telling the pilgrims that they cannot remove food from the breakfast room. There are moans of disappointment as fruit and tea-cakes are returned to the buffet.

One by one everyone takes to the road, each with their reasons, each with their own versions of the Camino, each with their own experiences to colour it, each with their own lessons from it; in the end it is June and I who are left and we are about to leave when Gene appears. He tells us that in the dorm where he had spent the night, there had been a pilgrim who had wanted all the others to sing her a lullaby as she went to sleep, and they obliged. He has dropped by for a spot of breakfast, and he is dining alone as we leave, reminding me a little of the guy at the end of *2001: A Space Odyssey*.

The path continues up the road past the hotel and then veers off, rising up through an oakwood lane of morning mist. There are oaks and heather and silence; no, not silence – there is the sound of the forest hissing, of crickets and birds, and the distant echoes of the sea in the leaves. It reminds me of the Sperrins back home and I pause at the top of the hill to look back out over the open space that I've crossed over the previous few days.

The trail through the woods broadens into a wide earthen path that looks like a dry river bed. It is the colour of cayenne pepper. It is flanked by flaxen grasses and then conifer forest. The sky is cornflower blue. There are cairns made by our pilgrim forebears, and at one point they have spelled out their names in rocks. We take a break by a monument to three hundred prisoners of war executed by Franco's nationalists. I wonder what had been said on that foul day; in what kind of weather had those men died at the hands of their fellow Spaniards, and what had their executioners talked about on their way back? A plaque on the monument tells the dead that the firing squads had been in vain. Democracy came to Spain, the dictatorship became something to read about in history books, and cyclists pass us by and we exchange 'Buen Camino's. The path drops and rises like a kite and in the rising path ahead we see a solitary pilgrim moving upwards, upwards, upwards towards the sky.

A little further on there is a pop-up cafe with pop-up totem poles and faces painted on logs with day-glo paint. It is harmless, but I feel that it is catering to a different constituency. Perhaps it is an echo of the Glastonbury festival, which brings to mind unpleasant memories of the muddy wastes of Olde Englande and watching a desperate party-goer paddling a lilo across a lagoon of steaming mud and shit to buy cider from a tiny striped marquee. I imagine the train coming back from the Somme was merrier than the train coming back from the Glastonbury festival. Muddied survivors stared into the middle distance with expressions that read 'I have seen things'.

Chills run down my spine.

*

Gene catches up. He asks if there is a quarry nearby on account of the heavy thuds he has heard. We say we don't know but that there are signs up to say that the forest through which the path runs is a hunting reserve, so perhaps the heavy thuds were shotgun blasts. We fail to convince ourselves, especially when we hear what are actual shotgun blasts far off to our left. A little later we hear the heavy thumps again. Perhaps there is a quarry nearby. Living in a city for so long has meant living away from most of the sounds of human activity. What is the sound of the city? Traffic.

We continue along the path down to San Juan de Ortega – Saint John of the Nettle, so called because this place was once the wildest spot on the Camino, plagued by bandits who would kill pilgrims for what little they had. It was at this spot that, after years of relative obscurity, the Camino returned to life. A local priest took it upon himself to clear away the encroaching undergrowth from the forest path and, with possible help from hunters, kept it clear so that it could be walked. At one point the whole Camino had fallen into disrepair and its modern state owes its existence to various fraternal societies – Friends of the Camino – from various countries, who clear the way, run hostels and *donativos*, raise money for improvements to paths, or create new paths that are safer.   And then there are the yellow arrows, which are either spray-painted on street corners or purpose built signs. The infrastructure of the Camino is the work of many hands over many years.

The church in San Juan de Ortega is interesting because it is seen as a fertility shrine. Spanish nobility used to pray here in the hope of having children. The tomb of San Juan is small and unprepossessing. I think of the tombs of Santa María de Real, where Spanish nobility was laid to rest. His tomb is off to the side of his own church, under a frieze depicting the nativity. The centre of the church is dominated by an ornate catafalque over which the strong light of the outside world spills through the door. He had founded his church as a haven for pilgrims travelling through such hostile territory, deliberately cutting himself off from the world by moving permanently onto the Camino.

I wonder about him and compare him to all those Irish saints. They existed in an age before the Normans came with their militaristic bishops and bejewelled clergy. I think of those saints like Brendan who sailed to Canada in a skiff of leather, or Colmcille who sailed to Iona where the Book of Kells was begun, or Saint Kevin of Glendalough who prayed by standing in the lake with his hands outstretched to greet the rising sun. I wonder if San Juan was like them, people who were constantly attuned to the divinity in the world around them, who did not see the elements of the world in conflict but saw the single being of which they were a part. I wonder what it must have been like to be a saint like that, living in such material poverty, discomfort, and danger, and to have arrived in a state of being in which they did not feel poor, or uncomfortable, or afraid.

There is a cafe by the church. Gene prefers to sit inside. June and I sit outside and are talking when a familiar figure emerges from the forest path in the company of two pilgrims. It is Andy, a bandana flapping on top of his head. The two pilgrims are from Switzerland, and have walked all the way from there. Two friends from school, they had started independently of each other and in full ignorance of each other's plans to walk to Santiago. They had bumped into one another on the way and had stayed together ever since. They dispense knowledge about avoiding blisters as I perform meatball surgery. Andy lets us know that he had veered off track in Nájera and had walked twenty kilometres to the monastery of San Millan. He was the only pilgrim there and the monks had said a special mass for him.

He and the Swiss order *morcilla* sandwiches. They don't touch them but flies are all over them as soon as they emerge from the dark interior of the bar. The sight of a single housefly anywhere near food would turn my stomach in Ireland. Here I have learned to accept their presence if I'm not to starve. The sight of the soft, crumbling *morcilla* being feasted on by flies still revolts me, but not a short elderly pilgrim with a grey moustache who pants as he speaks. He asks if anyone wants the sandwich. No, take it.

Is it nice?

It is smooth and soft says one of the Swiss girls, try it, it's good. The man sits down and giving the flies next to no warning, tucks in.   The Swiss friends will walk around Switzerland when they complete the Camino.

*

Andy and the Swiss pilgrims leave just before we do. I watch them walking away, him tall with his two hiking poles made from branches, them shorter almost hidden by their rucksacks. June says that Andy has some sort of issue with women, that he's nervous around them. She says this because he flicked crumbs at one of the Swiss girls as a joke. He looked sheepish having done this. He did something similar a while back, says June. On the way into Viana they went to see one of the huge haystacks and he threw some straw over her head.

I remember burping at my sisters to annoy them, of greeting female student friends by posing like a boxer. I did those things to be funny. And people want to be funny in order to be liked. I see Andy doing similar things, and am interested in June's assessment that these are the products of an insecurity around women. I wouldn't accuse him of it; I don't know him. But I'm not a woman and might not be so attuned to things like this. I tell June that I think he knows, because of how he'd looked sheepish, and maybe dealing with it is part of his Camino.

*

Before we reach Atapuerca we pass Agés. The signpost has signs for both towns, but it looks as though it is saying that Atapuerca is Ages away. It feels as though it is. It also feels as though we might not arrive at all as we have to proceed on the highway and the drivers all seem to have the most important jobs to do. They cannot wait and the cars and vans flash right past us. We walk on the verge when we can, past small copses of trees with signs saying they are actually hunting ranges, and abandoned picnic areas with funereal furniture made from slabs of concrete.

Atapuerca is announced via a large sign depicting a caveman rendered lovingly in pencil. He smiles over his shoulder, and with his tumbling locks I'm surprised the words 'Because I'm Worth It' aren't printed beneath him. He is there to commemorate the discovery of the remains of Europe's earliest human settlement. A fake circle of standing stones has been erected in a field, presumably to the same end. Andy and the Swiss pilgrims and some Italians are staying in the hostel. I see Andy cracking walnuts he has gathered in preparation for the pilgrim meal. He cracks them on the ground with a rock, something Europe's earliest humans would have understood.

DAY EIGHTEEN

Atapuerca has sunk to the bottom of a sea of fog.

It is a spectral morning with dim shadows in the mist. I can hear birds singing. The sunlight fills the thick air. Motes of vapour are like specks of dust. The buildings in the town square are two dimensional and matt grey. The cafe has rucksacks by the door.

They belong to Anika and Gene, who are downing coffee and apple pie. They stayed in Agés. We have breakfast and June joins us. When we begin walking, the mist is lifting. The path runs up a hill where, overlooking Atapuerca, there is a cross in a field of stones that have been arranged in whorls and circles. They remind me of the procession stones at Beaghmore in Tyrone. Indeed, the path assumes the form of the rocky stream-gully tracks of the Sperrins, and I am consoled with thoughts of home.

The others continue on ahead and I follow the path as it runs down the mountain and onto the highway. The open landscape reveals how few pilgrims there are, how vast are the distances between them, how isolated they all seem. One pilgrim asks me to take her picture, and she strikes a pose as though in mid-step walking away from the camera. Another pilgrim marches by looking like an extra from *Tron*, talking at the top of her voice into her phone. There are a few silent villages before I see a place where I can rest.

It is a small cafe, the kind of place which exists because of the ever-hungry, ever-thirsty Camino that passes by its door like an insatiable millipede. There is a group of Korean pilgrims drinking beer, and this is where I catch up with June and Anika, who are drinking coffee and, like the Koreans, are tapping on their mobile phones. I am no match for the allure of the internet, which is a trap, that's why it's called The Web.

I move on, meeting an English woman at the village *fuente* who is wearing a bandana and wants her photo taken by the *fuente* as she is documenting her journey for her husband. She had cancer therapy and is proving to him that there is nothing to worry about.

*

There is a tour party in the village. Posh women walk along talking about who met whom in Savanna. I wonder if they are soul-less or if I am arrogant. Are the motorists who flash by rude, or am I walking where people are not supposed to walk – part of a world where walking is now unnatural, where cars are legitimate? I look at pilgrims walking in the middle of the road, expecting no evil – but to the motorists they must appear as brainless as stray sheep. The path hugs the verge of the busy highway and I arrive at a fork.

I look around. In the distance is the urban sprawl of the industrial polygon outside Burgos. There are no yellow arrows here, but there is enough pilgrim graffiti to suggest that both roads lead into the city. As I am pondering which way to go, based on a scrawl that reads 'Río/Ind.', I see a strange John the Baptist figure approaching from the direction of the industrial polygon. He wears sunglasses and a bandana and is waving his hands above his head at two pilgrims I recognise as the Quebecois. It is Gene, and although the Quebecois continue on their way, he makes his way to the fork in the road to tell me that that they should have gone the other way. The English woman arrives and agrees. Her husband had walked the Camino earlier that year and has texted her, advising against the industrial route which is "long and boring". She and Gene go off in the direction of the river. I am still deciding when Anika and June arrive.

Two have gone to Burgos via the industrial polygon, and now five have opted for the river. We follow the others down to the river, which is arrived at by skirting Burgos airport. The tour party is behind us, a flock of white cotton and Panama hats. Ants have turned the heaped earth by the path into a shimmering delta as they course along their scent-trails. The path leads down to a village through which heavy vehicles thunder and snort along a main road. Across this great divide we break at a cafe where the Koreans are still drinking. They tell us that they want to visit Ireland to drink Guinness. I haven't the heart to tell them what I tell everyone thinking of doing the same; they look so happy at the prospect, and ignorance is bliss, especially when it comes down to such trivial things as this. They move on, some of them on painful feet, laughing as they wince. Anika, June, and I walk into Burgos though the long park by the river.

We are seeking Eumaeus.

*

Eumaeus is the name of a hostel in a convent. We think that this would be a good Camino experience to stay in a place that is explicitly religious, rather than a place that is 'spiritual' or 'well-meaning'. I find too much of what is described as 'spiritual' is a pick'n'mix of bits of different religions chosen for the attractiveness of their surface value: A 'spiritual' person can come across as a magpie, pinching the shiny salient ornaments of world culture and cobbling them together into a sort of Heath Robinson religion of their own devising. All those hippy beads and wig-wams, holy pictures and coloured kaftans owe as much to a person's notions about designer living as they do to a genuine quest for... what?

So a stay in a convent which is the home of a religious order would make for a change, and a change is as good as a rest. Religion, as any ful kno, comes from the word *religare*, which means 'to bind together'. It is where we get the words 'ligature' and 'litigate' from; the former something that is used to bind, the latter bound bundles of legal forms – the Red Tape that closet crooks are always complaining about. Religion binds a community together through common ritual, dress, social norms, conventions, and a calendar. There is precious little about one's inner journey in religion, but there is an awful lot about learning to live with others. I think that religion gives strength to the weak, it comforts the lonely by making them part of a community, it enables the lowly; but it is also a way for petty sadists to justify their cruelties, and it can be mob rule. It is no different to nationalism, communism, the class system, or team sports.

Eumaeus is tucked away behind the park. We are greeted at the door by the *hospitalero*, whose first words are to tell us to be quiet because there are priests in the chapel and they are praying. We understand. We are quiet.

Are we all Catholics?

We're Irish I say, which is a lie. Anika is not a Catholic, and has told me that she doesn't really know what Catholicism is. As far as the *hospitalero* is concerned Irish equals Catholic, an equation I dispute, but I remind myself that the priests are praying in the chapel and so I say nothing.

Welcome to Eumaeus. The dorms are segregated between men and women. It is a convent, so this is no shock. Gene is there, and Alex from Canada whom I met in Grañón. We are whispering because the priests are praying in the chapel, when June appears at the door and asks me to perform translation duties. Horror has struck.

June keeps up Lena's practice of scanning bunks for bed bugs, and today she has struck pay-dirt. There are bed bugs in their dorm, and they are alive alive-o. The *hospitalero* flusters and goes for the chief nun. She is French and won't speak Spanish when I translate June's request for another room. My French, nurtured through five years of grammar school, allows me to ask for coffee in Bayonne and tickets to Tangier at the railway station in Marrakesh. Beyond that: *je ne pais*. But if explorers can communicate with lost tribes, and Andy can negotiate his way through Spain using mime, we can describe the calamity that has befallen Eumaeus.

It dawns on the chief nun. There are bed bugs in the house. But she seems to take this as an affront to her efforts to keep the place clean. Suddenly the Holy Spirit descends on her and she receives the *charisma*, the gifts, and she can now speak in tongues – English springs forth from her lips like a font of sweet water.

"They weren't here yesterday", she says. "Look! There is the problem!" She grabs Anika by the face and begins pointing at her acne. "Look!"

Patience snaps. I could deal with every odd aspect of Eumaeus up until now, but bad manners are never excusable. We ask for our money back. The chief nun locks the women's dorm, after June and Anika have removed their rucksacks. They didn't unpack and there is no risk of carrying the bugs onwards, but some other pilgrim has her stuff locked in the room. We exit Eumaeus and make our way into the city to the Municipal, which is near the cathedral and across from a cafe where the *morcilla* eating man from San Juan de Ortega waves at us and points to the blink-and-you-miss-it (because-you're-tired-and-pissed-off) doorway of the Municipal.

The Municipal is modern, clean, quiet, private, and designed by people who know exactly what someone wants having walked twenty kilometres or more only to be assaulted by a nun. Not a bed bug in sight, we sort out our beds and have a nap.

Later that evening I sit in the common area and write up my journal. At the table behind me I hear someone ask another pilgrim: "Why are you doing this?" But the other doesn't say, and talks about what she was doing before coming on the Camino. To be fair, I have no answer to that question either.

DAY NINETEEN

Some people are awoken by the rays of the sun. Some are awoken by the crowing of a rooster. Some people are woken by alarm clocks. Today I am awoken by the Babel of sleepy pilgrims rising up from the depths of sleep to begin another day. The hospitalera shoos out those of us who linger by shouting "¡Vamos, Vamos, Chicos!" I am one such *chico* and I visit the cathedral for the first pilgrim mass since Roncesvalles. The mass is in a side chapel, and we pilgrims are a tiny group scattered around the pews near the back of the church. The front few pews are full of old ladies. There are as many priests at the altar as there are people in the congregation. Above them, crowning the retable is the odd image of *Santiago Matamoros*. I am now used *to Santiago Pelegrino* in his sou'wester with a sea-shell on it, his walking pole with its hourglass water-gourd on it, and his brown cloak. *Santiago Matamoros* is a different aspect to this figure: he sits up there on his charger, rearing up above the prostrate forms of trampled Moors. He wears a turban to rival anything sported by the sultans of the *Sublime Porte*, and he twirls a scimitar around his head. *Matamoros* means Moor-slayer. He doesn't look all that different from the Moors he is slaying.

It's as strange as a bishop in a chess set. What is a religious figure doing on a battlefield? *Santiago Matamoros* was the patron saint of the *Reconquista*, the triumph of the Catholic monarchs over the caliphate. You don't start wars with your friends; although the moors left a rich legacy in Spain, they did demand a tribute of one hundred virgins from their Christian subjects, destined for the harems. And given the choice between some fine looking buildings and the damnation of your daughter into sexual slavery or a war of independence, well... it's Hobson's choice, isn't it? Although the last Moorish city, Granada, was taken in 1492 (when Columbus sailed the ocean blue), the influence of the moors in Spain is deep. From the architecture, to the language, to the severe religiosity of the Catholicism of the south (which had to be more Catholic than Catholic to avoid the suspicion that they were really Jews and Muslims of questionable loyalty), the moors helped mould this country.

Not everyone is satisfied with their expulsion all those years ago. When I was in Córdoba, visiting the famous cathedral that had been a mosque made with striped Visigothic arches, I saw the security guards expel a group of men in white cloaks and green turbans. They had been making a film, and the red-bearded presenter had muttered angry descriptions in Arabic, rolling his eyes heavenwards and pointing upwards. Late that night somebody played the call to prayer from a window near the cathedral/mosque. The sound filled the streets. But then that's not just a Spanish thing; the same happened in Dublin on Camden Street.

*

Away from all this.

I have breakfast with June and we hit the road. As we leave the city a tree throws its yellow leaves up into the air as though throwing confetti. They rain down through the blue sky. At a small park we take a break, greeting the Koreans as they pass us, and then one of the other pilgrims from this morning's mass, and then Alex arrives with more tales from Eumaeus.

*

The Quebecois, whom I last saw heading for the industrial polygon despite Gene's warnings, stayed in Eumaeus last night. They went for dinner in town and so missed the mass in the convent. Upon their return they compounded their blasphemy by saying that they would not partake in the pilgrim meal because they had eaten.

Cue this morning, and when they sat down to breakfast they were told that there was no breakfast for them because they were not pilgrims. It is one thing to be given the brush off by an inbred bar-tender in the middle of nowhere, but quite another to be insulted by people who are supposed to be exemplars of the Christian message. We have met many people on the Camino, and stayed in a variety of hostels. We have stayed in vast production-line dormitories such as Roncesvalles and bare-minimum simplicity such as Grañón, we have experienced hospitality in the company of Dutch Christians, with foot spas and wine in La Casa Mágica, alone in Saint Jean, and together in Atapuerca, but we have not encountered such hostility as at Eumaeus. It seems that we are not the only ones to leave the place with bad memories to laugh over. Alex says he left before it was his turn to be insulted.

*

Just beyond the motorway there are fields of strange black plants. They are dead sunflowers. I'm used to seeing them when they are yellow and green, and round and standing tall. I have not seen them after their life has gone from the flowers to the seeds. The bowed sunflowers look like burnt matchsticks. I wonder how many thousands of seeds they have created. They are dry and rattle, rustling as they are pushed by the breeze.

Just beyond them, workmen are busy building part of the road system and the path is marked through it with traffic cones and plastic tape. This is also the Camino. The path runs under the colossal legs of the overhead motorway and through vestiges of woodland to continue parallel to the road on the other side of the barrier. Streams flow under the road. Weir water the colour of fresh champagne pours green bubbles into a black river, spilling out to flow away to the distant shores of Spain.

The towns here are off-season; hostels are closed or far away up country lanes. We find an open cafe and sit down outside. The Koreans are also there, unshod, their naked and blistered feet propped up on the tables. Inside the cafe there is a map of the world on one wall and people have written their names at their place of origin. We sit in the sun and drink beer and wine. There are no watches, no clocks or bells to chime the hour, and the day lives without their interference.

A little farther and we arrive in Rabé, a clean, pretty town where the hostel is a renovated house. The atmosphere in the house is so mellow and welcoming that it seems to act as compensation for our recent run-ins with the witch and the nun. The Koreans are there as is Beatrice and a South

African couple with whom we share dinner in the cosy dining room. At one point in the evening, with the washing machine churning our clothes, and June watching *The Fall* on her phone, I spend an hour at the local bar watching the light change. The town is serene and all for me, and the dog that saunters past.

The day ends with a trip to the local convent where the nuns welcome us to their service. They sing their prayers, and hand out miraculous medals at the end. What am I to do with thing? It is a small aluminium token, oblong like a penny flattened on a tramline, and is embossed with an impression of the Virgin. A string of pink wool runs through a hoop at the top. I have seen these may times in Ireland; I have seen them being handed out on street corners by elderly religious people, or tucked into the flap of a plastic envelope containing an icon, or tied to my childhood bed-post by my mother, or glittering on the folk-art of the Camino, on the crosses and cairns I have passed by on my way here.

What am I going to do with it?

Before catching that flight to Biarritz, this medal would have gone straight into the bin. I did, after all, burn a King James Bible just to prove to myself that it was only a book. Now I have it pinned to my rucksack. Why? As a sign of respect to those nuns? As a sign that things might be different now? Because I can get away with it? After all, where are the bar-room philosophers to mock it? Because it's not something I would do.

Somebody else would do something like this, so I pin the medal to my rucksack.

*

DAY TWENTY

Before going to sleep I had gone to set my alarm only to find that I had lost my phone. I must have left it in Burgos as I was being *Vamos Chico*ed out the door. Beatrice texted Pearl to ask for it, as she was staying in that hostel last night. I have groundless confidence that we will meet soon.

Sleep was sound, because there wasn't a sound until daybreak and the zipping and rolling and polyester scrunching of sleeping bags brings me round.

*

Today I walk up onto the *Meseta*. I look at the contour map that was given to me in Saint Jean and see the *Meseta* as a long straight line running west. It looks as though after the pulsing heartbeat of the previous twenty days, the Camino has suddenly flat-lined.

The *Meseta* is the plateau that constitutes the majority of the Iberian Peninsula. My only experience of it was driving across La Mancha and feeling as though I were being given an ant's eye view of a table-top. There will be no soaring peaks or deep river valleys, and any hills that do exist out there will assume a greater significance than if they were one among many in a range. The peaks will be higher for being singular; the valleys will be deeper for being in a land where nothing ever seems to change. I am looking forward to this.

I want to walk out there where there is nothing to distract me; I want to be in a place where I can scrutinize myself. I remember reading about Gordon of Khartoum and how he would annoy his bodyguards by going out into the desert by himself. As dawn would break he would get on his camel and vanish into the desert, retuning later in the day. He travelled with no companions, setting out alone and returning alone. When asked why he did this, Gordon replied that he was "walking before God". It did him no good, and he ended his days in the crook of a tree on his front lawn being used as target practice by the soldiers of the Madhi.

I don't want to wind up as target practice by crazed, slave-driving fanatics; but the phrase "walking before God" has caused me to want to be out there on the oceanic plain of the *Meseta*. I think that having no distractions will allow me to pare away the winding sheets in which I have buried myself. I seriously consider walking across this empty space to be akin to Lazarus walking across the floor of his mausoleum, towards the brilliant light of the open doorway in which he can see nothing but from which he hears a voice summoning him to return.

Γνῶθι σεαυτόν, said those clever Greeks. *Gnothi seauton*: Know Thyself. But is such morbid introspection good for the soul?

How am I supposed to know?

*

The daybreak path from Rabé into the *Meseta* is amber, sounds like a rooster, and in the cold blue of the young sky there are planes with candy-pink contrails high above its head; they look like meteors falling to earth. When I leave the town and walk up onto the *Meseta*, there is a single tree with leaves the colour of fire and there is glitter in the dells by the side of the path. It is frost, hard and white on dry flattened stems. The sun is the colour of molten metal, and it sends my shadow out ahead of me. This is how the light plays with me: in the morning I am following my shadow, in the evening my shadow is following me.

This morning my shadow reaches out to June and Beatrice, but it does not touch them and they are soon out of sight. I carry on until I see a small hikers' shelter down a track by the side of the road. There is a water-pump there which draws no water, and pilgrims have left their names and messages all over the stone walls. Lone trees stand in broad fields of stubble. The light warms my face. Now I am alone here on the cusp of the *Meseta*, thinking that if the life I have made for myself is not a pleasing life I ought to just throw it away and accept the life that was given to me at birth. I ought to be who I am and not who I want to be, because wanting is poverty; and the more I want, the less I have. Wanting to be myself has turned me into a pauper.

*

Back on track. I meet few people. In the distance there are windmills, modern and with tripartite propellers, like big white shamrocks. I wonder how Saint Patrick must have looked to the Irish, trying to explain his religion to them by using a shamrock. I like to think that the first emissaries to his mission returned to their spirit lodges to tell their druids that a Briton had arrived from Wales, whose sign was the crossed staff that Roman soldiers used to carry their kit, and his god was the God of Clover.

I meet Pedro, who had been at the hostel in Rabé. He is from Barcelona.

"So does that make you Spanish or Catalán?"

He laughs. "It depends who I am talking to".

He is sitting by the road and tells me that too much isolation is bad. He taps the side of his head. Further on and there is silence. The earth is yellow. The sky is blue and hawks circle a distant tractor that is tilling the soil. The air is filled with the smell of harrowed earth; it is the smell of roots, cool and plentiful, and of mould webbing the damp soil. Arriving in Hornillos having descended *La Cuesta de Matamulos* – 'Mule-killer Slope' - and the only other human being is driving a yellow post van that slips like melting butter along the edge of the fields.

Beatrice and June are in the cafe there, where June has left a note on the menu trestle on the outside pavement saying 'Stopping Is Always Good'. They leave ahead of me and I get to walk through the empty streets past an obelisk with a painted cockerel on top of it, and see a beaded curtain, like long strips of fusili pasta, rolling in waves as the breeze strokes it. I see the moon above the rooftops.

I think about the other two, again far ahead, again not waiting, again not wanting to wait, and I remind myself that yoking one's mood to the ways of others is never a good thing. How many others, on this Camino and long before it even began, went on ahead, went on without me, went on their own way? For how many of them had it been me going on ahead, going my own way, going on without them?

*

I step up onto the *Meseta* again and the land is even flatter than before. It stretches away on either side to a horizon as fine as a razor's edge. At one stage I am passed by a Korean man on a unicycle. Not long after I see a man in a Peruvian bobble-hat walking in the opposite direction through the fields. He is brushing his teeth as he walks. A Danish pilgrim falls into step beside me. She says that she walked this part of the Camino earlier in the year. She is walking the whole *Camino Francés* in instalments. Last time, she says, she stopped soon after Burgos. Now she has started in Burgos and will walk to León.

"The *Meseta* was different last time, says she. "It was green as far as the eye could see. But it was busier then, and pilgrims were getting out of bed at five in the morning to dash across the country to find a bed for the night. There were places where you could watch pilgrims going from door to door without any luck". I think of when I went from door to door in Saint Jean before finding a place. I wonder where all the pilgrims who left on that day are now: those cyclists, the English-speaking Germans, the Danish-American, Jesus, and the pilgrim who came bearing fun-sized Twixes.

We arrive in Hontanas, passing between two standing stones and descending a steep gravel path. The earth around this town looks burnt and there are crows circling the moon. The Danish pilgrim, Anna, is joined by another pilgrim Cristina, whom she had met earlier. Cristina had also been walking the Camino earlier in the year but had to quit. Her knee gave way and she had to fly back to Rome and go straight to hospital. Now she is attempting the remainder of the route, picking up from where she left off in Burgos. Pedro arrives at our table. He is wearing a beret and has had enough for one day. Anna and Cristina also decide to stay, the deciding factor being the famed *paella* of the local hostel.

I go on, back up from the canyon sheltering Hontanas and back onto the plateau of the *Meseta*. My toe begins to smart and I stop to repair the bandage on my foot. The blister still looks red raw, but the dressing comes away without sticking and is unbloodied. I wrap it up again, and set off through fields of white earth that blaze silver and gold as the sun strikes the flattened stubble.

The track now takes to the quiet road, and I walk under the shade of trees. Then, revealed bit by bit as I turn a bend in the road, the Camino presents me with San Anton, once a hospital for pilgrims suffering from *Ignis Sacer* – 'Holy Fire' or 'Saint Anthony's Fire'. This illness was ergot poisoning, caused by eating bread infected with the wheat fungus *Claviceps*, causing mania and gangrene prior to death. The Order of Saint Anthony ran hospitals to care for the afflicted. Their symbol, the Tau cross, is marked on a roadside bollard by the ruins of the cathedral-hospital. If the sea-shell is the symbol of the pilgrim as a walker and a talker through a landscape of places and people, then the Tau cross is the symbol of a pilgrim as someone whose spirit has been sickened by earthly fare and is in the process of recovery.

*

I arrive alone in Castrojerez. The dome of the church at the entrance to the town is tufted with scutch grass, blond and wispy like the scalp of a nestling. The town is a street that runs for two kilometres and it is oven hot as I tred the stone path up to where I see some of the others. June is there, and so is

Beatrice, and Mark, the musician from Grañón is there too. I stop and remove my boots. They are new. They are comfortable. But it is nice to be free of them for the day.

The hostel is across the street from a church that has skulls and cross-bones carved into it: *Memento Mori*; there is an ossuary in the crypt. The *hospitalero* books me in, stamps my *Credencial*, and then says *"go raibh maith agat"*. He says each word free of its neighbours, the way he must have learned it (from a pilgrim? From time in Ireland?), and he says it with a smile. This could be the first time I have been thanked in Irish outside of an Irish class, and it makes me laugh.

Dinner is in the local bar, and we four sit down to dine with local cats staring though the windows of the patio doors. I translate for the waiter and for the other three. Musical Mark takes out a little bag and unrolls a Neoprene keyboard upon which he starts to play the song we sang in Grañón. Mark is a Texan. He wears a woolly hat and a bodywarmer, but then soccer shorts and sandals. Although sartorial elegance is the first victim of the Camino, he stands out as particularly fashion-senseless and talks about buying some trousers "for when it gets cold in the evenings", something I've yet to experience even this late into the year; but Mark is Texan and Spain might be too close to the Baltic for him. After dinner we amble up the main street to the town square. The Municipal is up there, modern and marvellous, and there is a hiking shop; but the Municipal is silent, the streets are empty, and the hiking shop is shut. The newsagent's is next door and is still open and we buy bandanas, black buffs with grey sea-shells on them. We wear these into the local yuppie bar, where there are three women chatting and a dog wanders about. A quiz show hoots from the television; the contestants must defuse a toy bomb by answering questions. I feel pleased that I can defuse the toy bomb *en español*.

I lie in my bunk contemplating the wide empty plains all around and am thinking about going out to the edge of town to watch the stars when I am awoken by phone alarms and the sounds of the others packing up.

DAY TWENTY-ONE

Darkness, and the tapping and murmuring of pilgrims passing by the hostel. We leave in the dark like snails with our homes on our backs. Breakfast is in the cafe. Mark is the first to leave, braving the chill in his soccer shorts. The unicyclist passes the door and waves in. We wave back and I say that I saw him yesterday. Beatrice says that she spoke to him and discovered that she had seen him when he was a child – he arrived in New Zealand with his family, all unicyclists, and had performed as part of a circus. Now, years later she has seen him again cycling along the *Meseta* on the way to Santiago. It's a small world.

Outside, where dawn tints a veil of cloud, windmills blink camera flashes on the horizon. The path leaves Castrojerez, crosses a bridge over a dry stream bed and then rockets up up up to where there is a hikers' shelter. The shelter is a lean-to and it is covered in so many signatures, doodles, greeting, blessings, and cartoons that it has the appearance of having been stained. Beside the shelter is a cross festooned with beads, bracelets, and ribbons. I stand by it and look east to where Castrojerez rises like a Tolkien city or a depiction of Dante's *Purgatorio*. Men are planting trees by the cross and they chat to passing pilgrims. Their voices rise and fall in the cool clear air.

To the north and south the flat horizon smudges in the gloom. There are many windmills, blinking with the same camera flashes and the effect is that of a long glittering train of stars. The path runs west across this flat land and a flock of birds passes above the lone figures of hiking pilgrims. For a moment the flock swerves and I descry the shape of one great bird in the air, fractal to the multitude. Then, without tilting or listing, the horizon is below my feet as the track plummets. Far ahead of me are June and Beatrice, dots on the thread-thin path. The earth is in various shades of brown, from flaxen to chilli red. I hear squeaking and glimpse little rodents jostling in the ditch by the side of the road.

A jeep approaches, stopping and starting by individual pilgrims. It is the Civil Protection, and they are asking everyone if they need any assistance. They stop by me "*¿Necesitas algo?*"

"*No, no. Estoy bien. Gracias*". And I smile and wave them goodbye. They trundle away up the steep hill. I turn and I see them pause again at the most awkward angle, asking the same thing to another pilgrim. I reach the bottom of the steep downhill path and am walking towards a distance copse of trees when I hear an air-raid siren and then the distant snare-drum cacophony of an explosion. Smoke or dust rises to the south. Past the trees the path rises, crosses a road and runs along with a monotony that forces me to aim for a fencepost or a shrub by way of a marker to remind myself that I am actually making progress. The grey dry grasses on the verge click as though unsticking themselves. The rosehips in the bushes are blighted with mould.

*

"Are you Irish?" She has seen the tricolour on the belt of my rucksack.

I tell her I am. It is the half-truth of my life.

She is called Juliette and she has walked from Puy. Roncesvalles was her half-way point. She is from Brittany and lived in Galway, a city with which I am unfamiliar and so not in the position to field Juliette's questions as to how life has changed in that far-flung coastal city. We chat together as we walk past pyramids of sugar beets into Itero where the cafe is full of roaring Spaniards drinking beer. The sight of a group of Spanish pilgrims is a novelty, but one that soon wears off as their voices increase in volume despite them all sitting around the same table.

Juliette doesn't so much stop as pause; a swift coffee and she is gone again having only stayed long enough to reveal that French food is superior to its Iberian counterpart if the fare on offer in the cafes is anything to go by. When she is gone I am left, sitting in the middle of the courtyard, my boots off.

This is the exciting scene that greets Gene as he saunters into the cafe courtyard in the company of two other pilgrims. They all sit down at an adjacent table. Anna, the Danish pilgrim from yesterday arrives, saying that Cristina left the hostel late, but that the *paella* was wonderful.

Then she goes the same way as Juliette, which is the way June and Beatrice must have gone, and Mark before them, and countless others today, and yesterday, and all the yesterdays before it. And now it is my turn to see what they have seen.

The land that the Camino passes through resembles desert dunes. It is the colour of a hearing-aid. When I stop, I stop in the conviction that it is silent but I hear the singing of a lone bird or the drone of a beetle as it flies past. A cricket hisses in the dry grass. And it is not even a dead land: a row of bright yellow trees flare up like a sheet of flame through a fissure.

I meet up with June in Boadilla. The bar we break at has plaster crumbling off its walls and tables with glasses and plates that are crawling with flies. Some of the plastic promotional patio furniture is cracked, and the tattered awning is sunbleached. There are adobe houses crumbling at the edge of town. The barman is in a tracksuit and walks with his head slung low, wiping his nose with the palm of his hand as he and some friends lope away down the street. The bar is also a hostel but, this being the low season, seems to have given up the ghost.

June and I sit in the dilapidated beer garden. She sends a message to Lena who is now back in Copenhagen. I ask after her. She's fine, I'm told; she is finding the cost of coffee difficult to get used to. We walk to the hostel, a friendly-looking, a bit like *La Casa Mágica*, and I meet up with Gene, Anna, and Cristina. They are staying the night there and so is June.

I don't want to go on, but I do.

*

The path from Boadilla to Frómista is beside a river. After the dry lands I have spent all day in the verdant reed beds and trees by the path lend this place is an oasis. But the arid landscape of the Camino is still inside me. And as I walk I imagine other people walking with me: my father, my mother; I wonder what I would say to them if they were here. It has been a long time since I told them I loved them. It has been a long time since I had that courage. I think of them, but not of my friends, not of past loves, only them because I am their only son and I am a failure who has disappointed them. I wonder what they must think of me. I am growing old and am not married. When they were my age I was coming home from Primary school by myself, coming home on short winter evenings to hot stew and cartoons, and doing my homework on the living room floor with the flames of the fire dancing in the hearth. I have no house of my own, no career, no wife and kids, and for all the pleasing fictions I tell myself concerning freedom and independence, I am not happy about this, about how it must seem. I know they can't be happy with this.

The tress of the riverbank sprinkle the still water with leaves the colour of copper and gold. The silence amplifies every rustling tree or flickering dragonfly. A fish splashes in the water. I see a hut in a field and go to investigate. It is a single room with no door. There is a large nest of hay in there, and boxes of porridge oats beside the wall. Polish writing is spray-painted. Did a Pole live here during their Camino? For a night? For longer? Why longer? Frómista is not far. Did they stay here on a hot summer's night? Were they alone? I remember Andy telling us how he had spent the night above Orisson in a shepherd's hut. Had someone done the same thing here, so close to town? Perhaps they were happy in their own company. Perhaps they didn't want to go into town.

Neither do I, but I don't fancy sleeping in this little hut either. I go back on the path and follow the river to Frómista, where the river turns out to be a canal. It pours through sluice gates and sprays out from fissures between the huge stone blocks that clad the walls of the cutting. I arrive in town across a thin metal bridge and I think about the mill race at Sion Mills, back home, and how one winter the ice was so thick I accidentally walked out almost to the middle of the river before retracing my steps with the care of a man in a minefield. I was alone then too, but not lonely; I had stood on the icy rigging of the old railway bridge at Camus and watched a cormorant, like a little black dragon, fly along the length of the frozen river, right below my feet, with the snow tinged pink from the sunset.

Now I walk into Frómista along empty streets until I get to a series of marquees outside a series of bars. They are the pavement tables and a voice shouts "keep her lit!" It's musical Mark, and Beatrice, and others I do not know. June had taught him the expression 'Keep Her Lit' as part of a short-course on Irish idioms that had sprung up in Castrojerez. That was only last night. Why does it feel like last year? 'Keep Her Lit' means 'Keep Going', a farming expression for leaving an engine running rather than risk not being able to restart it in cold weather. Now it means 'Don't Stop'. But this is the end of my day, and I ask for directions to the hostel.

My bed for the night is a metal bunk around which is coiled a loop of electrical flex. The person on the top bunk has left their stinking boots under the bed. Wet socks droop from bed-rails and drip puddles of grey water onto the floor. Water, electricity, metal bunks – is this a hostel or a South American torture chamber? I remove the electrical loop, have a tepid shower and then wander outside where I meet the others. Is there a place I can just go for a pizza? They don't know. I go and check and find nothing but a monosyllabic bar woman who avoids eye contact as she scans the newspaper, and a distant line of Korean pilgrims carrying supermarket food back to their hostel. I think of ants bringing leaves back to their nest, and reckon that the Koreans have the right idea. But I go back to where the others are sitting down for the pilgrim meal in a hotel dining room.

Beatrice I know, but not the others. There is Alastair who is somehow involved in the hotel business, and I settle on the belief that he owns a string of hotels in Australia and California. This isn't the case, but perhaps he wishes it were. There is an Australian woman I think is wife, and I don't know if either of them wish that were true; and a Dutch couple, who look as though they have spent all their lives hiking in the outdoors and have hiked from Puy, making them the second and third people I've met today who have set themselves a task that makes mine pale by comparison.

"Don't compare", they say. "Each Camino is different". Nobody likes the food, and the others keep asking Alastair what he thinks of the wine. He is a wine-taster, that's why.

The hotel fills with locals, extended families ranging from babies in prams to elders of such advanced years that they look as though they have been freed from their pickle jars for a night out. Is it Sunday? Why else are they dressed up to the nines?

Back in the hostel, we sit in the common room. The *hospitalera*, who told me there was no church service in a tone of surprise that anyone had asked, has been replaced by an old gaffer in a flat-cap. He keeps looking into the common room, bearing witness to the spectacle of pilgrims sitting in silence, tapping on phones or leafing through abandoned books. I can't take the excitement anymore and say goodnight. I go up to my bunk, remove the flex again, and get into my sleep-sheet.

Every ache is amplified and I am in the grip of tonic annoyance: My sleep is disturbed by someone using a headlamp; My ears smart from the ear-plugs having to be pushed so far in to muffle the snoring; My feet hurt; My shoulders hurt; The cold pinches my toes; Sleep is insubstantial, short and broken, and both Navarra and La Rioja are far far away.

DAY TWENTY-TWO

Five O'Clock in the morning and the lights are flipped on. The noise of people packing begins a second later. I know it is pitch dark outside, and I know that they know. Yet I cannot understand the rush. It is a band of Koreans, racing out into the night; but there will be room in Carrión de los Condes, and there will be nothing but cold and dark for at least two hours yet.

Well, they are up and about. Others join in. I might as well, and I find myself leaving with flecks of rain still in the air and the dark streets dripping with the sounds of hiking poles. I go to the local cafe, the place where the bar woman was rude yesterday, and sit down for breakfast with Beatrice. Alistair the wine-taster is leaving. The Dutch duo are arriving. I don't remember their names, and when I ask Beatrice she says she calls them 'M&M' because that's their initials. If I didn't know who she was referring to I would think that she was walking the Camino with Eminem.

Pilgrims in the cafe are outnumbered by hunters. At first I take them for some form of local, paramilitary police force. They are decked out in camouflage fatigues and peaked caps, with their combat trousers tucked into marine boots. They are drinking brandy for breakfast and are perfect specimens of unhealthy living. For all that may be said about hunting and huntsmen, not one of them looks fit, confident or brave. I see one of them later, gambling and losing on the fruit machine in another bar, a place where I continue to wake up after Beatrice has left and the lack of sleep keeps me doped like a sluggish fish in stagnant water.

I spend two hours here talking with Wayne, whom I'd last met in Viana where he said that the Camino gave him time to "think about what might have been". He talks about Australia, about his family's role in two world wars fighting under the Union flag for a country they still considered a homeland. He had a long-lost brother, he says, with whom he has only recently been united and of whom he was ignorant for most of his life. When I ask him what it was like to meet this long-lost brother for the first time he says that it was "all good". I like this low-key response. It is honest and natural and the polar opposite of the fawning ham-acting that seems to represent happiness in our culture.

Wayne is staying in Frómista today. He says cheerio and walks off into town, his hands in his pockets. I sit outside where the late morning sun has dried last night's rain from the benches. Clouds tumble across the sky and a breeze scatters smattering drops from an awning. A few cars idle along the street. The pilgrims have all gone, and the town falls into the lull that perhaps all these larger towns fall into. They are big enough to house a number of hostels and are seen by many pilgrims as places to sleep in; they are destinations. The guide book I have has divided the route from Saint Jean to Santiago into thirty-tree stages, one for every year Jesus was on earth, and almost every English-speaker I have met is using this book and this series of stages to plan their Camino. Unlike the small towns with their one cafe and constant flow of customers, towns like this look like they have a circadian cycle of feast and famine. This is the famine.

*

It is almost noon when I begin walking out of town and onto the *senda*. This is a long runway of ground white gravel running parallel to the highway. At intervals there are bollards along which the *senda* runs. The impression is like driving through a tunnel with the lights flashing overhead with the regularity of a metronome. There is a choice, though. There is nineteen kilometres of this to Carrión, or I can take the scenic route by river.

*

The scenic route by the river is a broad metalled auxiliary track for farm vehicles running alongside low concrete viaducts. Copses of trees echo to gunfire and I wonder what the quarry is; small birds perhaps, quail maybe. Trespassing pilgrims?

Beyond a little village I turn off to investigate a field of wig-wams. The wig-wams are part of an out-of-season novelty hostel. A steer's skull is on a pole draped with dream-catchers. There are geese milling about the wig-wams, defensive and honking, their strangled yelping failing to attract the attention of a dog dozing on the inside window-sill of a house. There is nobody about, and I wonder if there were, would I stop for the day because the novelty of staying in a wig-wam is too good to pass up. This too is the Camino. The geese snake out their necks and hiss and honk, and one opens its wings to make itself appear more intimidating. It works; I walk back onto the track.

The track ends in a hamlet. There are no people. No cars pass through it. There are no cats or dogs laying claim to the empty streets. Old signs have shed most of their paint. Things rust. Things crumble. A zephyr puffs at the dust. I stop. Now there is silence.

I stand still and let the silence crowd in on me. I am so far away from anywhere I know, and the strange and sudden feeling of the Camino as a tightrope with nothing on either side of it grips me. What am I doing out here?

I turn back to the scenic route. The path runs alongside trees that run alongside a river. Far across the fields there is the highway and the *senda*, but I see no tiny figures walking the senda. I see no cars travelling west. I remind myself that I left late from a town where people were leaving at 6am. But, I repeat to myself, where is everyone? Where are you?

Where are you?

Again and again I stop and look back, and again and again I see nothing but the mirror image of the path in front. The silver undersides of the leaves flash into the surf-hissing wind. The breeze picks up and the trees begin to roar. It is the sound of white noise, as though the universe is detuned.

This continues for mile after mile; tonic white noise and not a soul to be seen. For some reason the simple act of walking now seems as laborious as if I were walking in lead boots. The absurdity of my life on the Camino overtakes me and I stop walking and take to standing there. I stop but my heart keeps walking on. What am I doing here?

What am I doing here?

Where are you?

There is nothing but the rushing trees and the empty fields and the barren path.

What the hell am I doing here?

Where the hell are you?

The answer is the dumb machine roar of the Camino.

That's enough.

I have stopped and will my heart to stop too: *Just stop, just stop, just stop it*. No more. That's enough. That's all. That's enough of me and you and everything else. Stop. What's the point of letting it run on?

I have stopped but I could stop, full stop. I could stop me and you and everything else by making a noose, a tidy hangman's noose with thirteen coils to the knot. And I could use any one of these turbine-hissing trees too. But all I can imagine are the coils in the bungee cord of my rucksack; a bungee noose, and my risible dead body being found, springing up and down like a yo-yo in the wind.

*

This is the Camino:

I am sitting at the chapel of *El Virgen del Río*. I am sitting on the verandah as though it were raining. I've tried the doors but they're locked, and the sound of the trees is gone. I am sitting here looking back across the fields. I have looked back before but with a sense of accomplishment. Now I look back with a sense of failure.

I don't want to walk along this Camino of theirs any longer.

There's no harm in admitting it: I don't know why I began walking it, and no reason has presented itself. I'm not even sure where I am; let alone what I'm doing here.

Well, what would I be doing otherwise?

I think back to the life I was living just a few weeks ago. I think of evenings spent drinking alone under the bottled light of a sixty watt bulb. I think of days that ended when work ended, and weekends that drained away as though they had a leak. I remember the rhythm of the working week, and how each five day stretch just seemed to fold itself up and vanish. I remember making the weekday evenings go away hour by hour by episode by episode of one box-set or another. There were rare meetings with friends who became acquaintances who became people on Facebook who never posted anything who became tiny postage-stamps of their faces by the side of the screen. I learned how to kill time in cinemas and cafes and pub corners with books, and in the gym; a well-toned mind in a well-toned body, and a withered soul like a child kept locked up in a cellar.

I mastered sarcasm. A smart wit, a trip-wire responsiveness to any perceived slight that had to be repaid in spades, an inchoate misanthropy, and yet too stupid to give it up because I was too dull to see any way out. A rut so deep it was a trench. My life in the trenches, dug in against enemies that were not there; a stupid, lonely coward. Perhaps I went on the Camino to get away from that person. Perhaps I just don't want to be like that. What is there to like? Haven't I stewed for too long in the same stale juices? What is so attractive about a person in a rut, who has not the moral strength to get out of it?

I look back along the track. There is not a soul, and those distant trees are silent now. I watch them pulsing, their leaves flickering green and white as the wind turns them. And it is as though a voice is telling me to look because I am meant to see something there. There is a great benevolence in the world; this is what I think and I do not know why. And it occurs to me that I have been brought here, as though I was not pushed onto the Camino by the person I did not want to be, but summoned here by a quiet voice I could not hear back in Dublin but which I had obeyed.

This quiet voice does not console.

It is the voice of a judge with a bitter judgement. It tells me that I am inert, as neon is inert, as is argon. It tells me that I am egotistical, that I am cruel; it tells me that I feed on myself and that is why I am starving. It tells me I am vain, thinking that in my godless life I am humane, that I am wise. All I have done, I see, is to lose faith in what I was taught in school. All I have done is to outgrow childish things and I strut the earth as though it were an achievement.

Why do I despair? Because the ego is thwarted, because it cannot get what it wants; it is selfish. I despair because I am selfish. I despair because I believe in myself.

Why do I feel calm all of a sudden? In my despair I have forsaken myself; and rid of such an illusion, the emptiness feels full.

This is the end of the scenic route by the river.

I sling my rucksack up on to my back. There is a hand-pump with Saint James's cross on it. It works, but there is a sign saying that the water is not treated so I judge the water in my flask to be enough and begin walking to the highway. The road from the church joins the highway and its attendant *senda* at a small town. I visit the church, a Templar church, and have my *Credencial* stamped at the door. The retable has been here for over a millennium. It is not as over-powering as that in Los Arcos, not as all-encompassing as that in Santo Domingo, but countless people have seen it, from ages beyond memory to the last pilgrim to enter this church before me.

Will I stay in this town? If I do I will never meet the others again. They are ahead of me and they will not wait for me.

Is that what I want? Maybe. Maybe not.

I walk out of the Templar church and walk though the town to where the *senda* runs towards Carrión. Fine; Carry on to Carrión. The *senda* plods up the long side of a hill. At the top I see it running on and on like a ladder laid flat on the ground towards the distant haze that is the city. One foot follows the other all the way along this thankless walkway. I decide to go to Carrión and book into a hotel, still in a mind to let the others walk far ahead of me. I pass a man sitting on a bollard listening to a football match on the radio. We wish one another a "Buen Camino". I've no idea if he is a pilgrim. There are people using the senda to walk their dogs, much in the same way that people at home use golf courses, and they too wish me a "Buen Camino". I notice that old Spaniards never do this, but say "Adios" as a greeting – 'To God'.

As I arrive in Carrión it begins to rain; there are light, sparse cold drops, but as I reach the town centre it is strong enough for me to step into the shelter of the tourist office porch. This light skiff of rain, this slight pause, changes the trajectory of the day. I continue along the main street and bump into M&M who are leaving a shop. "Your friends are in there!" They point through the window. It's June with musical Mark and Beatrice. I was on the way to a hotel at the far end of town, now I tap the glass and wave in.

"So you got here!" They are all smiles and handfuls of sweets.

"Where are you all staying?"

They are staying at the convent hostel, but not Beatrice. "I'm in Santa Clara", she says, "back down there". She points the way I have come. The convent hostel is run by singing nuns. I walk in expecting to register, but no-one is there because "they have gone to get their guitars". When they return they not only have guitars, but an autoharp and a set of bongos. They hand out song sheets and ask everyone to sing along. They sing 'Ultreia' the song I last heard being sung in Orisson and follow it up with *Guantanamera*, the nuns working their bongo magic before asking the pilgrims to sing a song in their own language. Mark sings his Grañón song, and the nuns sing a song in Korean for the Koreans who join in and laugh when it is over. It is lovely. They are lovely. But I am not in the mood, for this or for tomorrow, for Santiago or for people, for singing or for talking; I want to go.

The others are going to the pilgrim mass and we arrange to meet up at the restaurant further up the street. I turn to June and Mark: "Pray for me" I say. I feel like a weirdo. They are the words of a madman, but she nods and looks concerned. Mark looks concerned too: "Sure thing, buddy. We gotcha".

I follow Beatrice to Santa Clara where I meet the *hospitalero* in the gift shop. He blinks constantly from behind thick glasses and repeats the last few words of every sentence, of every sentence. He shows me up to my room, which used to be the cell where one of the nuns or monks lived. The tiny monastic community must be gone now, the place transformed into a hostel for pilgrims. I wonder about the community that once lived here, them and their world, but not for long; I return to the street and retrace my steps up to where the restaurant is warm with light and people and the street is damp in the shade of the dusk.

Only Beatrice is there. The others are still at the pilgrim mass which is "going on a bit". We order, but not the pilgrim menu. The pilgrim menu seems to be the same everywhere we go. For the same price we pick our way through the menu, and I even think the waitress is happy to talk to us, to recommend things, rather than to note down another pilgrim menu.

We are eating when the others arrive: June, Mark, M&M. The mass, it seems, left a lot to be desired. "That's the part of our church I really don't like" says musical Mark. "All that waving your hands around like you're doing a magic trick, casting a spell".

"And it went on for ages" says June. "I couldn't wait for it to finish". Mark tells a joke about a bishop and a ladle and M&M crack up; soon we are all smiling, eating and drinking, and the long lonely tramp towards Carrión is forgotten. When the meal is over I return to Santa Clara. The tumble dryer has left my clothes warm and damp. I take them out. Another pilgrim has left their damp clothes in a heap. I put their stuff in the dryer and pay for it. I hope it doesn't shrink.

I lay my damp clothes on the radiators in my room. The shower is luxurious compared to those in some of the hostels I've been in. The space and silence is palatial compared to the cramped dorms of metal-frame beds. There is a portrait of the *Pietà* on the wall above my bed. As I lie beneath it waiting for sleep, I think of earlier and the sense of how miserable my ego had become in the dawning understanding that it is just the shell of a seed, and it must yield to the new life within.

DAY TWENTY-THREE

My feet touch a warm rug. Bliss. The simple pleasures of life.

I make the most of this oasis by showering again and using up the little shampoos and shower gels that were on my bed in a gift bag, as was an individually wrapped emery board in a cardboard tube.

Decadent? Perhaps.

It is with a spring in my step that I leave Santa Clara and walk up the main street of the town. I buy postcards from a shop that is crammed to the rafters with Camino souvenirs, but I cannot find the post office, despite the shopkeeper's instructions. I wander back down the main street to where I see a *Correos* sign, but it is the sorting office. Some things will have to wait. I go for breakfast in a cafe by the sorting office and when I leave I ask a man smoking outside *"¿Sabes donde están los correos?"*

The man freezes, fear behind his glasses. *"No español"* he says. And nearly no teeth either. He is missing his upper incisors. He points to himself: "Irish".

'Tis an awful small world, to be sure. His name is Brian and he is walking the Camino having just recovered from a stroke. He has smoked all his life, he says, and is not in the best of shape. He puffs on his pipe as he tells me this. Today, he opines, is just a big walk with nowhere to stop.

Brian isn't wrong. Today is indeed a day without places to stop. The guide map looks like a blank page with a straight line drawn through it. I wish him luck. He wishes me the same, and I am away, back up the street walking past the place where I bought the postcards and feeling embarrassed for some reason, as though the shopkeeper might see me and wonder why I'm still loafing about town.

I turn the corner, fail to find another post office despite the directions of a man on the street, and then Carrión is behind me. I cross the bridge, pausing to look at the castle above the river, and then I pass the Parador, cross the busy roundabout, and am walking the road beside damp fields. There is a dirty fleecy sky, dour and overcast, and light rain begins to fall. It continues to rain like this for hour after interminable hour. It is too light to warrant a poncho. Where there is a rest area, there is a well and a few concrete picnic tables dripping with rainwater. The well is a small cement tomb from which juts an overflow pipe. Behind it are the depressing heaps of toilet paper and human waste that seem to inhabit every secluded spot on the Camino.

There is only one person on the path here.

"Hello", he says, "I'm Bertrand from Switzerland."

I remember Andy's pilgrim friends. "You walked from Switzerland?"

"No, no. Saint Jean".

"Me too"

Bertrand risks a wet backside by sitting down for a break at the picnic tables. I say goodbye and walk on. And I am alone, totally alone, for seventeen kilometres of strict-straight Roman road, now paved with beaten soil and gravel. The faint rustle of the rain is the soundscape of the landscape, broken only at one point by a flock of birds taking flight from a field. The burr of their wings sounds like a propeller.

I feel as though I'm on a treadmill. The road is ironed flat. The landscape is a series of blank slates in brown or beige. Are the retables of the churches in this part of Spain so phantasmagorical because the people who lived out here for generations went crazy? These are the blank lands that foster visions; living Rothko paintings where every horizon is the edge of an opening door, an opening window. On it goes, and when I see a hikers' shelter by the side of the road I find Cristina there with another pilgrim. As with the shelter on the hill after Castrojerez, it is a lean-to covered in graffiti. Bertrand catches up with us. We ponder the significance of a brand new pair of hiking boots sitting by the side of the road in the rain. Everyone wants there to be at least one bend in the road, a curve, a lost horizon that might set the imagination racing. But there is only the gentle slope up ahead and the unfounded promise of a proper place to have a break beyond it.

I leave and walk up the slope. There is nothing but the blank stare of the wet road. It just continues on ahead, and so must I. Hours of walking. Hours. And hours, and then the spire of a distant church. This must be how the mediaeval pilgrims felt: elation, joy, relief. The church and then a small cluster of buildings: civilization. The road gives up before I do, and drops like a stone, down down down to these small buildings. A Guardia Civil patrol car cruises by and I hold my hand up by way of saying 'hello'. They return the gesture and then are gone.

The road stops by a cafe and I find Beatrice, Gene, and June preparing to leave. They are all glad of the break. The waitress is rude to the point of having a personality disorder, but I don't care. Having slogged across so much nothing, sitting down out of the rain and having something to eat feels like some sort of small victory.

The others leave and there are good wishes and 'see you later's all round. As they go Juliette appears asking me if I saw the police. Indeed I did. I waved to them.

"And did they catch the man?"

"What man?"

"The man up there". She points out the window, at the road. "He was at the shelter".

I don't know anything about a man at the shelter.

"Yes. He was looking at the women there. He was behind the shelter. I could see him. He was masturbating". And at this point Juliette, standing in the middle of the cafe, mimes a pervert masturbating behind a hikers' shelter. "I shouted at him and he ran away. When I saw the police here I told them".

He can't be hard to spot, I think. There isn't so much as a fig-leaf to hide behind up there. But the story is disturbing. The empty roads and isolation of the *Meseta* have not been what I expected. But I have only ever been threatened by myself out there.

But who knows? We have created a world in which friends of mine walk home alone with their keys poking through their fists like knuckle-dusters in case they are attacked. One friend in London told me of a plan to have women-only train carriages. These already exist in some countries. Once I was in a Dublin gym locker room, drying myself after a shower, and a massive steroid-crazed hulk was wandering about muttering in German and staring at me. "I felt like I was in prison", I told Agnieszka, "it was terrifying".

"Women get that all the time" she replied. "More often than you'd think".

More to the point, despite the Camino feeling like the safest place I've ever been, where the greatest crime seems to be petty theft, there was an incident the year before where a pilgrim was attacked in an attempted abduction. Prior to this another pilgrim went missing. Both pilgrims were women. It turns the stomach to think that there are men out there who do such things, to women and to other men, so making light of the pervert up at the hiking shelter is not an option. The Guardia Civil must have felt the same way as they went straight up there after having been alerted.

The fate of the pervert is a mystery. But his punishment is not. Good people are rewarded by being good people, and bad people are punished by being bad people. A pervert's punishment is to be a pervert.

*

The cafe is beside a hostel, and must be how the hostel maintains an income during the low season. I leave it and walk along the street of a small village, my eyes peeled for a *Correos* but there is not one to be found. There does not seem to be much life in the town, and I have reached the end of the street without meeting a soul when I hear a wavering cry behind me. I turn and see an old lady in her nightgown. She faces the door of a house and wails the way a lost child wails. She reaches out and touches the door, then wails again.

What can I do?

She upsets me the way the homeless upset me, not so much because of their predicament but because there is nothing I can do about it. Living in a city has put me in such a situation so many times that I have become callous. Yet I remember going to Manchester for the first time when I was eighteen and seeing a person sleeping rough for the first time in my life and being so horrified that a person could end up in such a situation. I have seen people in that situation hundreds, maybe thousands, of times in Dublin. And they no longer horrify me. They just ruin my day, and I hate that. I hate thinking that, hate admitting that, hate the world for creating that situation, and I hate being part of that world.

I walk on, with the old lady still by the door. Maybe she is frightened the way a child can be frightened. Maybe she is alone. Maybe, in her dotage, she feels as though she has lost her parents and wants to go home.

*

The road meets the motorway again at Ledigos, and I continue on in the belief that Terradillos is not far. Compared to how far I have walked today, it is not much farther, but I am tired and when fatigue sets in time and space seem to stretch. There is a *senda* running under trees up to a point where I think I have either taken a wrong turning or walked past Terradillos. But I do not remember doing either; there has been no opportunity to take a wrong turn, and I have seen not so much as a kennel on my way since Ledigos. Then, I see the top of a roof and feel that I am nearly there.

If fatigue stretches time and space, then disappointment stretches patience. There is a hostel, but its gates are shut and two Alsatian dogs prowl the grounds. I keep going and find myself inching down a short steep street to where Templar flags herald my destination: a hostel named after Jacque de Molday, the last leader of the Templar Order. The hostel, run by a friendly *hospitalera*, is themed on the fabled warrior-monks with each room named after an illustrious knight, and a big Templar cross in pride of place above the fireplace in the dining room. When I arrive she knows my name and shows me up to where my "friends have you in their room, yes". As they do. Gene, Bernice, June and I are in the same room, and we are joined by two Koreans, and later two Spaniards.

Dinner is with the four of us and Alastair, M&M, and a Chinese pilgrim who speaks little or nothing of any European language. She is walking the Camino with the remaining time on her visa having come to visit her daughter who is studying in the UK. She looks half her age. I ask Alastair about being a wine-taster. He is on a bus-man's holiday, researching wine for hotel wine lists as he goes. He will continue his travels down into Portugal. I ask him about the wine we are drinking with the meal and he says "some wines are better talked over than talked about".

It's a neat response, a smart response, a witty one too, but comes nowhere close to the response I got from a priest when was a student and he was the university chaplain. He had just officiated at a funeral.

"That must be the most difficult part of being a priest, doing the funerals".

"No. Confessions are the worst".

"Is that because of all the terrible things people tell you?"

"No, it's boring". He shrugged. "You've either heard it before or done it yourself".

DAY TWENTY-FOUR

Today presents the blistered pilgrims of the Camino with two options: the *senda* by the highway, or the 'green route'. As soon as I set foot on this green route I feel that it should be called the red route as last night's rain has brought out the rich red colour of the soil. This red soil, tilled, turned over and over releases the overpowering scent of damp, rich, subterranean realms of gestation and decay. Puddles of rain water change colour as I pass by them: Electric blue, purple, burgundy, beryl ringed with orange.

This beautiful red carpet is rolled out before us – June, Beatrice, myself – and we walk and we talk, and we listen to one another. This is the Camino. For the first time in what feels like an age, I remind myself to Pay Attention. 'This too shall pass' I tell myself: this is the eternal truth. Bad times are not permanent, so do not give up. Good times are not permanent, so don't take them for granted. Appreciate them.

Appreciate this moment. I think of the world as something that wants to be appreciated, something that manifests itself as a vision of beauty. I dread to think that this is something I will forget when I am back in 'reality'. So I enjoy the walk. The world is as much there for me as it is for anybody else. Be slow. It needs to be appreciated, it needs to be admired.

Thoughts:

Pay Attention to this moment. This moment is on loan, these beautiful things are on loan; just as everything is on loan. The time of my life is borrowed time. My body was loaned to me at birth and is to be returned at death. Family, friends, the things I say are mine, they are all on loan. Who or what are they on loan from? Call it the Great Beyond, the Universe, call it God, or the Cosmos, or Life – it doesn't matter what I call it: It gives, and it taketh away.

*

To the north of the track are the Cantabrian Mountains. Caesar Augustus drove his troop across this Martian soil when he set himself to war against the Cantabrians. There are mines in the mountains;

wealth sprang from them as water from wells. The mountains appear on the horizon as a tsunami, its crest bitten into by the hot blue sky. I hear a crow call. I can hear its wingbeats; they sound like shears on stiff fabric, they sound like a slow steam train.

*

We meet no-one else on the track. Only when we stop in tiny hamlets do we meet people: people from Alaska, people from Italy, no-one we have met before. Nice people that we don't get to know better. We stop to look at the bodegas in these villages – sunken wine-cellars like hobbit houses, their ventilation chimneys poking up from each tumulus with its tiny bolted door. When we are walking, there is only the three of us, flung together by chance for this one day, and the only signs of life are the distant barks from a series of silos as a siren wails. At one point a train rumbles past, dragging wagon after wagon of raw ore.

We arrive at the outskirts of Sahagún. There is a quiet little chapel and a path that runs over a bridge and between two statues. The statues remind me of something from *The Lord of the Rings*, and the significance of this spot becomes apparent when the inscription that runs across the ground between them tells us that we are at the geographical halfway point between Saint Jean and Santiago. So, we ask ourselves: How do we feel about that? Happy to be closer to the end than the beginning? Sad for the same reason?

In Sahagún we meet Danny and Liam, taking a rest day because of shin-splints. Their calves and ankles are swathed in sticky blue bandages. Further in town, in a bar, we catch up with Gene, Anna, and Cristina for a very long and very good humoured lunch. There is plenty of wine, and *liquor de hierba* to finish. The waiter mimes everything on the menu. He might have been at the wine and *liquor de hierba* too judging by his rabbit impression. We buy stamps and postcards and send greetings home. We leave Sahagún late in the afternoon and arrive at our hostel, Via Trajana, late in the evening. As we arrive, the dense golden light of magic hour coats the countryside. The hostel is cosy, a country house, and the food is country cooking and complements a day that absolves all those tough days I allowed myself to have. In the dining room there is an oil portrait of some farmers slaughtering a pig. We share our dinner table with a Finnish couple, Armo and Milla, who say they have travelled the Camino before and choose their accommodation based on the quality of the food.

The day ends with the sunset searing the clouds, bats flitting by the window, and the stars appearing over the peaceful world.

DAY TWENTY-FIVE

The sun walks with us along the red road. To the north the irregular serrations of the mountains appear distant and unreal, as the moon appears unreal in the noonday sky. The three of us continue along the Roman road to Religioso. Here we stop at Bar Elvis. I am used now, because of the *Meseta*, to see every salient feature of the countryside as possessing a singular distinction. A lone tree, a prominent farm silo, a shrub in a field; all of them assume a degree of importance because they seem to have been singled out by the landscape. There is no anonymity on the *Meseta* – everything is exposed and set apart.

But Bar Elvis is a smack to the back of the retinas.

Inside and out, the whole place is scrawled over. Doodles, names, initials, stick figures, cartoons, slogans; the cave art of the Camino tribe is everywhere. This is as much a part of the landscape of the Camino as is a retable underlit by candlelight. Every square inch of the place has been scribbled over: the walls, inside and out, the tables, the bar, the ceiling, the pillars propping the place up. A 'No Smoking' sign covers a bald patch like a toupee, which is its only function as the patrons pay no heed to it, puffing away like chimneys as they glug beer and shovel *patatas bravas* down their throats. The owner has *The Walk of Life* blaring on the CD player. By design or by accident, it is stuck on repeat, and the song plays in a loop for the time we are there. Perhaps it has been playing in a loop all day. Perhaps it will play in a loop for the rest of the day. Perhaps it has been playing in a loop since the dawn of time, and will play until time ends. Perhaps this is one of those places from *The Twilight Zone*, where some cosmic truth is represented as a guy in a beret whistling like an untended kettle as he throws knives around like juggler's clubs before hacking slices off a ham-shank to make sandwiches. He too smokes, and glugs from a bottle of beer, and when there is no-one to serve he lounges outside on the patio furniture. Even when there is someone to serve he lounges outside on the patio furniture, and only ventures to the bar on the 'kill two birds with one stone' principle. This is how I get to be standing at the bar beside Beatrice wondering how it could be possible to open a place like this on the Camino, and just live out here, half-cut on light beer, and kept alive on cured ham.

"You could", she says. "Why don't you?"

*

There is another choice of paths from Bar Elvis: to the *senda* and into Mansilla, or continue though the countryside past the prison, and again into Mansilla. For some reason a lonely path by a prison holds little appeal to the others who opt for the *senda*. I have it in my head that the senda is to be avoided, and it doesn't register that by avoiding the dreaded *senda* I also avoid the company of the others. By taking the *senda* they go on without me. They don't change their minds and follow me down to the prison. I don't change my mind and follow them. I do manage to convince my ego to take to the road with me, however, having abandoned the poor thing outside Carrión only a day or two ago. Without it I had better company. With it, I tramp up past the bodegas and gravestones of Religioso, and turn downhill at the crossroads to where the prison is big, alien, and industrial.

I can hear the tannoy from the prison. It is the voice of a robot. I feel that it is not a voice from the prison so much as that it is the voice of the prison itself. It is a strange thing to walk this stretch of road, all alone, with the open and empty fields to one side and the closed and crowded prison to the other. Here I am, one free man who can go where he pleases, and just a short distance away there are scores of captive men who can only pace the exercise yard when they are not cooped up in their cells. I wonder if it is possible – if they are permitted – to look out of a prison window and see the path. If so, who is watching me, and do they envy the freedom I have? Or are they imagining that they are snipers?

I cannot say that those prisoners are shut away from the world, like the cenobites in a closed convent. They are part of the world. It is a world I tried to step out of when I came on the Camino, only to discover that I had brought that world onto the Camino with me, because I was part of that world. It is a world that brings me no pleasure.

When I think about returning to Dublin, I think about returning to Dublin and then I don't want to return to Dublin. I think of that sepulchral city and how it has given itself to the dumb world, and how I gave myself to it in turn. It is at one with the world, and the world is a world whose people have been trained by proxy violence and by vicarious cruelty to be vile. The world is tutored by television and the internet to accept the extremes as normal and the base as admirable. The world has able-bodied people leading sessile lives in thrall to foolish fictions. Given a little time, the world transforms day-old children into square-eyed idiots with no critical faculties.

Long before the Camino I was trying to get away from the world, but if I am as to the world as a cell is to the body, then I was not liberating myself but encysting myself. I was foolish, with the foolishness of the world, and in my foolishness I considered the world to be some external thing that was bad for me; but I was part of that world, and so I was bad for me. So I walk past the prison, the great penitentiary of León, and being foolish with the foolishness of the world I cannot see the other prison that is there this day.

*

The path past the prison runs alongside a drainage ditch in which there are red dragonflies. They gleam with a ruby glow and they sound like someone fanning the pages of a book when they fly past me. They are the only sound that comes from the world beyond the confines of the prison until the road joins the highway. There are trucks here, lots of trucks, and they roar and leave clouds of cement dust in their wake.

I walk along the hard shoulder, wanting to leave the highway and get away from the fast, thundering metal of the trucks and lorries. But their road and mine only divides at great earthworks where men are rearranging the landscape to create a motorway bridge. The bridge has no road lying across its back. No road runs under it. There is only the ploughed earth, the searing sunlight, and many thousands of gossamer threads that glimmer as they drift in the air.

There are no yellow arrows now. Only hot, dry dust and the sounds of machines. I can see the town in the distance and it is nice not to be guided by the arrows but by my own wits to get there. I walk into the outskirts, past a graveyard, and am wondering if this is indeed Mansilla and not some other town when I see the old city gate and arrive. As with all such towns, the open, white-washed suburbs are replaced by cramped streets, cancerian plazas, and a shift on the spectrum into a palette of greys and pale browns.

I find the hostel. The *hospitalera* stamps my Credencial and remarks that it is "busy". I go to the dorm and am sorting out a place to sleep when Beatrice says hello. I move across the dorm to where she is perched on the edge of her bed. She says she wants an early night, but is going to find a supermarket to buy food for tomorrow as she doesn't think there will be anywhere open so early. I ask her why not, and she replies that "there doesn't seem to be much to the place".

She's not wrong. The shower, when I find it behind an unmarked door is little better than a hosepipe sticking out of the wall. There is a window in the shower cubicle, and directly on the other side is a table of pilgrims. I recognise some of the voices, but they sound boorish and annoying now. I shut the window to shower. All the while I keep reminding myself that it's all about perception, that things are as good or as bad as we allow them to be; but I feel treated like dirt by the standards in this place, and I cannot see why I should feel good about it. It may be my pride that is offended by this, but the effect is to send me out of the place to find a bite to eat where there are no pilgrims with their quests and ego trips, but normal locals leading normal lives in the way that I should be a normal local leading a normal life somewhere far from this place, it's hosepipe and its braying pilgrims.

So I go. I go and I go and I go, far far far away out into the suburbs, the quiet unwound suburbs, where I find some normal local bar and sit with a beer and *Living Water* as parents and kids with their normal lives come to spend time together and go. I return, helping a man with directions to the hospital as I go – for which I use my guidebook map – and then I simply sit in another bar, reading the Spanish newspapers which are full of chat about what the new government might do to the place.

Back in the dorm, two Korean pilgrims are packing for tomorrow when one of them collapses. There is only the three of us in the dorm. Her friend reassures me that it is fine; it is epilepsy and they are together because one of them is watching out for the other. The pilgrim who collapsed comes round and gets to her feet. Her friend points to the top bunk.

"Really?"

"Yes".

I help her guide her friend up onto the top bunk where she lies in the recovery position as her friend reassures me again, "is OK, OK, OK. Is OK". She is calm, smiling, patient; I wonder how many times she has gone through this before.

DAY TWENTY-SIX

In the morning I leave before anyone else. In the courtyard I look up and see a red light moving past the windows on the upper floor. It is a pilgrim getting ready for the day ahead. The main door is locked, but I open it, close it behind me, and am away. There is a crescent moon and around it, the whole universe. They make the walls of the city seem splendid, ancient, noble, and charged with tales of all they have seen. I cross the bridge, and then the road, and then fish my headlamp out of my bag, switch it on, and slip down the steep verge to the track. I stop many times to stare up at the stars, allowing my eyes to get accustomed to the dark so that more and more stars become apparent. With time, the sky becomes velvet rolled in sugar.

The sun rises behind me. I stop to turn, to look, to walk on, to stop and turn and look again. The sunrise is burned by halogen colours, bromines and chlorines, and the sky behind it is Marian blue. I am soon walking in the pale morning sunlight, under the trees that separate the track from the road, and then it turns, over a short wooden bridge, and then into a park by a long Roman bridge, arched like the Loch Ness monster. There is a cafe by the end of this bridge, 'The Green Dolphin', and I stop for breakfast. I am the first customer today. The waiter says that in a week all the private hostels will start shutting down because the busy season will be over. In summer, he says, there is a constant stream of pilgrims, but in winter maybe one or two a day.

I take my breakfast to a table. On the television there is a travel show about Andalucía and I'm wondering what life would be like if I had stayed there when outside the window I see M&M, who glance up at the cafe. I wave at them through the glass, and they smile, and I thank God that I can make someone smile despite all that I am feeling. I open the door for them, sweeping the way before them with my free hand as though I were a footman. The air clears, and we laugh. We sit down to breakfast together. Then, I see Mark, musical Mark, still in his freezing soccer shorts. I call to him out the door "come in and have coffee with us!" He smiles too and we pull two tables together and breakfast continues. Then Beatrice joins us, and the Chinese pilgrim from Terradillos who has only a few words of English, and amazes us all again just by virtue of the fact that she is tackling this. One by one the breakfast party drifts off, and then I too am walking in the warm morning air along a broad pavement towards hills of singing pylons.

It is on the slope of this hill, where birds nest in the holes in the concrete pylons, that I stop to fill my flask at a *fuente*. I meet Beatrice again. We continue along the track together. She talks incessantly about all manner of things from New Zealand wildlife to the issues experienced by the students she teaches. I gather that she is also a counsellor, offering career advice to students. She sometimes has to tease out underlying crises that are affecting their performance in school and she says that resolving these issues gives her the most satisfaction.

We see the urban sprawl of León away in the distance between the hills. A motorway roars like an engine, drawing lorries filled with all manner of things towards it and spewing forth an equally burdened river of merchandise. The path rises up to where it overlooks the motorway. Here, through the wire mesh of the fence, people have woven crosses. I remember them from Logroño, in what feels like a lifetime ago. Beside the fence someone has set up a lemonade stand. Cans of lemonade are in plastic boxes, kept cool by big blocks of ice laid across the top of them. A tin on the table beside the boxes is marked 'donations', and a sign hanging from the front of the table tells us that we should pay a donation for a soft drink, so that more soft drinks can be bought for future pilgrims. There is nobody around to police this. Someone could have made off with the lemonade, but no-one has. Somebody could have made off with the tin of donations, but no-one has. Beatrice and I put our donations in the tin and take a lemonade each. It is cool and pleasing, and tastes good for the way in which I came to be drinking it. We pause to drink. On one side of the fence there is the slow world of the pilgrim with all the trust involved in this lemonade stand. On the other side of the fence is the speed and clamour of the world, with all its buck-making, muck-raking, back-breaking work, and stress, duress, and ferocity. The fence is the tenuous veil between them; the crosses, the spell that keeps them apart.

I still cannot say why I am walking the Camino. In fact I am less sure than ever. But I do not want to leave it, not when it can create places like this, places that I will never encounter in that world on the other side of the fence. We continue into the city, over a bridge and into the old town through an arch in its venerable double walls. I have not thought about where to stay but I walk with Beatrice until she has found her hotel, almost invisible as the sign is a tiny plaque the size of a postcard on the door-jamb. By the time we find it, I cannot be bothered going off to look elsewhere and I ask the *hospitalero* if there is a room. There is, and at a discount because it is not *en suite*. But there is nobody to share the bathroom with as all the other rooms are *en suite*. I wash my clothes and hang them to dry on a bungee stretched across the railings of the balcony.

León is stranger than Burgos, which was itself stranger than Pamplona. It seems that the further along the Camino I go the less of a city person I become. It has not even been a month, yet the new habits of waking to walk, and living off-line have set me apart from the throng of citizens and tourists that now surround me. They photograph the illustrious buildings; I do not. They all seem to be busy; I have nothing to do here. I have no reason for being here. Neither do they.

There is a small square just outside the hotel and I am sitting there, talking with Beatrice when we are joined by M&M and then Mark who has finally found himself a pair of trousers. The cathedral is close by and Mark and I decide to take a look. It is being repaired, which helps me imagine it as it was during the time of its construction. The entire thing was erected in fifty years, and must have been quite something to pilgrims who arrived at it from a world of tiny, rudimentary villages. The cathedral is impressive to this modern day pilgrim in that it is a building over which much care and attention is being lavished, yet it serves no function necessitated by modern city. It is not a hospital, nor a bank, there is no office space here, nor does it make the kind of money a nightclub would, or a cinema. It is a great shell and its windows are panels of coloured light. Tourists, myself included, wander around staring upwards with audioguides pressed to our ears.

*

Outside the cathedral, Mark offers me his opinion on it. He does not like the cathedral because it is bombastic; it is showy and dead. He describes it as a museum piece, rather than a church, because a church is made of people not blocks of stone. I agree with that, but it is not enough for me to dislike it. I do not see a choice between big monumental structures like this, and a community of people. They are aspects of the same thing, different atoms in the same molecule.

He doesn't think you should have to pay to see inside the cathedral. "It was six bucks to get in there", he says and he's not wrong. I'm of the opinion that these six bucks help repair and maintain one of the great gems of Western culture, which is a bargain considering you could spend twelve bucks going to see *Transformers 2*, which is an artefact of Western culture that doesn't need to be maintained. Why complain about viewing something like the cathedral for a knock-down price when nobody seems to mind paying through the teeth for tickets to have their intelligence insulted?

He laughs and this and we wander about a bit more before he leaves to continue his song-writing. I buy stuff at a supermarket and go back to the hotel. One important thing I have to remember is to enjoy a long night's unbroken sleep when I can.

DAY TWENTY-SEVEN

At 8am builders begin drilling in the street outside. I leave the hotel and go for coffee at the plaza in front of the cathedral. I watch the people drift past. An elderly Chinese man passes with quavering Chinese music wafting from a transistor radio he has hidden up his sleeve. A group of teenagers begins to gather. They are dressed as characters from *Suicide Squad*, *Slipknot*, or wearing the 'Anonymous' mask from *V for Vendetta*. Hallowe'en is just around the corner. My good sense deserts me for a moment and I feel a pang of defensiveness. Hallowe'en was an Irish festival and it revolts me to see a folk festival from my childhood harvest countryside debased by these idiots. They're only ignorant, I tell myself; think about something worth employing your brain on. One of the teenagers, dressed as a nun, clowns around in front of the cathedral to cackles of mirthless laughter from the others. I try to remember the experience of being twelve and going to Rome on a school trip; I try to remember the feeling of encountering the sheer mass of people on that scale for the first time.

I hang around town until it is noon seeing Beatrice and Mark as they are heading off, and then June who says she is taking a rest day. We wander for a bit, settling at the table in the plaza where I had met with the others yesterday. And that is where we stay for most of the day, eating, drinking, and talking. We go for ice-cream. And in the evening we go for pizza in a place that is putting up Hallowe'en decorations. At the next table there is a guy stuffing a hamburger into his mouth. He sits across from a young woman with a wasp-waist who glowers at him as the sloppy, disintegrating hamburger falls in gobs through his fingers.

I say goodnight to June outside the cathedral. It is late and I need to find a hostel. There are no plans to meet up tomorrow, no destination agreed upon, just two pilgrims going their separate ways. And our separate ways are in the same direction.

I go from door to door. It's late and each hostel is either full or closed for the night. There's nothing else for it, and so I fall asleep in a hotel room as someone on the street outside shouts "*¡España! ¡España!*" over and over again.

DAY TWENTY-EIGHT

The urban world rises and falls and stacks up through an industrial estate to pass by bodegas and become the suburb of *El Virgen del Camino* where I stop for breakfast before taking the path via Fresno, which veers away from the main road running west out of León. Where the path forks there are a group of French pilgrims mulling over which direction to take. Yellow arrows shoal in both directions. They ask to see my map and then decide on the *senda* and the main road. The route I take runs through scrubby hills and chaparral. Green holm oaks are great globes on fields of red earth and by the side of the path ants have made chimneys for their vascular cities that look like high collars of Demerara sugar.

A note on oaks: It is important to remember the importance of oaks. The oak, as you doubtless are aware, is represented by the seventh letter of the Ogham alphabet; a vertical line with two shorter parallel lines of equal length branching off to the left from the upper half. This corresponds to the Latin letter D. The oak is also represents the ninth month of the old Irish tree calendar, which is roughly from mid-June to mid-July in our Gregorian calendar. As such, it is my birth-tree.

It also lends its name to my birth-city. In Irish, Derry is translated as *Doire* – an oakwood. *Daire* is a single oak tree. It was at *Daire Calgaich* that the city of Derry was established many moons ago. At its inception the city was a small religious settlement known as *Doire Cholmcille* – Oakwood of the Dove of the Church. This 'Dove of the Church' was a man, Colmcille, who would later go on to found the monastic settlement on Iona where work on the Book of Kells was started. It is said of Colmcille that he feared the sound of axes in the forest more than he feared death.

Colmcille was made a saint, but he was not the only saint smitten with the mighty oak. Saint Brendan became known as 'The Navigator' owing to his heroic voyage to North America in a boat made of leather. He tanned the leather for his boat by soaking it in water together with oak bark, the tannins preserving the hide and making it sea-worthy.

Further back in time we go and we find that the oak was long associated with kings, with eagles, and stags; the stag also being a familiar of King Donn, Lord of the Underworld, and an aspect of the Dagda, the 'Good God'. Although it has been quite some time since people in Ireland believed in the Dagda, it was a god in the pantheon of my ancestors. Honour thy Father and thy Mother. Respect your forebears.

*

At Chozas there is a café that plays Mexican guitar pop. I leave in the wrong direction and three people wave to me and point me to the path. One of them is in a wheelchair, twisted around in the seat with her head tucked into the side of her neck. She smiles at me as I thank them and I leave Chozas thinking of her and all those others who will never walk, not the Camino, not anywhere. I remind myself to stop sometime, to stop and be grateful for what I have, what I can do, rather than be angry about what I don't have and what I cannot do. Or what others have, and what they can do.

Outside of the village I walk towards the far, high violet watermark of distant mountains. I imagine that up there somewhere is the *Cruz de Ferro*, the Cross of Iron, the highest point of the Camino. Down here there is a path that runs straight through fields of maize. The road is so straight and level it is inhuman, a machine-made track made for machines to travel along. There is something here, however, that is beautiful to behold: the drainage ditch between the track and the maize fields is filled with water that has the consistency of gravy. A milk-skin of green algae covers it. Across this mire flit bright, shining dragonflies: blue ones, red ones, I see a black one, black like polished jet. In the trees above the water there are spiderwebs. They are caught in the prongs of the branches where they hang like dreamcatchers. There is one open field where the maize has been cleared. Countless lines of gossamer glimmer among wild grasses and dandelion globes. The dandelion is the most beautiful flower in the world; it turns from a sun into a moon and, when the wind whispers to it, it becomes a constellation of stars. In the distance is a line of trees shaped like feathers balanced on end, and a plume of smoke is rising behind them.

But I cannot stay there forever.

The walk is interminable and whatever thoughts my mind might turn to, they are replaced one by one until I am fixated on that vanishing point where I want to be. Once again, the false ending stretches the final part of my day beyond endurance. What I think will be a stroll through a small town becomes a long trek around a sewage treatment plant and then towards an empty crossroads. A solitary cyclist passes me, shining gossamer trailing behind him in the late sunshine like speed trails in a photograph. There is one resident who sees me limping along the street and he tells me that Órbigo is not far. I don't believe him, but when I have reached the end of the street and turned the corner all is forgiven: the mighty span of a Roman bridge rises and falls like a ship on a sea-swell, and I see the end of my path for the day.

*

Now I am in Órbigo. The bridge was the scene of jousting tournaments in the past, where a certain Don Suero challenged over three hundred knights. I picture him, the sounds of the hooves on the stones, the clash of lances on armour, and the whinnying of the horses. These were chivalric jousts, and silence had to be maintained throughout. The rule on this was so serious that a boy who shouted "go on!" was condemned to having his tongue cut out. The knights, when chivalry really wasn't dead, objected and the boy kept his tongue.

I cross the bridge knowing I am elated but not having the energy to really feel it. I find my hostel, a *donativo* run by a group of Germans. They give me a cup of water when I arrive. I have walked thirty kilometres and don't provide them with much in the way of witty banter.

The hostel is a renovated house with a courtyard around which are rooms and an upper floor. There are forty families here today. There are five pilgrims. One of them is Juliette, but she is staying in a room, not the dorm, and vanishes behind closed doors for the rest of the day. The dorm is shared with a woman from Sarria, in Galicia, who tells me to expect nothing but bad weather, a German student, and a Spanish man who insists that we all have dinner together. He has bought bread and ham for sandwiches, fruit, and alcohol-free beer. The meal is quiet, the Galician saying very little beyond how cold it is at this time of year, and the student insisting she is not hungry. The Spaniard tells me that he is retired. He was a bus driver who carried people from Algeciras to Madrid. "Moroccans, mostly", he says, "looking for work".

He extols the virtues of eating bananas: "Potassium!" And he flexes his shoulders by way of demonstrating how potassium keeps you healthy. They are nice people, but I think back to the riotous meals in Zubiri and Pamplona and compare them with this. This too is the Camino, but it is so different in its temperament. I remind myself that I have walked over thirty kilometres to be here, am tired, and feeling lost.

I wash my clothes by hand at an outdoor sink and drape them over the line, but there is no chance they will be dry. The sun is going down and the air is already chill. I leave them hanging and go a little way down the street to where the pilgrim mass is being said.

*

When I enter there are a few rows of old ladies saying the Rosary. The Rosary is something I associate with old ladies, and something I view as a relic from some bygone age I wasn't a part of. Like the old ladies themselves. The prayers seem mindless, murmured in a way that reminds me of cattle chewing hay, and the aim, if there is one, seems as mysterious as the Mysteries they invoke prior to each prayer cycle.

It's easy to think this, and never bother trying to fathom why they do this. So, I sit in the back half of the church, the only pilgrim in the place, and listen to them chanting in Spanish, over and over again. It occurs to me that given enough people this would sound like an all-female version of those Tibetan monks who chant in unison in their high temples. And would I ever mock them?

Once again I am struck by how exotic this religion is and, with the retable, the inscriptions around the roof, and the paintings on the walls, I am struck by how European it is; there is so much of pre-Christian Europe in Catholicism that I see again how Protestants and Muslims might see it as idolatrous, pagan, even Heathen. But I see this not as a weakness, but as a strength.

The priest walks up to the lectern, singing as he goes, and mass begins.

The question some religious people ask is: What makes people want leave the Church? The question I ask is: What makes people want to stay?

*

After mass, I put a stamp in my *Credencial*, and wander up and down the street. It's a small town and I'm passing through. I return to the dorm. It is pitch dark. My clothes on the line are still wet, but the morning damp will make them wetter, so I take them in and hang them off the end of the bunk. The place is still half empty. The Galician pilgrim is sitting crouched in the corner with a woollen hat on. She is glued to her mobile phone. The German student is buried in her sleeping bag, waiting for sleep. The Spanish pilgrim is lying in his bunk too. I step outside and look up at the stars. I could have looked at them forever.

DAY TWENTY-NINE

Throughout the night the others snore like old men sawing through sad trees to the accompaniment of a depressed tuba. I cover my sleep sheet with a number of the blankets stacked by the door, and when I decide that morning has arrived, sun or no sun, I stick my damp clothes through the bungees on my rucksack, pack up and go. Tonight I want to sleep in Astorga.

When the sun does rise it feels like compensation for the night. The clarity of the light is so pure that everything it touches looks as though it has been washed clean. There is a short walk through farmland that gleams like rich fabric before breakfast is reached in the next village. The café has a television and news of the American election race is being discussed by a studio panel of people I don't know. I wonder what their debate is supposed to achieve seeing as how none of their viewers is an American capable of casting a vote. The pint-sized electronic, daytime ghosts of Hilary and Donald drift across the screen. They grin. They wave. Big crowds of smaller electronic ghosts wave back. They all look happy. I wonder why.

*

The sunrise sends beams of light through stands of slender trees and it causes the ground to steam. The vapour rolls in coils of brass and silver. The track is broad, orange, earthen, and it rises through hills of holm oak and conifer. I walk up to the ridge from which I can see the village of Santibáñez. The path runs down to meet it. At the entrance to town a tractor guns its engine. It has just sunk its claws into the earth and is beginning to plough. Above the snorting and farting of the tractor there comes another sound: it is the sound of singing. The singing is cheerful; it is jolly voices singing Christian pop songs from a bygone age. As I get closer the music becomes louder and its words more distinct. It is not a choir, but a recording. The streets are empty and through these empty streets the music flutters and slides. I follow it to its source: it is being played from a loudspeaker shaped like a bullhorn attached to the belfry of the church. I step inside, but the inside is as empty as the outside. Only one man stands at the far end of the church, his back to the wall, staring at the ceiling. The music plays on.

The music follows me up the hill out of town, past cattle sheds and empty fields, and then it stops. The air settles still.

A little further on and a mannequin is standing by a bush. The mannequin is fully dressed in mis-matched clothes, including a trilby hat. A tiny wooden statue of *Santiago Pelegrino* stands by its feet. On the other side of the bush there is a cross wrapped in strings of beads, ribbons, and bracelets. A man is squatting by the foot of the cross, getting up only to take a few steps back and go down on one knee beside the mannequin. A bike decked out with panniers is parked beside him. I walk up to where he is kneeling and ask him if he wants me to take the photo for him.

His camera has a roll of film in it, making it kin with the coelacanth and the bristlecone pine. The man poses with his bike, grinning with expensive teeth, his face radiating the vigour of the outdoor sportsman. He is one of these Spaniards that don't know when to quit and must be in his sixties at least. He is Catalán and has cycled eight different Caminos over the course of his life. He reminds me of the old Italians who sang '*O Sole Mio!*' – one of them had told Lena, June, and I that he was sixty-three and had plans to walk the Camino three more times in his life.

The cyclist is short, wiry, tanned, and there seems to be nothing of the pilgrimage about him; but he too is on the Camino, and he is happy, and it is a sunny day. After I take his picture, he turns to the mannequin. It is the ropiest looking thing on earth with its oddest collection of clothes and its trilby hat. "*Es muy bonito*" he says, appraising it with a satisfied smile. It's all in the eye of the beholder.

"¡Adios!" He speeds away. "¡Buen Camino!"

*

The path passes sandy cliffs in which birds have made their burrows and then runs up past jeeps beside which lounge hunters with big guns and small dogs; they smoke, and occasional gunshots can be heard from the forest. Beyond them is '*La Casa de los dioses*' – The House of the Gods, the gods being some friendly hippies who have erected hammocks and a *donativo* food stall for passing pilgrims. The stall, and the shelter, and the little room that sits open to the road have all been graffitied over, as was Bar

Elvis, as were the shelters above Castrojerez and on the road to Terradillos. I still don't know what to make of places like this. There is too much of the wilfully 'spiritual' in them for me, but I remember the polar opposite in Emmaus in Burgos, and I settle in accepting that this too is the Camino, and if I am not enthralled by it, the other people here are; tearing into apples with big smiles and repeating "this is amazing!" in English.

The path runs on through conifer trees and then there is Astorga.

Just like that.

I arrive at a cross on top of a hill, and beyond it I see the city.

Just like that.

All around the cross there are children reaching up to try and touch its arms. A few adults shout things at them, warnings against falling over, telling them to watch what they are doing, but the kids are sending up such a racket and none of them are paying attention. The path down from the cross is a long concrete runway and some of the kids speed down it on bicycles. It turns into the road through San Justo, where I check to see if my washing has dried. It hasn't. The yellow arrows point the pilgrims onto a track behind some industrial buildings, over a stone bridge and then winds up and down a corkscrew of zigzag steps on a green walkway over railway lines. The path crosses busy roundabouts, through which the Catalán cyclist zips, waving and grinning, a green bandana flapping; and then it is all up hill, steep, steep , steep, until I step through an arch and I am in Astorga.

*

The Municipal is just inside the city. The *hospitalera* is Danish, grinning and welcoming me with a map of the city and questions about my day. She shows me to the dorm; it is bright, over-looking the city rooftops, and so well cleaned I feel like its first ever occupant. There are washing machines here, says the *hospitalera*, a kitchen and dining room should I want to use them, and a patio. Sunlight fills the place.

Two Australians have arrived, having left the Northern Camino because it was too cold, misty, and half-closed. Their days had been excruciating tramps, going on into the night searching for a place to stay. I wonder if this is what the pilgrims of yore had to do; or did they sleep rough? And did that explain why they died in their droves?

In a typical Camino cost-cutting exercise my still-damp clothing goes into the same washing machine as theirs, and we split the cost. I buy the washing powder and leave half of it for someone who will come afterwards. 'Free Soap Powder' I write on a scrap of cardboard with arrows pointing to the

Free Soap Powder. As the machine runs its course I leave my guidebook with the Australians to help them plan their way to Santiago, and I go for a walk.

In the town square, I bump into Beatrice who is drinking with Gene and another American, Rachel. They are all staying in the four star hotel. I walk around town, looking for a hiking shop. My walking trousers, which are the trousers I was wearing when I walked out of my flat for the last time, are about to fall apart. All the hiking shops are shut. I see the Chinese shop and get there as the owner is locking up.

"When do you open again?"

"Never".

So I sit in a bar and have a *tortilla* and a beer and let time flow away. Still better than work.

*

I return to the Municipal to find that my dried clothes are folded on my bunk. My guide book is hidden under them. I pack them away and then go out to look around the city. Near the hostel is a public garden looking out over the city walls. A plume of coal smoke begins to rise from right below them. It is green-grey and segues into the darkening sky. The mountains on the horizon look like rough seas, and there is one star above the sunset. The city below the walls is in shades of black and there are voices, there have always been voices, so long as there have been these walls there have been voices; there have been centuries of talking here. The voices fade, just as the lives fade, just as the days fade.

I return to the city square where I run into Beatrice again, and go for dinner in her four star hotel restaurant. We ask for the *Cocido Maragato*: the local dish. The waitress says one between two would suffice. She reappears with the first course, which is a huge platter of meat, and nothing but meat. 'Ten different types', boasts the menu, and we try to figure out what those ten types might be. One of them looks like an ear.

The second course is chickpeas, chickpeas and cabbage. Desert is soup, soup with pasta. I don't know what the Maragato people were thinking of when they put this menu together, but I like it just because it is so different from the usual. It is obvious, and Beatrice agrees: the Camino is a luxury.

The Camino is a luxury, a holiday for the bored, the disgruntled; it is a holiday for people looking to trek on the cheap and have pocket money left over for fripperies such as this. I remember speaking to Mark in León, saying that I saw little evidence of the Camino being a pilgrimage. He agreed.

Well, what can we expect? I am not the only one who has brought the world with them onto the Camino. I dare say that every soul from Saint Jean to Santiago is a product of the world they want to leave behind, and so we are all fish out of water but fish nonetheless – we are adapted to one element, and this is not it. We are adapted to a world that squeezes humanity into unnatural forms. We have retained these forms even here, even after all this time and all these kilometres we are no different to the people who started out.

Maybe the Camino is just a luxury and nothing will come from it but sore feet.

DAY THIRTY

I think it was Anthony Burgess who said "laugh and the world laughs with you; snore and you sleep alone". I thank God for ear-plugs. I have a bag of them and am happy to give them away to fellow pilgrims. Today I have to buy new trousers. It's an exciting event in anyone's life, but I manage to remain calm. I pack up my bag, wish the Australians a "Buen Camino", and then I am back on my own Camino, and get as far as the nearest cafe before I stop for breakfast.

At the next table there are a bunch of foul old men who fart and hack up phlegm and call the proprietor 'niña'. They provide the mood music to a stream of pilgrims looking for coffee. None of them make the effort to speak any Spanish. I wonder if that is because they don't know any Spanish, or if it's because they are too nervous to try what they know. The cafe also sells religious trinkets. I buy a little laminated Icon: *Nuestra Señora del Perpetuo Socorro*. I buy it because I want to carry it to the *Cruz de Ferro*, but I have no idea why, except it reminds me of my mother and I am her disappointing son who is all alone in the world, and I am ashamed that I am who I am. I am a failure and a fool. Or at least, that is my *persona*.

*

Breakfast after breakfast. I have drunk so much coffee I feel that if I start walking I'll run into a wall. They are putting up the stalls for the market, out in the square under the clock tower where two Maragato puppets strike the hour. I notice oak leaves on the city crest, oaks by the cathedral, acorns on the ground.

The hiking shop opens about two minutes before I arrive to ramble off exactly what I am looking for and why. I cut quite a dash in my new pantaloons, and despite the high price, what must be done must be done. "Adios" says the shopkeeper throwing my worn-out trousers into the bin. Since I'm there and throwing my money around like the Monopoly Man, I also buy a rain jacket, anticipating nothing but rain in Galicia.

I leave Astorga with an old lady wishing me "¡Buen Camino, pelegrino!" There is a short walk to the edge of town and then I am walking back out into the countryside on a pavement where there is a memorial to a pilgrim who was killed by traffic. I pass by a hermitage where there is a *fuente*, and in the adjacent garden there is a tree decorated with sea-shells, each with the name of a pilgrim on them. There is also a sign asking people not to defecate. I presume this prohibition refers to the garden and not for the rest of our lives. A picture speaks a thousand words, and to underline the gravity of the message there is a drawing of some faeces that looks like a weeping ice-cream.

I am in Maragato country now, and take every opportunity to stop and rest. The Maragato people have numerous creation myths associated with them. They are either the descendants of a Christian enclave in a Moorish kingdom, or vice versa, or a people like the Basques but who lost their language to that of the Castilians, or they were brought here by the Romans and resettled having been banished from some far-flung homeland. In the silence of a red stone Maragato village I reflect on how even a banal street can be beautiful if you allow it to be. The sun makes it gleam; it polishes the cars, the kerbs, the flagstones, the pillar boxes. I leave the waymarked route, opting for a visit to a renovated Maragato village, getting to which involves inching down the unsurfaced hard shoulder of a highway in a state of tonic paranoia, before crossing to a *senda*.

In the renovated Maragato village, where they are selling honey and textiles, I am no different from the rubber-necking tourists who wander the main street. I am reminded of the tourist on Abbey Street, Dublin, who was photographing a destitute woman who had fainted onto the tram-tracks. People are not scenery. They are not souvenirs. If I were to ask any of the tourists here why they are here, it would be like talking to myself.

The village is pretty, but I feel bad about reducing people to a tourist attraction, so I go. The path out of the village runs through scrubland. It was between Astorga and Rabanal that a pilgrim went missing and some others were intimidated by strangers on the way. Those tales are all the more upsetting because the world here seems so peaceful, and not at all a stage for hostility. When I get back to the main path of the Camino there is a *senda* of white gravel. It leads to the first in a series of semi-derelict villages, where I take one break after another, until I find myself drinking beer outside a place called 'The Cowboy Bar' which has a painting of a horse on the wall. Gene strolls by. He had the cold in Astorga and is fighting off the after effects. We have a beer and chat about nothing before he moves on. When I do decide to leave I meet two Italians, one of whom has a birthday today. She perks up when I say I'm Irish because she is interested in druids. She was born on Hallowe'en. *It's Hallowe'en! Tanti Auguri!* She is interested in how druids believed people born at this time of year were seers who found it easier to contact, and be contacted by, the other world.

There's no proof for this, but it adds to the gaiety of nations.

*

There's no proof for God either, right?

Right.

This is the truth that I hold self-evident: He's just somebody's imaginary friend.

But that is normal: Everyone has imaginary friends.

When a celebrity dies people mourn the death of an imaginary friend. People, from teenagers to adults, defend singers, writers, actors, directors, and a whole host of entertainers from criticism as though they were defending the reputation of a friend. People identify with fictional characters, including superheroes, sometimes going to the extent of dressing up as them for fan conventions.

Having imaginary friends is the norm for human beings.

So to call God somebody's imaginary friend is a feeble insult.

So what? So what if it is a feeble insult. It's still not true. If there is no evidence for something, I don't have to accept it. And so I don't accept the existence of a Big Man in the Sky if I see no reason to. Things we call miracles all have explanations, or will have as our knowledge of the world improves, and so they cannot be demonstrations of divine power. The idea that God has made us and has given us our lives, as a craftsman makes models, and that he will alter our lives in our favour if we ask him with enough heartfelt desperation, exists because of a human desire for things to be different.

There is no proof.

And I have not been given any proof. And I will never be given any proof.

But this isn't about proof.

I don't accept that there is a Big Man in the Sky who makes everything. I don't think most adults believe that there is. I do not accept that Creation is distinct from Creator.

Thoughts:

What the waves are to the sea, Creation is to the Creator.

The waves are created by and from the sea. They rise and they fall. Creation comes forth from the Creator, living and dying, coming forth and returning. The waves are not separate from the sea. Creation is not separate from Creator.

*

The *senda* from the Maragato village runs under heavy boughs and between verges of brambles and wild grasses. The landscape is rusting oakwoods and a snake runs across my path. It is the first time in my life I have seen one and there is a strange power in how it flows across the path, a beautiful ripple. It makes me feel lucky.

Along this path are small billboards advertising a country guesthouse, complete with stables should you want to do part of the Camino on horseback. When I pass the entrance to the driveway to this guesthouse, two big guard dogs appear from under some bushes. One of these dogs walks down the short track from the gate to the *senda* and begins following me. It reminds me of the dog from *Cujo*. Its lower eyelids droop so much it looks as though it has blank red eyes. It does not speed up or slow down, but it plods along with the dumb insistence of a shark. From time to time I stop to look back over my shoulder, and it is always there, far now from its country house with stables. I keep going and it does too, and a line from *The Rhyme of the Ancient Mariner* begins to run through my head:

Like one who on a lonesome road,
Who walks in fear and dread,
And after having once turned round walks on,
And turns no more his head,
Because he knows a frightful fiend.
Doth close behind him tread.

I remember this from *Night of the Demon*.

I'm sure I'm not being hunted. This isn't some starving hyena. What if it's rabid? I saw none of the famous foam frothing around its chops. Is it just some friendly country dog, then? It hasn't walked up to me, only paced, paced away behind me. When I cross the road, it crosses the road. I'm certain it is following me. When I get to the edge of Rabanal, I stop by the door to a cafe and see the dog emerge from some bushes just ahead of me. The thought crosses my mind to step into the bar as though I want to drink a nonchalant beer when the dog yelps, a strange yodelling sound, and runs away as though running in reduced gravity, its jowls rising and falling in time with its ears. I turn to see what could have startled it, but there is nothing there, and when I look back at the dog is has vanished. I look up and down the road, but it is nowhere to be seen.

*

I meet the Australians from Astorga as I walk into Rabanal. They smile, praising the weather, saying how glad they are that they found a place to stay. But I don't think I'll find a place to stay – the hostel is full and so I continue on up the long main street until I decide to stay in the first place I find, which turns out to be a hotel. There is no reason for this except some unspoken desire to be alone and not have to bear the brunt of another night kept awake by snorers. Dinner is in the hotel dining room. And my neighbours are Armo and Milla, the Finns from Via Trajana. The presence of Armo and Milla indicates that the food here must be good.

Times change. I chat to them throughout the meal, telling them about the haunted dog and they joke about the symbolism of the animal. "It is your past", they say, "something that bothers you. And now it's gone!"

It's Hallowe'en after all, and they tell a story of their own, about walking through a city when a man runs past them telling them that the way ahead is clear. When they turn the corner there is no sign of him and no sign of any way he could have left the street. They are the only people I've spoken to all day in any normal, human way. The dinner is delicious, but it is their company that makes it enjoyable. They remind me that good food is any food eaten in good company.

After the meal I go to the church across the way. It is closed and I call in at the adjacent hostel where an English *hospitalero* is eating potatoes. I ask him if there is a pilgrim a mass on. He isn't sure, telling me that there had been singing at seven, and since there were only two monks they might have turned in for the night. I wait outside the closed church in the dark.

Nothing happens.

*

Part Three: Cross Roads

Breakfast is in another hotel, taken there in an effort to escape the freak economics of the menu in the hotel where I have spent the night. It makes no difference. Fish in a barrel, the cost is just as high. Mustn't grumble; I sit and eat as a the television blares a show compiled from camcorder clips of domestic accidents; and as the hapless victims slip, skid, are hit, fall, are shocked, scared, or narrowly escape a cruel death, zany saxophone music honks and squawks. A swany whistle hoots whenever someone gets hit by a car. Oops! Silly!

The swany whistle toots as a group of pilgrims pass by the window. They look very monastic in the cruel light of dawn, their heads bowed, attentive to whatever one of them is talking about.

*

The path out of Rabanal is pock-marked with ant chimneys. Their colonies are great abstract animals, where each insect is a cell in an organism. They are part of the universe of the soil, and what a great alchemist the soil is; it transforms everything that touches it. It turns seeds into plants, and plants into mulch. It turns iron to rust, and wood into fungi. There are whole worlds beneath my feet, an ocean of soil, and as rich with life as the oceans of the earth.

The world turns and we are being moved more and more into the shadows. The short days have told the trees that winter is on its way and they are in their autumn colours. I think of my familiar childhood landscapes where everything had a name, even if it was a name I gave it: this large rock, this bend in the river, this particular tree. I named them as I named pets; as my friends had names.

For a while the path runs above a forested slope and below a hilltop of scree and heather. There is a sign written on a rock: "Go up there for a great view" and there is an arrow pointing to the right. Why not? I go off the path, high up, and alone I see the world spread out below me. It is silver and gold. The globes of yellow trees float on the low mist. Sheets of cloud, the colour of salmon flesh, the colour of marble, wash the sky. The world that I considered hard and cruel is soft and placid. It is oblivious to the turmoil that fills the ether, ready to be picked up by a phone or a television.

*

Now I am in Foncebadón. I arrive at the village with the chill of the mountain air clinging to the ground. There is frost here, glittering in the dells. I cross the road and walk into a town that appears to be

119

crumbling away. Buildings are roofed with variegated sheets of corrugated metal. Walls are shored with rough beams. One or two buildings have caved in. Goats wander the streets in Foncebadón. The cafe is a *donativo* with a self-service just inside the door. Coffee comes from a push-button flask, and I give my donation and take the coffee outside. I sit at a table by the side of the cafe, eavesdropping on a group of Americans. They sound like the American Christians who were at the Dutch Christian hostel, and they are talking about the pilgrimage to Jerusalem. I've seen a few stickers up on signposts advertising this and wonder if many people do it. I can't imagine it to be popular today, what with the Syrian part of the eastern Mediterranean being a war-zone.

Their conversation gives way to goodbyes as they leave in ones or twos and then I am there by myself, sitting sipping coffee as a few goats with their horizontal pupils and long clueless snouts clatter onto the patio. I look back down the street to where there is an empty, unadorned cross. The cross says that I am supposed to be alone; I am supposed to be alone up here. This is the way things are meant to be. Here's my lot.

It's an unpleasant thought, and I don't know if it has been brought on by the chill of sitting still, or thoughts of a cruel, war-like world. I go indoors where there is a log fire, tended to by a young hippy who is never off his phone. The hearth is plastered with photos of saints and gurus, and quotations from people like Rumi and Mother Theresa. Letters and postcards from all corners of the world overlap one another. There are candle stumps and trinkets of all sorts along the mantlepiece.

With another coffee I sit and watch the flames of the fire. A log fire is one of our first and best inventions. I can imagine the prehistoric community at Atapuerca feeling this good when they came in from the cold to the heat and life of the flames. I do not plan what to do next. I do not plan on sitting here forever either; but right now, I watch the flames and drink the coffee, and that is as good a plan as any. On the mantlepiece, mixed in with the trinkets and candle stumps, there is a tiny brown book. It has to be a Bible, because this is the Camino, gurus and Rumi notwithstanding, and I have seen Bibles like this before. When I was at school people from the Gideon Society came and gave out such Bibles to all the students (our Little Red Book). I remember them because we all got something for nothing, and the man from Gideon looked like Abraham Lincoln. I take the little book down off the shelf and open it at a random page. I read this:

Romans 12

[1] *Therefore, I urge you, brothers and sisters, in view of God's mercy, to offer your bodies as a living sacrifice, holy and pleasing to God—this is your true and proper worship.* [2] *Do not conform to the*

pattern of this world, but be transformed by the renewing of your mind. Then you will be able to test and approve what God's will is—his good, pleasing and perfect will.

I don't want to offer my body as a sacrifice, holy or otherwise. I've seen *Apocalypto*. I've seen the *Kingship and Sacrifice* exhibition in the National Museum. But I do want to be transformed by the renewing of my mind.

How will I transform this mind of mine, then?

I jot down the reference to this quote in my notebook and place the Bible back on the shelf. I go back to finishing my coffee when familiar voices greet me from the door. It is Armo and Milla. If they visit the places with the best food, I wonder what has brought them here. I wonder no more when they ask for the homemade cake. I join them and their good humour is as cheering as the fire. They are reporting back to their Spanish teacher as they go, reporting back to their social media group in Finland. The group retaliates, sending them pictures of snowy birch forests and frozen lakes. I imagine Finland is always like this, but they assure me that snow is unusual in Finland at this time of year.

After the coffee, cake, and company, I decide to buy a *palo*. It is little more than a stout staff capped with a metal spike and with a loop of bootlace threaded through a hole at the other end. There is a stand of these by the fireplace at six Euros each. I have avoided using hiking poles so far, but if it helps take the weight of my back as I cross the mountains into Galicia it will be worth it.

Armo and Milla go ahead, and I sit on. Then it is my turn to go. I stamp my *Credencial*, and thank the people who run the cafe. The hippy is on his phone by the fire now, but the proprietors, perhaps *hospitaleros*, smile and thank me in return. I feel like I am checking myself out of hospital, and I'm reminded of the *hospitalera* in Grañón who said "this is not a hostel but a hospital for the spirit".

I am not far from Foncebadón when a man comes jogging down the path towards me. "John! John! It's raining! It's raining up there!" He laughs as he says this, then stops beside me and confides "no, I forgot my sticks", before adding: "You look just like a friend of mine back in Switzerland. He is called John. How do you say it when a person looks just like another person?"

I feel like saying *doppelgänger* – double-walker, but choose "spitting image" instead. My resemblance to John of Switzerland is so uncanny that he asks if he can take my picture and email it to his wife for a laugh. Why not? I stand there, smiling for the camera, as my freakish similarity to John is captured for posterity. The man thanks me and continues on down the mountain; from where he remembered his sticks, back to where he had forgotten them.

*

The man returns, hiking poles working overtime and he canters up the path like a four-legged creature. "We met before", he says "back some days ago".

He's right. He is Bertrand, the Swiss pilgrim from the seventeen mile trek along the Roman road when I was walking to Terradillos. How is my Camino?

I just blurt out the words: "I'm sad".

"Oh? Why?"

"Because I feel like I have wasted my talents. Because I have worked so hard, for so long, for other people, and have nothing to show for it".

Bertrand tells me of how he came to be walking the Camino, of how he got burnt out from running his own business; of how he woke up one day and just had to take a break. He tells me that he felt sad too, but the Camino has made him happy again. We walk up the path, chatting and then, out of the blue, the *Cruz de Ferro* is there before us.

The cross is small, a simple affair: two metal bars, no figure of the crucified Christ, no inscriptions, insignia, no colour beyond black. It is fixed to the top of a tall pole like a telegraph pole. Around its base there is a massive cairn, set there one stone at a time by the thousands of pilgrims who have passed this way before me. I have four small shells given to me by Agnieszka. There are three small shells and one large, flat shell the colour of gunmetal.

I rifle through my rucksack and find the shells carefully wrapped, and I fish out the three small ones. I arrange them in the shape of a shamrock in a clear space among the stones of the cairn. I take a picture to show her when I get back. I take the icon I bought in Astorga and look around for somewhere to put it. I settle on a crack in the wood caused by weathering and I wedge the icon into it. I look straight up and see the cross high above me, and nothing above it but infinite space.

I look around the cairn. The stones were carried here by pilgrims. They represent wishes, regrets, fears, memories, worries; they represent all the sadness and hope of thousands of lives. And there are other things. There are my shells, and there is an old black and white photograph of a man holding a toddler's hand. The photo is held amidst the stems of a small flowering blush of yellow daisies. There is a fishing rod, there are medals, Rosary beads, photos of people, family photos, there are names, names, names written on the stones, written on notes. Ribbons have been pinned to the lower part of the pole.

Bertrand photographs the cross and its cairn. I offer to photograph him, and he stands at the foot of the cross as I take a few pictures. He takes a few pictures of me. There are a few other pilgrims there and they want their photos taken too.

"I'm going on" says Bertrand. "I'll send you the photos". I give him my email. I promise to reply with his photos. He wishes me luck and is on his way, off along the broad *senda*. I stay a while longer, looking at the stones and other things around the base of the cross. In ones and twos the other pilgrims leave and then there is nobody there but me and I go and sit at the shelter near the closed church. Here, there are only the sounds of flying insects. Behind the rest area are old, weathered sanitary pads, and paper, and sods of overturned earth.

I sit there and ponder my sterile life. "Time's eunuch" was how Gerard Manely Hopkins described it in his poem *Thou Art Indeed Just, Lord*. There was a man wondering why, despite his efforts, he had nothing to show for his time on earth. And now, I am another one. Another one of Time's eunuchs: no wife, no kids, no home, nothing to my name, nothing with my name, no relics or footprints of me ever having been here. Famous for nothing, infamous for nothing, and little chance of one or the other now.

I am sitting there lamenting my missed opportunities and my lost futures when a car pulls into the small car park near the cross and a family get out; a man, a woman, and two small boys. The adults wander about at a distance, but the two kids run up onto the cairn and begin jumping down it. They leap as far as they can, in competition to see who can get to the bottom in as few jumps as possible. I can hear their girlish shouts and their laughter.

Why does God never show me a sign?

Why are you so blind?

Why does God never speak?

Why are you so deaf?

The two children jump and play on that monument to worry, guilt, longing, and pain; they have no such spectres haunting them. They are called by their parents and the family drives off. The *Cruz de Ferro* is the geological high point of the Camino. Now it is time to come down from the cross. There is nowhere else to go, and nothing else that can be done.

*

The *senda* runs past orange and red tinted oak forest, down, down, down to El Acebo. There is a billboard on the way advertising a plush new hostel. Across this billboard someone has spraypainted the portmanteau *Tourigrinos*. I wonder if this is the same person who wrote on a shelter wall: *A real pilgrim walks in silence*. To which another hand had added: *A real pilgrim doesn't judge*.

El Acebo is tidy, swept-clean tidy, named after a holly bush, and all the stone houses have upper stories that jut out, creating a verandah on the ground floor. I see some pilgrims from the *Cruz de Ferro*, and am almost at the end of town when I see the new hostel. It looks like a ski resort. I ask the receptionist about rooms and bunks, and opt for a room, because I don't want to speak to anybody for the rest of the day. This is almost immediately thwarted by Armo and Milla calling to me from their table out on the patio. They had booked in elsewhere but the booking had been messed up. Now they have been booked in here by the other place as compensation. They will still dine in their original choice; because that was the reason they had booked in there in the first place.

There is shared laundry, but they will not accept the cost of this. Then away they go. I stay for dinner in the hostel, in a dining room with wall-sized windows that overlook the mountains of León. At sunset they deepen to black and the light is blood orange and smeared with distant rain. It looks like Mordor.

The meal is shared with an Austrian man who has walked from Vienna, the Camino being a lifelong ambition he is fulfilling now that he has retired. The road has given him the look of an explorer; tanned, toned, and he says that the nature of the hostel is irrelevant to the pilgrimage as in mediaeval times the hostels and inns were Big Business, and there were guidebooks at the time warning against unscrupulous tavern-keepers. There is a pair of Anglican sisters, who are from Zimbabwe but who grew up in Australia. They have the impeccable cut-glass English accents that are only ever heard in Commonwealth countries, but never in England itself. They tell me that they are grateful that the Catholic priests will give them communion during mass services because it is so important to them. There is another pilgrim, an American, who is a cross between an air-punching jock and a born again Christian. He is a nice enough fellow, but I keep expecting him to finish each sentence by bellowing 'Hoo-Ya' like a marine.

When I get back to my room, which counts as a bridal suite compared to some of the places I've stayed in – over the course of my life, as well as the Camino – I fish my tablet from where it has lain dormant at the bottom of my rucksack and switch it on. I see the photos Bertrand took of me earlier at the *Cruz de Ferro*. I email him back, thanking him.

There is one photo he has sent me that gives me pause for thought: I am smiling, my sleeves rolled up, the *palo* held as though I'd just pulled back a lever. This was taken at the cross. At the high point of the Camino, I was at my lowest; yet I look confident and collected.

I would like to thank the Academy...

*

"Holly burn it fresh, or Holly burn it old,

Name the worth of any tree, Holly is ten-fold"

- From a poem sung by Laoi Iubhan, in 'The Death of King Fergus'

El Acebo means 'The Holly-tree', a tree associated with warriors, their chariots and lances, clubs, the violent beheadings suffered by their foes, the display trees for those heads (for my forebears were head-hunters). It is the tree of the tenth month of the old Irish tree calendar, placed just after oak in high summer, and is therefore the tree of Lughnasa (modern-day August). Lughnasa is the time for chariot races. Holly is also a letter in the Ogham alphabet, a vertical line with three short lines branching to the left. It corresponds with the Latin letter T, and in Ogham it is called *tinne*: Iron Bar. It is fitting then, that it was at 'The Holly-tree' that Don Pelayo's sword was forged.

There, on the map: a forge in the forest. It is a pale blue dot arrived at by a path that looks like a root fibre. All the way down there, I think. That is where I will go today.

I have a long, luxurious breakfast, with plenty of coffee, and then I leave the hostel. I turn off the Camino, my heart singing as I do so, and walk away down a road without *sendas*. It is dangerous to walk a series of blind, hairpin bends, down, down, down into the valley where there is the forge. The sky is clear blue. The air warms the forest in its finery.

I am glad to get off the road and be down at the bottom of the valley, where I can hear and then see the small river giggling and tumbling around boulders beneath the overhanging branches. The path hugs a cliff and is strewn with leaves. I am walking along it when I hear the sound of an engine. I step in to the side of the path to allow a tiny motorbike with a fat man in blue overalls to trundle past. The motorbike clears its throat and carries on with its hornet's whine.

The path forks above the river. One tracks leads up, the other down to some stone houses. This is the forge. I can hear dogs barking from inside one of the buildings and the heavy scrape and rumble of metal being moved over stone. The motorbike is parked outside. The blacksmith in his forge. There is a sign on the door detailing times and days of the week when it is possible to see him at work. I would like to see this, and I would like to ask to use the hammer on the heat-softened metal; and I would like to stay here, hammering horse-shoes and fixing ploughshares, and never have to surface from deep under this sea of leaves ever again.

But I do not know the time. I do not know what day it is. I do not want to check; I feel free as an animal is free without time divided, with only the here and now. I know nothing other than that the doors of the forge are closed to me when I arrive at them.

I walk around the buildings that make up the forge; this is the forge of Compludo, where legend states that the sword of Don Pelayo was created, the sword with which he began the *Reconquista* at Covadonga. The mill race pours off the roof of the forge and into the stream. After so many days of desert conditions the world of the forest is liquid and flows across the earth. The breeze sets the canopy nodding and the leaves are bright green and flashing orange, gold and red, and all of them blazing up above the ferns, moss and murk of the forest floor. Some ferns are half-furled and resemble the prows of longships. I go back to the fork in the track and then continue, deeper, further into the forest. I am the only one here.

*

I walk through the valley, up, up, up along its far side, its southern side, as away to the north the Camino bears all its pilgrims away like leaves on a stream. The thin forest track is all for me, and I have only the very vaguest of ideas about my whereabouts. No-one on earth knows where I am.

I have shaken off the world. No clocks or calendars here, nor schedules, deadlines, appointments, or timetables. The feeling of not having to deal with people is the feeling of shrugging off a straight-jacket. I am Harry Houdini; watch this vanishing act.

And I like trees; I like the smell of trees, the sound of trees. I like how they feel, how bark can be rough or smooth, or the leaves like satin or paper. I like the dizzying variety of their seeds, of their flowers; I like how their roots can push up a pavement or undermine a wall. I like the way a tree can be a whole world to intricate ecosystems of arthropods, epiphytes, fungi, molluscs, and worms. They house birds as crowns house gemstones, so that the surf sounds of trees in the rocking breeze is gilded by the songs of those that can fly.

They are the paths taken by squirrels and martens. They are lignified sunbeams: they conjure themselves out of thin air. Earth, air, fire, water; these are the things that trees are made of. Photosynthesis is a power greater than any spell in any story. Trees eat sunlight and pull lakes of water from the soil into their trunks and up through their leaves in a ceaseless exhalation. Here is a forge of rare power: a tree moulding sunlight into an acorn that can grow into another tree. Such a thing done once is awesome. Such things are done by the millions of millions, and have been done for millions and millions of years.

The falling leaves reveal the neural architecture of the forest: the branches fork like nerve endings. Trees communicate by releasing chemicals into the air as nerve cells communicate by releasing neurotransmitters into a synapse. I imagine myself to be so small that I am walking through the nerve endings of a brain that houses a mind I cannot begin to contemplate.

Why are you so blind?

The trees did not evolve to please me, yet here they are and here am I. And they please me.

What have you done to deserve this?

Don't I have the health to walk in these woods? Don't I have the time and money, the ability, to take to the Camino? Do I know what I have been given?

*

The track twists upwards and crosses a landslide marked with candystriped tape. The river rushes below me, rushing west, and as I climb higher and higher its rushing hushes then sighs with the breeze. I see the valley, the trees baking in the silent sunlight, before the path turns away and I can see the village of Espinoso on a distant ridge.

I walk into Espinoso past the allotments at the edge of town. Stands of Brussels sprouts and rows of cabbages are alien lifeforms ripe with life. As are any one of the chestnut trees on the road into the village. As are the burrs of the chestnut trees that scatter the road like green sea urchins. As are their seeds, polished wooden teardrops that the people here gather for a feast-day.

Espinoso, like El Acebo just across the valley, is neat and its houses have upper floors that jut out over verandahs. Everything is stone. The only sound is the quiet scraping of someone plastering a wall. Some of the houses are well-kept; others are shells with '*Se Vende*' signs pinned to their doors. I walk the length and breadth of the village, but see only one road connecting the place to the outside world. I wonder if this is a commuter town, and its silence is caused by its population being away in Ponferrada where they are busy at work.

I walk to where the road in Espinoso both begins and ends and see two young women getting out of an SUV. I ask them how I can get to Ponferrada. They point to the road: "Follow it all the way".

"Thank you".

I follow the road all the way.

On the road ears are more useful than eyes, as the corners are blind and approaching traffic is a shift in gears or the revving of an engine long before it is a car or a lorry bearing down on me. When all is quiet I find I have the time to ferry bristling caterpillars across the road on a twig, pause and watch some form of giant cricket eating the remains of crushed insect roadkill, hear chestnut burrs crash to the forest floor, watch butterflies, watch grasshoppers flash blue and vanish as they fly and settle, wave away tiny flies that have taken to orbiting me like satellites, and watch an ichneumon fly move through the air like an aristocrat with murder on her mind. I see rove beetles roving, and a bright yellow and black bird which might be an oriole, before I have left the forest behind me and am on the descent towards a Ponferrada that looks like it has been spilled rather than built. High on the slopes a shepherd corrals his flock by whistling and shouting at his sheepdogs. At one point all his sheep run down the hill below me in an avalanche of bells.

From now on the road is hemmed by a cliff and a crash barrier, and I avoid being hit thanks to the road being quiet enough for the oncoming traffic to move into the centre of the road to avoid me. This is not the Camino and there is no facility for pilgrims: no *fuente*, no *senda*, no *flecha amarilla*. I'm just a pedestrian in a place where pedestrians are not supposed to be. I press myself into the crash barrier and stop walking as traffic roars by. When I can, I get onto the other side of it, but only when there is no precipitous drop. Even then I cannot walk on the other side of the crash barrier; the brambles are like bales of barbed wire.

I arrive in the villages of Salas de los Barrios and Villar de los Barrios. Renovation work is taking place and lanky workmen covered in cement dust don't reply when I say hello to them. These workmen drive at speed, their trucks testing gravity as they tilt around corners. Time and time again I step off the road, and stand well back in the dry, weedy embankment as the traffic speeds by. At one point a woman stops and offers me a lift.

"¡*Estoy caminando*!"

She shrugs, she smiles, she nods and drives off.

As I walk I wonder if she was not so much offering me a lift as rescuing me from a dangerous predicament.

*

Now I am in Ponferrada. There are starlings dotted on the powerlines making them look like sheet music. I set foot on a pavement; a dusty, dirty Spanish city pavement made from concrete griddles. I am so relieved to be away from the traffic that I could kneel down and kiss it. I sit on the first bench that presents itself and feel the muscles in my back open in relief. I cross into town via a bridge which is the hang-out of a gang of gossiping pensioners and once on the other side, a man asks me if I am looking for a hostel.

I do not trust him. Why?

I tell him that I have my guidebook, and I prove this by showing him the sorry, dog-eared corpse of what had once been the splendid and shining thing I bought in Saint James's church, Dublin. All the same, the man gives me directions. I thank him, wait for him to go away, and then go off looking for another place.

It's closed.

But the directions the man gave me are correct and I arrive at the *donativo*. Perhaps all of those who have walked from Saint Jean or further feel the same as me right now. Maybe we have all bitten off more than we can chew. I think the *hopitaleros* here know this. They joke with the newcomers, whoever they are and irrespective of language. The *hospitalero* working the desk is French. Few of the pilgrims are. When it is my turn to register he asks me where I am from.

"Ireland".

"Kerry?"

"Further north. Near Derry".

"Near Conemarra?"

"Further north".

"Sligo?"

"Further north".

"Donegal?"

"Close enough".

It's some achievement to wring a laugh out of me, but he succeeds. He says there is an Irish pilgrim from Belfast in Bed Eight. Every time I see the *hospitalero* he says "Bed Eight".

I am not going to introduce myself to Bed Eight.

*

There are few people on the streets of Ponferrada. Cars drive past in short queues, having been ushered through by the traffic lights. There is very little noise and the furniture belonging to the pavement cafes is stacked up in front of the cafe windows.

I walk to the old city, where the Templar castle glows in the light of spotlights trained on its walls. It is how castles are supposed to look: it has battlements, turrets, a drawbridge and portcullis. It has flags, windows for archers, a moat, and looks down upon the city around it. Its presence has created a souvenir industry selling Templar related trinkets: key-rings of the Templar cross, t-shirts, model knights, bracelets, necklaces; there is very little Camino merchandise on sale and, on a day where I left the world of the yellow arrows, the absence of the Camino continues. I feel like a tourist now, strolling about this place, looking at the stuff, with nothing to do but wait until daybreak. Perhaps it's thinking like a tourist that has me avoiding a whinging junkie beggar-woman. Not a fellow human, not another soul sharing this earth with me, but a junkie. A pathetic loser. A pest. And maybe it's thinking like a tourist that has me seeing littering doss-heads and aggressive drunks in a bar and wishing they would just disappear. Perhaps I have stepped off the Camino in more ways than one.

I circle the city streets finding nothing but closed restaurants. Then I meet Armo and Milla, who are sharing a drink with the two pilgrims I saw at the *Cruz de Ferro*, and who waved at me as I entered El Acebo. They are mother and daughter, and they began in Saint Jean a week after I had left it. We learn that the restaurants are closed owing to a feast-day, which is rare logic, and we wind up in a pizzeria.

*

The two Americans have also been weirded out by the empty streets and shouty beggars, so I offer to walk with them as their hostel is close to the *donativo*. We say goodnight and good luck, and I make my way to my dorm. There are four bunks. Two of them are occupied by Spanish cyclists who have come here via the *Ruta de Plata* – the silver route, from Sevilla. The other is a Canadian who half-jokingly calls me a bastard when I ask him what part of America he is from. I don't take it to heart; I can be half-jokingly considered a bastard if I go around someone else's home town thinking that they are 'whinging junkie beggar-women, littering doss-heads, and aggressive drunks'. I wouldn't like it if a Spaniard came to Ireland and did likewise.

The Canadian snores like the Queen of England, which wakes the cyclists who strike up a conversation. I wish them all well and carry my stuff into the library of the *donativo*. The sofas there give every indication of doubling up as beds. I fall asleep surrounded by books I cannot read.

DAY THIRTY-THREE

"¡VAMOS, CHICOS! ¡VAMOS!"

A *hospitalero* with a name-badge proclaiming him to be an 'Ángel' is ringing an old school bell and roaring at the ranks of drowsy pilgrims. The sun will soon rise on another day in my world and theirs. The *hospitaleros* will strip all the beds, sweep all the floors, clean all the bathrooms, and prepare themselves for another influx of pilgrims. I will pack up my belongings and take to the road, west towards Villafranca. My big plan is to arrive there and then continue on though the forest, again leaving the Camino.

Priorities: something to eat. I make my way into the city centre, which remains as quiet as I left it the night before. A Belfast accent calls out: "it's that way!" A speed-walking pilgrim in Lycra sportswear minces past, his hiking poles tapping before him. "I got lost getting out of here last time!" He points with one of his sticks to an arrow pointing the way out. "That wasn't there last time!"

I tell him I'm looking for the cafe that's right in front of me and wish him a "Buen Camino". So, I think as he recedes down the hill, that must be Bed Eight.

Breakfast taken care of, I return to the Camino and as soon as I'm on it I'm off it again, hiking up into a housing complex of apartment blocks by a school. I retrace my steps to the river. I did exactly what the map told me, so how did I get lost?

I think back to see where I could have gone wrong. There was the steep street, then past the surly teenagers, and then the modern bridge. There was the view of the Templar castle, high on its cliff overlooking the river steaming with morning mist; as Wagnerian a scene as you could wish for, if you wish for those kinds of things. Then the city park with the happy kids wishing me a "Buen Camino". Then this eponymous Iron Bridge – *Pons Ferrada* – but no, no, no... all wrong. And of course I was told just as much, by a man in a ropey track-suit and goldie-looking chain who looked like he was on his way to see a man about a dog. And, as with his fellow citizen yesterday, I nodded and grinned, and ignored the man, because the guidebook knows better than the people who actually live here.

I see a yellow arrow right where the man said there would be one. I don't know what Ponferrada ever did to me to warrant such mistrust in its citizens, but they taught me a thing or two about being so wary. I follow the arrow, along by the river, up to a roundabout, and away. There is mist on the river, mist in a fine band on the hills, and mist melting in the sky above me.

I meet Armo and Milla when I pause for a coffee in a village just out of town. This is Bierzo country they tell me, famous for its food and drink. Certainly, as I walk along, the landscape bears more of a similarity to that of distant Navarra or fecund La Rioja than it does to the tough, dry *Meseta*. I think about this: 'distant Navarra'. How far have I travelled? It is a strange thing, to think that I am nearer the end than the beginning, and that sooner rather than later all this will be over. And with all these thoughts of endings and finishings in my mind I notice an old woman with a sickle walking down through her back garden.

I meet Almo and Milla again, in a cafe again, but I sit outside and I suddenly feel embarrassed as though I am constantly invading their space. A little beyond this and I am met by someone I thought I'd never see again. It's Anika.

*

Anika is fed up with the Camino primarily on account of a caddish Portuguese who abandoned her after a fling. We walk along, and I ask her why she is on the Camino. She is learning Spanish, and after Santiago she wants to go and volunteer somewhere in the south of Spain.

"Anywhere in particular?"

"There is a nudist colony looking for volunteers".

It's an odd ambition, but we are all different, though as far as the Camino is concerned Anika is more different than others. She has had little or no experience of Catholicism growing up in Sweden, and has found pretty much all of this to be perplexing. I can only imagine that, like a lot of non-Catholic Europeans, it all looks like an expensive anachronism; something from an age before democracy, where a woman's place was in the home, the love that dare not speak its name never spoke its name, and the poor were either cannon fodder or livestock. I don't press her on her take on the beliefs of the people she has met, but she ventures forth into the conversation anyway, saying that she has no idea how people can believe such things.

It's refreshing to meet someone even more like a fish out of water than I am. She smiles a lot through a jeremiad concerning the insipid quality of Spanish food, which is an issue I have learned to live with but, if meeting Almo and Milla taught me anything, it's that there is plenty of good food if you know where to look. Again and again, she returns to the subject of the Portuguese who jilted her. I'm sorry that happened to her, and she keeps mentioning that she might meet him again a little further along the way, just a little bit on, at the next town, or the one after, do you think so?

By a copse of trees there is a man roasting and selling chestnuts. He runs this stall on a *donativo* basis. He makes cones out of newspaper and fills them with charred chestnuts. I 'buy' some and share them with Anika. We wander along, peeling the chestnuts and deciding that it was fine to throw the shells into the verge because they are organic. When we get to a small town Anika roves from cafe to cafe, looking for a place that serves salad, and we wind up sitting outside a bar where I'm admonished by an old lady for using an adjacent stool as a footrest while I loosen my bootlaces.

"Her worries are light" says a voice. It is Danny. He and Liam have emerged from the cafe and are polishing off their coffees before moving on. They rested longer in Sahagún because of the infernal shin-splints. "They're not so bad now", says Liam. "Hurts a bit". They are back to walking about thirty kilometres a day. We are talking about these medical issues when Almo and Milla walk past with a nod of hello. I feel sad that they won't stop, but perhaps they are also embarrassed at constantly running into me too. Either that or the food in this cafe is terrible.

*

I leave Anika to finish her salad and continue out of town. Bierzo country is all vineyards and orchards. The heat brings a constant sweat to my brow, and the path is steep. There seems to be so much abundance here that not all of it has been harvested. I smell the sour cider of apples that are split and rotting on the bough. In one sunlit vineyard I see quails walking between the low branches of young vines, and in the empty window of a barn above Villafranca there is a huge wasps nest; it is a massive airy paper lung, and the insects flit in and out of portholes that look like upside-down pockets.

*

There appears to be a great sluice of topaz dust pouring down the side of a mountain into Villafranca – 'French Town', on account of all the pilgrims coming from France – and I never find out what it really is. It catches the light and gives the town the appearance of a place where something magical is being mined. I walk into town down a long empty road, eating the last of the roasted chestnuts from the crumpled remains of the paper cone. I arrive at the Municipal to find that it is closed and so I rest for a moment, wondering who was the last pilgrim to leave and who would be the first to arrive again. I walk further down the steep streets of Villafranca, avoiding a hostel before which people are playing ukuleles and maracas. I also avoid going in the right direction and am striding past the Red Cross depot when I realise that I am heading south out of town. I retrace my steps and then make for the river, where there will be the bridge and the old part of town: therefore, hostels.

And my reasoning bears fruit. Sweet, sweet fruit, as it happens. I arrive at Leo's, a hostel converted from an old Bierzo town house. It is clean. It is warm. It is friendly. It is an inn insofar as there is a pub and a parlour with an open fire on the ground floor, and all the rooms are upstairs. The *hospitalera* is the daughter of the owner and she runs the place with her sister. She is engaged to an Irishman and this explains why Christie Moore is on the stereo singing *The Voyage*. The Irish ambience is completed by the spectacle of Danny and Liam sitting at the bar drinking pints of stout. They are talking to the owner in Spanish. I speak with an English pilgrim. She is Anglican and asks me if I know what time the service is at. I check with the *hospitalera*. Seven O'Clock.

*

I arrive at the church but there does not seem to be a service. One or two people are wandering around in the shadows and I wander too, wandering and wondering. Then an old lady taps me on the elbow and points to a mysterious door. I push it open – and there is a church inside the church.

It is small, the pews pushed close together and the first few rows are full of people saying the Rosary. I find a place at the back and am sitting there, pondering the Russian Doll trickery of having one church inside the other, when the priest appears, walking to the lectern singing as he goes. At the end of the service I feel like thanking the priest, as during it I began to think that it must be a thankless task doing this every day of your life. I wait for him to finish talking with a group of Colombians, a conversation that must have touched on every topic known to humanity, before thanking him and remarking that the best thing about the Camino was that you have all these people from all these backgrounds and they all get along. There are no politics.

To this he responds by pretending to poke me in the eyes and stab me, before saying "¡Bah, Politicos!" and then flipping the bird. He is smiling as he does this, so all must be well.

*

Having lost contact with everyone I walked with, I now find myself part of a new group of pilgrims. English is our common language, but they are Polish, French, Brazilian, English, Irish (myself), and American. The others are not what I have been trained to think of as religious people. This after all, everyone knows religious people are the root cause of fundamentalist terrorism, cruel social doctrines, and boring attempts at popular music. I remember telling some friends that I was going on the Camino and adding the caveat that I was only doing it for the hike. And I remember that evening when Agnieszka spoke of her revelation and how I my first thoughts had been of the 'oh, bollocks' variety.

We gather in the cold and dark outside the church in Villafranca. The pilgrim meal is in a local restaurant, and when I walk in I see the barometer of culinary excellence, Almo and Milla, at a corner table. In another corner sit Danny and Liam toasting the day with raised glasses and a "Sláinte!"

The food is good because the company is good. The fact that trout is on the menu is such a novelty that we all order it, but when they arrive the little fish look so sad that I reckon they were happy enough catching flies in the river without a thought as to winding up on the dinner table. The wine, on the other hand, doesn't look sad at all. Neither do we when the bottles are empty and we wish each other a "¡Buen Camino!" for the following day.

Back in Leo's, where I have been given a room to myself, I sort out my rucksack. Bierzo country has felt like the mirror image of La Rioja, and I feel that these regions have bookended my walk through Spain. Prior to La Rioja were the Basque lands, and beyond Bierzo country is Galicia. I feel that when I hike over the mountains into Galicia, I will leave Spain and enter into a small country governed by Spain. I will begin my trek over the mountains tomorrow. I look at the map in my guidebook and dream of leaving the Camino again, of taking the remote route through the forest, and if it takes three days to reach Galicia so be it.

DAY THIRTY-FOUR

No. Bad idea. The remote route through the forest is a no-no.

The weather helps decide this, but it is the owner of the hostel who convinces me. The first stop on the remote route is Dragonte, and the owner here is helping to establish a hostel there. The *fuente* at Dragonte, pictured in my guide book, was her idea. But there is a problem, as she explains:

She and her husband had gone through the woods painting yellow arrows to help direct pilgrims to Dragonte and beyond, but 'the Camino provides' and hostels on the main route were not too keen on having customers siphoned off into the woods. The hostels, cafes, bars, and shops of the Camino are like filter feeders; they cannot follow the pilgrims, they can only be in their way. If the flow of pilgrims is diverted, they starve as filter feeders starve should the ocean currents change and send their food elsewhere.

So the villages and hamlets of the main route between Villafranca and O Cebreiro sent emissaries into the forest to remove the yellow arrows. The owner of Leo's is in the process of working with the council of the next jurisdiction, wherein lies Dragonte, to set up concrete bollards with vandal-proof arrows. As it stands, the remote route is unmarked, isolated, and the weather is set to turn for the worst. It'll rain today or tomorrow. It could even snow.

She is adamant that it would be a bad idea, and having snubbed good advice twice in Ponferrada, I'm not going to do it again. The main way it shall be.

Goodbye Villafranca, and goodbye Bierzo country. I set out in the light rain, staying close to the crash barrier around the twisting road out of town. I arrive at a highway junction up the verge of which is an arcade of bowed trees painted electric blue. This is not the way, but I walk up through this strange installation to where I can look down over the Camino. Here it is the hard shoulder of the highway, and above it is a motorway leading into a mountain. There is a loud suction noise every time a truck goes by as though they're being hoovered up by the tunnel.

This is the Camino out of Villafranca, and it is shared with a few Japanese pilgrims with their bright ponchos pulled up over their heads. They look like apples and oranges with legs. They and I, we, walk through the rain, alongside the river, alongside the motorway, alongside the highway, just a few people walking in the same place at the same time for just a few hours.

Danny passes me, saying hello with his headphones in, and then Liam, who chats a little about the steep climb ahead into O Cebreiro, the first town in Galicia where people overnight. He goes on ahead. For people who had done themselves an injury with their thirty-a-day regimen, they are fleet of foot. Or I am slow slow slow, sauntering slow, along the side of the road listening to the high motorway flyover boom and crack as heavy vehicles pass overhead. The hills all around are covered in dense, deciduous forest. The rainy mist catches and snags on the tops of the trees, and I am reminded of living in Wales, half a life away, when the hills where I lived in Ceredigion were like this. But it is not good to think too much about the past. These are not the Welsh hills, but the Galician hills. They stack up, one on top of the other, and soon the sky is pushed away by a close and high horizon.

I walk through Pereje, and stop for a break in Trabadelo, where I stamp my *Credencial* in the knowledge that the last part of the Camino requires two stamps per day in order to qualify for the *Compostella*. That's a thought: I am on the last part of the Camino. As important as this feels to me, signals from the outside world tell me that nobody will care; the Spanish king is greeting the new members of the Spanish government. Everyone is smiling and courteous, and Felipe VI looks like he hasn't got a care in the world. Which is how a man should be. In the cafe, bar-flies horse around, shouting stuff at one another and laughing. Pilgrims come and go, adding precious Euros to the till.

I am ambling along when I am overtaken again by Danny, and a while later Liam walks by. He keeps pace with me long enough for us to have a conversation about how there should be a Camino system in Ireland, with the existing hiking routes liked up and lots of hostels, and *donativos*, and Municipals run by every county after their own fashion. But the pipe dream ends with a shrug, because we know the Irish won't go for something that won't turn them a quick buck. "Sure listen to us", says Liam, "Irish dreamers and Irish schemers". And with that wistful utterance he says he'll see me later, and walks on.

He's right though. There is a curse on the Irish. The Irish are Esau's clan. We took the soup. Now look at us, British in all but name. No tongue of our own, no mind of our own, nothing of our own. A country in hock to foreign banks. Universities kept afloat by foreign students. And our children still drifting away to serve foreign powers.

The road takes me past a crowded motorway service station, the diner of which is crowded with families having lunch. Claustrophobia stops me from going in. There is a stall outside selling fruit and roast chestnuts. I buy one apple because I need to justify the visit to myself. The apple looks like a khaki potato, but it is the sweetest apple I have ever tasted. I wish I had bought more and when hunger pangs arrive, I make do with yet another in a long line of ham sandwiches, which I buy in a roadside hostel which contains a shop that sells little more than walking poles. A reminder of the arduous path ahead.

There is also a *bruja* in the cafe: a witch. She is perched on her flying broomstick and seems to be having a right old time of it. As well she might. I heard that the 'flying broomstick' was originally slang for a type of dildo marinated in the juice of psychedelic toadstools. The *bruja* is a common figure in

Galicia, and seems to fulfil the function of a leprechaun in Ireland. If the leprechaun promises good fortune with his crock of gold, the *bruja* sweeps away misfortune with her broom.

I leave the cafe, and then the highway, walking up the steepening slope to Ambamestas where cows are being herded through the streets. The ringing of their bells sounds like an old fire engine. When they are not being herded through the streets they sit out in the pastures, the rattling of their bells acting like heavy wind-chimes in the otherwise still countryside. Ambamestas offers a sea-change in so many things: gone is the desiccated wilderness of the *Meseta*, replaced by an arboreal world of hills and valleys. The houses, with their slate roofs and thick stone walls resemble petrified dinosaurs, and the Olympian span of the motorway with its mighty struts seems to frame this new world as a secretive place overlooked by the world of speed and deadlines.

The rain relents, and then stops and the forests steam. There is the animal stink of wet yet-flowering undergrowth. I buy stamps for postcards in Vega de Valcarce from a tobacconist with pumpkins on the wall and cats in the garden. There is a break in the clouds and the sun reaches me for what feel like the first time in my life. I have to hike in a t-shirt, and I need to put on sun cream.

I continue along the way. There is nobody else on the road until I am in Las Herrerías. There is a path that runs downhill into Las Herrerías, and there is a tavern on the hill. And walking up to the tavern in a black dress with a white apron, with her hair in a bun, is a woman who works in the tavern. She reminds me of a figure from a Goya painting, with her dark eyes and pale skin, and for an instant I feel as though I am watching a ghost – not a luminous spectre, but a fully fleshed apparition of a bygone age. The tavern, the woman, the landscape, they give me the impression of a window into another world. And then she is indoors again, and it is getting towards the end of 2016 again, and I am a stranger in a strange land again, but I'm not the first and won't be the last.

At the bottom of the hill, in the ox-bow terrace of Las Herrerías, there is a tree fletched with hundreds of bits of paper. They look like untidy blossoms, and they have been skewered onto the branches. A sign at the base of the tree reads:

¿Que son tus sueños?

Well, what are my dreams?

I don't think about this too much. I rip a leaf from my notebook and scribble 'to Be Not Afraid'. I pin this on the tree with all the others. There: I've just told the world I'm afraid. I've admitted it, and I've heard that one of the first steps in solving a problem is admitting that there is one.

I have no idea what the other steps are.

*

The road sweeps through birch forest, and their leaves land with a tap each time. Fields of pumpkins, bright yellow and alien, tilt at the river rushing ringing below, and having turned just another corner in a series of corners, the road leans back and I am marching up a mountain. This is it: the road to O Cebreiro. The sudden change of pace necessitates a brief pause during which I can feel gravity tugging at my rucksack. Far below me there is a paddock with behemoth bulls grazing.

*

Focus.

The steep incline grips the knees and forces the lungs to the point of heaving. Ahead of me are four pilgrims who look like turtles in their ponchos and hiking poles. Ahead of them is a soaring green mountainside dissolving into high mist. I follow the turtles up the hill and meet them where there is a fork in the path. They are French turtles, neither teenage, mutant, nor ninja, and they are deliberating whether or not to stay on the road or take the track. The road continues ahead, but the track runs through a holloway. A sign on a bollard at the mouth of the holloway informs us that the road is for cyclists and the holloway is for walkers. We begin along the holloway.

The landscape is now wet chestnut trees, all red and green, and the path is a cascade of russet leaves and chestnut burrs. They gather in such numbers that it looks like a path of embers. The dry stone walls are furred with moss. Water drips from the leaves and the forest streams with water as though it has just been lifted free from the depths. I walk higher and higher and the word 'enchanted' recurs as a way to label this place and this experience. Further up and there are local people gathering sweet chestnuts in big net sacks. A metal pot sits on a pile of smoking branches, and a man starts up a small chainsaw and slices up bigger branches that he adds to the fire.

The turtles take lots of pictures and ask me to photograph them, which I do. I don't want them to photograph me, though. Why?

*

The path runs by the hamlet of La Faba, and the road forks again.

This is the way to the top of the mountain. The path rises and flecks of rain touch my skin. Just as I touch the underside of the clouds, I pull on my rain-jacket.

I reach Laguna, and the manure and slurry smells of farms in the misty rain. If I walk a little further, I tell myself, I will be in Galicia. The path above Laguna is the path above valleys of copper shavings and dragon green. The path snakes into the clouds, and then there it is: A marker.

I am in Galicia.

The marker is tall, made of stone, with the cross of Saint James and heraldic crests. There are names names names of pilgrims who invested this marker with the significance I do. It means the final days of the Camino. It means entering a new world. It means that all will be different.

As I stand there admiring it, two Italian pilgrims arrive. I recognize them from before – the pilgrim whose birthday was on Hallowe'en, who was interested in what the druids thought about people born when the worlds of the living and the dead overlap. I take their picture for them as they stand grinning in the rain by the marker, thumbs up. Then they walk ahead into the rainy fog.

The rain sets in, and the fine blizzard of cloud is now fat pearls of water. Small mercies: I am glad I bought the waterproof trousers and the rain jacket back there in Astorga. I walk and listen to the whispering of the plastic fabric as it rubs against itself, the clicking and tutting of the rain as it falls on the brim of my hat, the chewing succulence of the mud beneath my footsteps. The cool water on my face is revitalizing after the weeks of Spanish sun. I am walking, listening, looking out over the misty slopes, and then there is the grey stone wall of what looks like a byre on my right hand side. A little further, and then the odd, stone igloo that is the cupola of the church appears. This is it, this is it, I think, I'm here, I'm here, and so I am as I step off the track by a cross and find myself on the road running past O Cebreiro.

Thank God I get to see this:

O Cebreiro watermarks the rain. The solid stone of its buildings is shadowy and secretive. And what buildings these are – *pallozas*, idiosyncratic bee-hive houses with thatched roofs and low doors. The Roman world has given way to the Celtic world. I stop and enjoy the rain for a moment. I see the warm yellow lights in the small, deep-set windows in the *pallozas*. Galicia seems cosy; it is rainy, foresty, streamy, green and bracken brown, stony in its highlands. It reminds me of the other Celtic lands. It reminds me of home in a way. *Nach bhfuil áthas orm a bheith abhaile arís?*

I step into the church. It is unlike the overwhelming churches of Navarra, or the gleaming vaults of León. It is cool, spare and neat. They have Bibles in different languages, but not Irish and I wonder if I should post them a copy when I get back. I buy postcards to send home, and postcards with Saint Francis's 'Canticle of the Creatures' on it, and the woman at the desk also stamps my *Credencial* with the date upside down. This was the church of Elías Valiña, the local priest who began painting yellow arrows along the Camino. When asked what he was doing he would reply by saying he was preparing for an invasion.

I walk through the village without a soul in sight until I see the Municipal up ahead. This is the Galician *Xunta*, one of a series of brand new utilitarian hostels that dot the Camino from here on in. A few windy beggars are bobbing towards the door. They are pilgrims and the gale that is picking up on the exposed side of the mountain is filling their ponchos and they look like massive balloons. The *hospitalera* works in what looks like a ticket office, accepting the few Euros it takes to stay there from each pilgrim and providing those that didn't visit the church with their first Galician stamp in their *Credencial*. I go and set out my bed sheet, shower and then go out to find somewhere to eat.

Somewhere to eat is the bar in an inn, and I have a coffee, which counts as something to eat, before going to the pilgrim mass. Danny and Liam are in the bar too and as I head for the door they say "don't forget to pray for us sinners, will you?"

And I say "If I started that, I'd never stop". And they laugh, and I laugh, but a little over a month I would never have entertained the idea of going to mass. Even the term 'going to mass' reminds me of charmless Sunday mornings spent bored in pews stuffed with half-assed parishioners. But this is the Camino.

I go up to the church. I meet only two other pilgrims at the door. I recognize one of them from Villafranca and the pilgrim meal. He is Alvar, from Brazil. The other is Mandy, an American. We sit in the church as another four pilgrims arrive for the service. The *Xunta* has quite a number of pilgrims, as do the other hostels in the village – but there are six at the service. The priest hands me a Bible in English and asks me to read.

I read: Paul to the Philippians 3:17 – 4.1, and I enjoy reading this thing that has been around for about two thousand years and has been read in different lands, by different people, and in different languages. I enjoy doing something I have not done before. To the list of Life Experiences, I can now add 'reading at a Galician mass' to Sky Diving and Seeing That Band I Like. I get the thumbs up from Mandy when I am returning to my seat. Five of the six of us then go for dinner.

The restaurant has low beams and a hearth that holds a merry fire. We push two small tables together and sit. With Alvar, Mandy, and me, the group is completed by Charlotte and Francois, both French and both on their honeymoon. For no better reason than it is Galicia, Alvar orders the *pulpo* – the octopus, and it arrives, a platter of steaming tentacles sprinkled with paprika, together with a bottle of Albariño. He asks us if we want any.

It is good to try new things, so I try the Albariño.

Alvar describes for us his Buddhist meditation exercises wherein he observes strict silence for a week. I mention Andy, the silent pilgrim I'd last seen in Atapuerca. The others know who I'm talking about, proving that the world of the Camino may be long and varied, but it is small nonetheless. Without saying, Alvar pays for everything. The owner gives us all *liquor de hierba* to round off the meal and we all return to the *Xunta*, bar the honeymooners who are staying in a hotel.

DAY THIRTY-FIVE

I don't really wake up this morning as I never really went to sleep. The cavernous dorm in the *Xunta* echoed with the demented rasping of moribund pilgrims. At one point I woke up one of the offenders, just to get him to stop snoring, just to catch a few hours sleep. As a result, I am getting dressed and rolling up my sleep sheet in a fug of jet-lagged stupefaction. It is easy to think well of people and be kind and forgiving when they are not there, but a person who snores provokes such wrath that I wouldn't be surprised if it was one of the leading causes of murder around the world. Nevermind. Fetch your boots from the stand downstairs, by the window that fizzes with windblown rain, and tie them on by the light of your headlamp. Once you are ready, get steady, and go.

The wind and rain push against me as soon as I set foot outside. There is not one light in the village. There are the stone walls of the buildings, dark and cold, and the horizontal rain whipping through the light of my headlamp like sparks of silver; I feel like I'm walking along a mineshaft. I shelter with a few others in the church porch until the inn opens for breakfast. I sit in there drinking coffee as pilgrims come and go, including Danny and Liam, Charlotte and Francois, and Mandy, and Alvar, and too many others so that at one point the bar is full to overflowing, and then it settles down and I order a breakfast of toast and more coffee. And then I go.

The cloud and rain reduce the visible world to a short stretch of dirt track in front, and a wake of the same just behind. The path rises until it meets a road and runs alongside it. On the opposite side of the road is a statue of a mediaeval pilgrim, braced against the rain, his hat clamped down on his head with one hand. All around him there is only thick fog and cold wind. Two foggy apparitions pass me by: Danny and Liam, whom I thought would be far ahead, but they saunter past making jokes about the view, and then the fog turns them into tiny grey smudges. The path rises then falls through mist and rain and a soaking Celtic world of farms, ferns, trees, and lees.

I go down down down, all the way down, and the cloud begins to lift free of the path, lifting higher higher higher, and I can look out over bright green fields, reticulate hedgerows, and the peaks of the mountains lost in the cloud. In one town, which is little more than a farm, the locals are slaughtering pigs. The animals are already dead and lying in a barn. In the doorway, one of them is hanging up by its back legs. It is as white as milk. On the concrete ground beneath it there is a pool of bright red blood and large black clots that gleam like port jelly. A man in wellies is steadying the pig. In one hand he has a large knife, and there are other men standing with the heap of carcasses. They are smiling and talking, because they enjoy one another's company on a cold day doing a dirty job.

I pass by this unexpected vision and then meet another. An old lady stands by the door of a house at the far end of town. She is offering pancakes to passing pilgrims, sprinkling castor sugar on each one as the one above it is peeled away. She is offering them on a *donativo* basis, and I give her a few Euros for this, not because the pancakes are worth a few Euros – why not? They are in Dublin – but because she is standing at her door on this cold morning offering them to people.

She also reminds me of a story told by Jack Kerouac. Kerouac, many moons ago, falls in with a jive-talking student of Buddhism and they go to climb a mountain in America together. On the way to the summit, the student extols the virtues of Buddhism with all the zeal of the newly converted. He pours scorn on the people of America for not getting with the program. They are blinded by their nine-to-five jobs, cars, lawns, and Tupperware parties. They are not, and will not be, enlightened. Kerouac is thrilled. He descends the mountain brimming with enlightenment, and decides to return home to visit his old mother. He walks through his home town sneering at the unenlightened ones as they mow their lawns and wash their cars with their unenlightened hands. As he reaches the garden gate, he looks up and sees old mother Kerouac at the kitchen window. She is peeling potatoes. Why? Because she is preparing a meal for her son who is coming home to visit her. She is doing this out of love. In a flash, Kerouac realises that he is not enlightened after all. He is just a cruel man, because he cannot see the humanity in those around him.

*

I stop at a cafe, saying hello and goodbye to Danny and Liam who are just leaving it. Over a coffee, I read the local paper. The main story is a trumpet-blast of outrage against teenage drinking. The boozy adolescents have become emboldened by numbers and now their *botellón* – knacker-drinking – is on the steps of Lugo cathedral. Something must be done!

The path dives off the edge of the village of Biduedo, and it is an effort not to slip on the descent. This continues all the way to Triacastela, where the entrance to the town is marked by an enormous chestnut tree. I wonder what Europe would be like if we had learned to live with the forest and not at its expense; and how trees like this would not be unusual because of their age and size, but familiar. By the time I meet this tree I am walking with steps so small that I am almost putting heel to toe. The broken night's sleep and the long downward hike have made me a dull, witless seeker of food and shelter, and I follow signs to a hotel with all the energy of a bottom-feeding fish following a scent trail.

I don't make it to the hotel. As I wend my way through the streets a voice from a doorway shouts "¿Albergue?" Fine, I take it and the laundry service too. I set out my sleep sheet and then go for dinner. There are no other people on the streets – no pilgrims, no locals. There is no sound from houses; no radios, no music, no sound of speaking. The local church is closed; the only service today being a funeral for someone I didn't know existed, and will now never have the chance to meet. All the graveyards along the Camino have given me this sense of there being secret worlds, and how my presence is transient not just on the Camino, but in the world too. Whoever is being buried would have been a baby, a child, they would have grown up and tried to make sense of the world and take part in it, and then, perhaps, they made an accommodation with it, and then they lived out their life until it was their time to go. Who decides when you will come into this world? Who decides when you will go? Who determines the span of a life, of any life: this person's, mine, that of the chestnut tree at the entrance to town? How much life was I given at birth? How much of it is left?

I find the local restaurant, and order the pilgrim menu. The place is quiet until a perfumed, leather-jacketed incursion of the local youth storms the bar. Country kids – 'culchies' - this must be the happening place. The waiter, despite the public outcry, plies them with all the booze they want, and then he takes my order.

The food has altered having arrived in Galicia. There is the *pulpo*, but there are a few other things I have not seen elsewhere in Spain. One of these is the Galician soup; a sort of broth made from potatoes and cabbage. It sounds drab, but it is tasty and filling, perhaps juxtaposed to weeks of tooth-blunting sandwiches. Perhaps also, I have spent the last years of my life in a city that heaps praise on anything that removes it from the stigma of Irishness. Potato and cabbage soup might shame the self-hating Irish, but it is seen as something special here.

*

I am finishing the wine and flicking through my decomposing guidebook when the Italian druid and her friend wander through the restaurant "looking at places". She tells me that "everyone else" is staying at another hostel, just down the street, and that they are going for dinner soon. I've just eaten, but I like the company of my fellow pilgrims and so I wander up the street and see them standing outside a hostel. There are a few familiar faces, those from O Cebreiro, and a few new people too. We walk right back to the restaurant I've just left, and rather than be embarrassed by this, act as though this was my plan all along. The service is smilier as a result.

More and more pilgrims come to join and tables are pushed together until it looks as though we are at a banquet, and I find myself at the head of the table. There is a lot of talk about how wonderful the Camino is, talk tempered by the jaded take on the scramble for stamps and certificates as seen by an English poet who is a dead ringer for Ted Hughes. There is talk about the weather: Alvar says he is going to spend all day tomorrow here, as part of his Buddhist meditation. The added advantage, he says, is that he will be able to walk through the snow which will settle in this area.

I don't eat, but buy a bottle of Albariño to share, and at the end of the meal I buy brandies for those who remain. These are served in such quantities that I reckon there is about half a pint in each glass. Again Alvar pays for the lot, but I manage to pay for the brandy.

I say good night to them all, and make my way up the silent streets to my hostel.

*

There is an old, sick guy snoring in the bunk in the corner. Or is there? Because as soon as I think this, I know I'm wrong. This pilgrim was sneezing earlier, and I'd felt resentment then. But he told some others, some Japanese pilgrims, that he was happy to "see my Japanese friends". Beyond them, he seemed to be travelling alone, and was ill.

He is not a sick, snoring old guy who could make me ill with his sneezing. He is most likely a nice person, and I am most likely not a nice person, because I see only a sick old guy and no-one else. I go to sleep thinking that if I am only going to be a nice person when all is well, I need to get it into my head that 'all is well' needs to be more often than I think.

DAY THIRTY-SIX

Up and out. I'm filling my flask in the hostel kitchen where a frying pan of roast chestnuts indicates a pilgrim meal of rare distinction, when an English pilgrim asks me if I have seen her green t-shirt. I have not and check the laundry room in case it is lying in there. She finds it mixed in with some of her other stuff. "I know it's not important", she says "but you get attached to silly things".

*

I have breakfast in a cafe run by a woman who is must have done this a million times before and must have had it with making toast every morning. I sit a few tables away from the Japanese pilgrims who sit to attention and talk about something in low, urgent voices. Some locals come in, but I don't know why. They do not order anything or speak to the owner. They accept a bundle of newspapers from a deliveryman, but don't open it. They are not speaking Spanish, but Gallego, a form of Portuguese and of which I have learned little beyond that 'O' and 'A' and the male and female versions of 'The'.

*

Away: Lush, wet boreens of rusting leaves and chestnut burrs. Rain rustles in the hiss of streams, the road rises through grey hamlets, and then the sun breaks through and I see silhouettes of treelines in the mist rising from the forest. Passing the low, shingle-roofed houses, and the fresh air is scented with hearth smoke.

It is hard to accept that this is the same *Camino Francés* that I have followed ever since Saint Jean. I became so used to the dry dust and the dun stone of Castille that this land of green fields and rainy trees feels as though I am not on the Camino anymore, but on some other path, in some other part of the world. There are times when the countryside here looks just like that of my native West Tyrone.

Some stretches of the path are deep gullies and I wonder if, during periods of heavy rain, they are impossible to use; they look as though they could channel all the water that falls on the mountain as though they were gargoyles on the walls of a cathedral. Along the way there are small hamlets and here and there they show signs of life in the form of *donativos* offering biscuits and fruit. And then, out of the blue, I see Pedro, whom I'd last seen in Hontanas, sitting by the door of a closed cafe. He has taken his boots off, part of his plan, he says, to preserve his feet. He tells me that he has a cold coming on. He is the last of the people from earlier in the Camino whom I bump into. Everyone else has either left the Camino or is ahead of me. I wonder what they made of this landscape as they passed through it.

*

The path runs down down down to Sarria. The meadows steam with mist and it hangs before the wooded hilltops. Chestnut burrs litter the path in places, as do the long red needles from pine trees with bark like tractor tyres. For a while, up ahead of me, a lone Japanese pilgrim begins to sing a quavering Japanese song. I wonder if he knows I am there, as he sings, high on this hill road, far from his home, lost in his thoughts.

Sarria is the town where many pilgrims begin their Camino. It is from here that the *Credencial* must now get stamped twice daily in order to qualify for the *Compostella*. I don't quite follow the logic of this, seeing as how I have proof of having travelled from Saint Jean, but I don't make the rules and I fail to see why I should make a big deal about it. So I collect my first stamp in Sarria at the hotel where I get a room, to have some peace and quiet.

Oh, yeah? Make plans and God laughs.

*

Sarria is quiet, its churches are closed and there are only a few people around. I walk up the Camino that runs through the centre of town, past the busier hostels and up to where they are dismantling an open air market. There is a view-point over the town and I look down at the clusters of old buildings, and the modern apartment blocks, and the buildings that are as yet unfinished. There are so many of us on the earth, and each one is so much to cope with and has so much to cope with.

Further up the road and there is the convent. It begins to rain and I shelter in one of its porches. A bead-curtain of rain begins to fall from the eaves; each rain drop is fat and white, like a mistletoe berry. I wonder how long it would have to rain to erode this monastery away. The rain rustles and sends circular pulses cancelling one another out in the puddles. Across from the monastery there is a cemetery with a place for urns and I can't help but notice how the clouds above it look like smoke.

The rain passes and I return to the hotel, popping into a minimarket to buy a few things to eat and get the second stamp. The hotel room is small, spartan, but *en suite*. The Ritz could not have felt more of a luxury. I lay out the things I got from the minimarket, switch on my tablet to play some music, and wonder what the hell I'm doing here.

I look at my email. June has written, telling me what she's doing. She is travelling with Gene, Beatrice, Alastair, Cristina, and others. There is a photo of them all at their own pilgrim meal. On a whim I also look at Andy's blog. He has been posting updates on his adventures along the way, and it is interesting to read about his experiences of places I visited but had a different experience of. But that's the way it is: we don't all see the same thing, because we don't have the same perspective. I leave him a message, asking him to look out for my note on the tree in Las Herrerías.

The Camino is touted as a cultural itinerary, and I know that in the past I would be all over Sarria, but the Camino is not a cultural itinerary for me. As I sit in my room I become aware of the vast emptiness in the life I have made for myself, and again I recognise the cowardice that has made this possible. It's not about being clever, it's about being better. It's about finding out what's wrong and putting it to rights.

Like in *Groundhog Day*.

*

Nature abhors a vacuum, and so into the silence that I sought in this room come the sounds of a movie. I'd forgotten that Spanish walls are one atom thick and that any sound carries right through them. Cars screech, guns blaze, men speak in some weird underwater language, something blows up; it's the whole circus of nonsense and it's being funnelled straight into my head.

A knock on the neighbour's door gets no response. How about a few knocks on the wall then? No? How about one big psycho thump powered by impotence and rage at the damn television in your room? No? How about more loud knocks on your door? Louder ones?

It opens. A man who looks like a badger wearing reading glasses is standing there, the blue-grey flicker of the movie flashing behind him. He peers at me over the top of his glasses.

"*¿Puedes bajar la televisión?*" I ask.

"You speak English?"

"Yes".

"Where you from?"

"Ireland" I say, omitting the 'Northern' prefix that I use with friends and well-wishers. "Can you turn it down, please?"

"No. I pay for this room. Twenty-five Euros."

"Ok, but I can't sleep."

"You can get another room."

"I paid twenty-fine Euros too."

"You American?"

"No."

"You hit the wall?"

"Yes."

"OK."

"OK. Even just a bit."

"Ok. A bit."

"Thank you."

"Goodnight."

DAY THIRTY-SEVEN

Leaving the hotel I see Pedro in the cafe at reception.

"*Hombre*" he says, incredulous at just how small the world is. He had stayed there too. I tell him about the noisy neighbours over breakfast. His head cold still lingers and he wonders if he should stay here an extra day and rest. I tell him to "feed a cold, starve a flu" and then explain what that means. Science interests him, and he hangs on every word.

We say cheerio again, and then I retrace my steps up through Sarria and then past the cemetery, walking down a hill dotted with dead fire salamanders. Why they are there? I have no idea. It looks as though they have crawled out onto the road to die. Coming from a country where wildlife is a mystery for most people, to see such a profusion of this charismatic animal, and all of them dead, feels like being served with a blessing and a curse at the same time.

I walk wondering about how different the world would be if people walked as pilgrims through their own country and through the countries of other people; not as hikers, not as tourists, or even *Tourigrinos*, but as people who consider the path to be a privilege and all they see and do a blessing.

And being here is a privilege; it is the luxury that Beatrice spoke of over the Maragato meal in Astorga, but it's much more than that. It is a privilege to be. Full stop.

It is a privilege to be.

I think about the unlikelihood of being here at all. I think of the chance encounter that brought my parents together, and multiply that by the chance of their parents meeting. And I think of how any deviation from their life histories would have resulted in some other outcome, an outcome in which I would not be born. So, there is the chance meeting of my parents, and their parents, and their parents, and so on, and so forth, right back through my ancestry. Everything that happened had to have happened; otherwise I would not have been born.

And yet everything did happen as it did, and I was born – but life is not long, and time ebbs away. Whatever measure of life I was given at birth, that is all I have. Before birth and after death are unknowable, but I cannot see why they are not just mindless obscurity with this brief, unlikely chance of life being all there is to experience the world. A chance of life with which to experience life. Being here to experience being here.

Life gives me life so that I may love life. Is this what Christians mean when they say that God makes people to adore Him? My Atheism is the rejection of the God for Children. I'm still an Atheist in that respect; but now I walk towards Santiago with this inchoate Faith in this new God who has been waking me up for who knows how long. And perhaps in the process of being woken up it is easier just to sleep on: five more minutes, five more minutes, five more minutes...

*

There are few people on the road who are not pilgrims. I see a farmer with an axe over his shoulder talking to a cow, and later I meet Crystal again, whom I'd last seen in Logroño with tendonitis. She tells me that she could run the Camino now; she is feeling that much better. She has three friends with her, one of whom has taken a 'vow of silence' and also a 'vow of baseball' as he uses his *palo* to hit chestnut burrs and wild apples lobbed at him by the others. Crystal is turning her hair into dreadlocks, and does this as she opines on how it's OK to steal farmer's fruit. They are all American and will Vote Trump, making them the only Americans I meet who support him, or admit to it. I give them a pin badge and the story of how I got it: I was just out of Sarria when I saw a shop and stopped to get one of my two stamps out of the way. I bought one postcard. The guy behind the counter thought this wasn't a big enough purchase so blagged his way into selling me a pin badge of a 'Camino flag' crossed with an Italian flag. He swore blind it was the Irish flag, but I wasn't going to argue with him, because such an argument would have been pathetic in the extreme, and it must be tricky enough living off selling tourist trinkets during the off season.

I didn't give a toss about the badge. Or him. Or his shop.

All the same, I have no use for it, so I give it to the Americans in the hope that they can pass it on.

*

There are no cafes. This grim fact weighs on me. It also provokes an outbreak of gurgles and proclamations from my stomach which has not greeted food since breakfast. Then: a cafe. I'm not the only pilgrim in the vicinity and those who have arrived before me are besieging the place. Piranhas have less of an appetite during a feeding frenzy. There is one woman running the place, aided by a man who appears once in a while proffering a plate of bacon and eggs. She is so busy taking orders from impatient pilgrims that I decide to leave the place and see if there is anywhere further on. There is.

It is practically empty, and I dine in regal fashion at the outside table, looking up at the green hills of Galicia. As I am eating, I watch pilgrims in ones or twos, or in little groups, pass on down the Camino. Then, a door opens and an old man totters out. He steadies himself against the door jamb, and feels his way with his foot before stepping out onto the porch. It is hard for me to believe that time can do this to people, to all people, and that once there had been a day when he could have kept pace with these hikers breezing by on the way to Portomarín. We don't all get to be so old, I think. But is that a blessing or a curse?

What have you done to deserve your health? What have you done to deserve this freedom?

I bring in my dishes and thank the staff, and they stamp my *Credencial*. I ask the waitress if she has ever done the Camino, and she laughs at the idea. I might as well have asked her if she has ever walked on the moon.

Through rough lanes across streams, between palisades of chestnut trees, and then a bollard with a magic number: 100,000. Not one-hundred thousand kilometres to Santiago, but a mere one hundred made to look terrifying by the continental comma. One hundred: it feels like the start of a countdown. I think back to Roncesvalles and the ludicrous roadsign promising/threatening seven-hundred and ninety kilometres until Santiago de Compostella. Now there are one hundred remaining. I think of what the last six-hundred and ninety kilometres have brought me: people, places, sights, sounds, and all I have thought about. I expected none of it. I have no idea what lies ahead.

I can't be the only one who has thought this. The bollard is coloured in with names, slogans, signatures, and hearts. And there will always be those who are just happy to see this. The Americans I had pizza with in Ponferrada, with Almo and Milla, are there. They pose by the bollard, smiling from ear to ear.

The final stretch before Portomarín is a steep drop that levels out by a reservoir. The town lies on the opposite shore and to get to it I must cross a tall, narrow bridge. I've never enjoyed seeing nothing below my feet. Even at a distance, the thought of standing above thin air makes me queasy. I remember those occasions when I visited Fuente De, in Los Picos de Europa, and took the cable-car one kilometre up onto the cliffs. There was a walkway there, suspended over the void, and stepping out onto it caused my insides to curdle. Even sitting in the cafe, looking out at the railings I felt uneasy. Now there is this bridge I must cross to reach Portomarín. What was it I wrote in Las Herrerías? 'to Be Not Afraid'. OK, then – I was thinking of something else, but it'll do.

Far below me I see my shadow walking across green beaches of low-tide algae. The last time I Paid Attention to this was leaving Orisson, on my way to Roncesvalles. There are fine gaps between the flagstones and I catch glimpses of the Earth's surface far below me. Rivulets streaming into the reservoir have carved deltas into the mud. It is a strange, drunken feeling, crossing this bridge, but when I am across it, I climb up a flight of Roman steps to an arch and pass into Portomarín. I sit in a bus shelter and check my guidebook map. My hostel is by the cathedral, so I put on my rucksack and march up a steep, arcaded street to where the cathedral stands. It is a monolithic cube with a blue rose window above its main door. It has no spires or buttresses, and the effect is that of a Norman keep – strong, dominant, securing the landscape.

The hostel can wait. I pop into an adjacent cafe for a glass of cider. There are a few familiar faces in the cafe, including Charlotte and Francois, and a few outside too, as the couple from the hotel in Sarria wander past. The badger-man's wife is petite and South American and she is listening to him as they stroll along.

Pedro is outside too. I bump into him on the way to the hostel. He is still labouring under his head cold and has taken my advice on feeding colds and starving flus to heart, tucking into a bag of Doritos and explaining how he has gone far enough and that this is the end of his Camino. We agree to meet later to discuss this further, but first I need to book in to the hostel. It's another night with a single room. The snorers of the world are expensive to avoid.

I meet Pedro again and go to a cafe overlooking the reservoir. There is a rainy sunset bleeding above the hills. Pedro, still feeding his cold, opts for Galician soup and gets a tureen full of the stuff. I am determined to have the pilgrim meal after mass, so I pass and have coffee instead. He launches into a lecture on the deforestation of old Spain. He calls this the *Desamortización*, a period when there was a land grab of church property, which was then overworked. In the distant past, he says, Spain was owned by the Spanish. There were no kings or governments, and the land sustained those who worked it. All that has changed.

*

The mass in the cathedral segues from the Rosary that is ongoing as I go in. At the end of the service, the priest invites the pilgrims into the sacristy to receive a special stamp on their *Credenciales*. Afterwards there is the pilgrim meal in the local Italian restaurant, pizzas all round, and a conversation about what makes a pilgrim different from a tourist. The Camino was created by pilgrims, not for pilgrims. It was the endless flow of pilgrims to the shrine of Saint James that necessitated all these pit-stops and hospitals, all these hostels and the whole industry of sleeping, eating, drinking, paving, way-marking, and safe-guarding that went along with it. It is a pilgrim who does this for religious or spiritual reasons, but they are not alone. Tourists like the food, the buildings, the people, the experience. And perhaps all that differentiates the most part of them is that they too are on a religious or spiritual journey, but they don't know it. Or they are a part of a pilgrim's journey, with neither knowing it.

We can agree that we have met with no danger, and that tales of crime are so rare as to be recounted in stand-alone detail. Neither have we encountered bad manners anywhere like those we find in cities, or are guilty of ourselves. People are calmer, perhaps wilfully so, but calmer nonetheless. And we have met so many good people, generous with time, patient and good-natured people, that we cannot think of tourists as 'wrong' and pilgrims as 'right'. We are part of the same great transient city of souls.

On a practical level, we remark again on how the tourists, the majority, keep the hostels open and the villages with a future. And if there are many thousands of people doing this for fun, for their 'Bucket List', as a life experience, so be it. The Camino is for all people. If only all people were for it.

It is here in the company of Charlotte and Francois, of Mandy, and a few others that I say that I am not afraid of the future. I said before that I am not worried about it, many times, to many people, in many places. But now it feels different saying it.

"Because you have Faith" says Charlotte, as though the reason is so obvious she can say it before I can. The F-word.

And I agree. It's true.

DAY THIRTY-EIGHT

Breakfast in the cafe where I spoke with Pedro about Spanish history. In the bleary dawn the world outside the window is still half-asleep. I browse the morning papers. Whereas newspapers in other parts of Spain dwell on the King and his government, Galicia concerns itself with more important matters. Previously it was the scourge of binge-drinking teenagers. Now, it is the scourge of 'macho violence'. Macho violence is another way of describing what English speakers refer to as 'domestic violence', which sounds cosier. The Galician press place the blame where it is deserved – angry men. The front page leads with the shock statistics of wives beaten and murdered at the hands of their angry men. It's sobering stuff, first thing in the day, and I wonder if people will see sense on this issue.

I fold up the paper, pay the barman for breakfast, and shoulder my pack. Once more unto the breach...

*

Farms. Cows. Pigs. Chickens. Tractors. Cats. Dogs. So much for their being no place like home. The path is sweet in the morning light and its greens and browns are smudged against the snow blue of the mist. There are long stretches of today's walk where the Camino is a slender *senda*, or a dirt track, or a muddy lane, or even just a beaten path skirting by a dry-stone wall. How could hundreds of thousands of people pass through these little byways and leave no trace but their footprints?

Then their legacy appears. A cross, for instance, by the edge of a forest. It is covered in so many ribbons, beads, and cards that it looks as though it is padded. It is colourful, catching the light that fails to enter the forest, and so it glows. There are photos of people tied to it, and strewn on the ground. The base of the cross is heaped with pine cones and pine cones hang from its arms like the weights of a cuckoo clock. There are personal objects, beads, mementoes, and there is silence. Not even the trees whisper.

Then the world reasserts itself: I pass an animal feed plant, with its stench of stale gravy. It reminds me of the animal feed plant near the school I attended in Omagh. It brings back memories of a lost world. Proust had his tea and madeleines; I have animal feed.

And then the Camino returns with a bollard scrawled with pilgrim graffiti, and prominent among the tangle of letters and words is: Joshua 1:9, which I make a note of, because it was important enough for someone to place it on a sign-post and I want to know why. I hear the sound of woodpeckers in the forest and remember the time I followed one as it hopped from branch to branch through the Polish woods until I reached the border checkpoint at Byelorussia but it did not, carrying on into a place I could not go because it had no border checkpoint. I see fungi blossoming on orange wood, and hear a whole tree of birds singing; it sounds like someone moving up and down the dial on a radio, so many squeaking and swooping sounds.

And then there are the pigs. I see them on the edge of a village where I speak with an old lady who is harvesting vegetables. This is the original Camino she tells me, indicating the road that runs along the edge of her farm. She is smiling and her eyes squint behind her big glasses. This original Camino passes by a sty, a muddy little enclosure in which sit pigs. They are white, and sit on their haunches the way a dog sits. I get the impression that they are sad naked people sitting in the mud, and that the pilgrims they watch pass before them are the ones who will eat them one day. I have not stopped to look at pigs before. I have seen them, in a bright paddock of wild flowers enclosed by trees, one sunny day in Donegal. And I remember them sleeping in their pens inside a byre in which my cousins locked me. I stood up on the wall dividing the pens so as to avoid them, and I looked down on them – snoring bladders, the colour of cigarette smoke, and one spotlit by the high window so that it glowed like a planet in space. But these Galician pigs have bright eyes, and they are silent. To think that they would be killed, to have the life fall silent within them, dismembered and eaten as a snack; and there they sit, like prisoners of cannibals, reduced to food, their lives marked for extinction.

I have always marvelled at living things simply because they are alive. There is a sort of magic in that, as though every living thing is a dead thing brought to life. But I have never looked at the food I eat in this way before. I cannot promise myself restraint when it comes to eating the dead, but I walk away from these poor souls wondering what we have gotten ourselves into.

*

At the next stop I have a ham sandwich. Hunger is the best sauce.

*

Palas de Rei, a staging post for royalty, is most welcome. My body has adapted only so much to life as a tramp and I end the day aching from head to foot. Especially foot. My blisters have healed, but there is an ache within my feet. I walk though a succession of small hamlets, some only one or two houses by the side of the road, until I see signs for hostels, hotels, and B&Bs. I call in at the first place I see. It's modern and a little bit snazzy, with *hospitaleras* who are running it as though it's a posh leisure centre. There is no sign of any religious decoration here, only an impressive map that runs the length of the cafeteria. I ask for a private room, and I get a twin room to myself. It is downstairs, dug in underground, and it is an ice-box, but then I hear the radiators creak as they come to life. Someone up there is thinking of me; someone up there in reception.

I hand wash clothes and dry them on the radiator. I check my email. June and the others are in Arzúa. Her plan is to walk to O Pedrouzo. The day after that she will be in Santiago. She has sent photos of some things she has seen along the way, including a man who runs a *donativo* offering stamps made from red sealing wax for the *Credencial*.

*

By the hostel there is a church with a stamp but no service as there are small children playing big guitars in practice for some forthcoming celebration. I wonder what it could be, and then I realize that Christmas is little over a month away. I wander into town, the Camino being a flight of steps that cuts across the main roads. I am almost out of town again when I see someone who counts as a familiar face turning a corner and entering a shop with t-shirts in the window. He is the man in the photo June sent me, the wax stamp man. I go into the shop.

There are t-shirts everywhere. There is a big table with a roll of fabric unfurled across it; there are outlines of hands drawn on it and messages. The man appears from a back room.

"*Hola. ¿Eres el hombre con los sellos de cero?*"

Yes, he is the man with the wax stamps. He is also the man with the artificial leg. He raises money through the *donativo* for the wax stamps and through the sale of t-shirts. The money goes towards paying for artificial legs for children. The t-shirt design changes after every so many thousands of sales, and he asks visitors to his shop to leave a message on the roll of cloth across the desk. When the roll is finished, he says, he will use it to decorate the ceiling of his shop. I get a stamp, embossed with a pair of footprints, and trace my hand on the sheet. In it I write what I wrote all those days ago when I left a message in the tin at Pic d'Orisson. I write: *Beannachtaí gach lá ar an mbóthair*.

He cycles between Palas de Rei and Melide every day, meeting people on the way and raising money for his cause.

*

I pop in for dinner at a nearby restaurant. There's nobody else there and the waiter's smile fades when I order the pilgrim menu. The same old, same old.

An American couple come in and sit at the next table. Their mission this evening, they tell me, is to try the *pulpo*, and ask me to take a photo of them eating it so they can show the folks back home. They are Rebecca and Mike, and I tell them to keep their eyes peeled for the wax stamp man the next day. We are joined by a jolly pilgrim in a day-glo yellow t-shirt and a top-knot. This is Matt, who sounds as English as English can be, but he's Swedish. As the evening wears on, Rebecca and Mike leave and I am chat to Matt who reveals himself to be the reincarnation of a Templar knight. He discovered this a few days ago in Ponferrada when he was perusing the battlements and had the eerie feeling that he had been there before, a just knight fighting for the honour of a damsel who lived up a tower. He died, confides Matt, many years ago in the Holy Land, at the battle of Hattin where his "bones still lie in the dust, scattered about the place".

*

When I get back to my room it has warmed up. I email June about the wax stamp man, telling her his story. Then, looking through my notebook I see 'Joshua 1:9', which had been written on a bollard. I Google it:

> "Have I not commanded you? Be strong and courageous. Do not be afraid; do not be discouraged, for the LORD your God will be with you wherever you go."

DAY THIRTY-NINE

Breakfast in the cafeteria, where I sit beside the turtles that I met on the way to O Cebreiro. They are French Canadian and it is from them that I learn "c'est Trump". They are shrugging and raising their eyebrows as they scan their phones for further news. One of them turns to me and adds in the slow, deliberate words of an unfamiliar language "it is not finished. We will see". It's as disquieting as the Brexit result, when the whim of a few clammy Englishmen became the unplanned mess that everyone was suddenly burdened with. Once again the world leaks into the Camino. It's as is as welcome as water leaking through the Perspex tunnel in a shark aquarium.

Out the door, and down I go, down a side road flanked by fences and hedges. A speeding white van does not slow or make accommodation for pilgrims and is snarls by, sending up dust and grit. The sunrise makes it look as though the town is on fire. I walk though one small Galician village to the next, through long, winding lanes that look like tunnels formed from trees. Each house comes with its own outdoor larder, an *horreo*: a tiny stone shed up on stilts that I mistake for little chapels until I see one with its door open, and stacks of corn cobs inside. Each village also has a Galician cross, a *cruciero*, carved from stone, with figures on both sides.

Beyond one village I smell eucalyptus. The trees are growing by the side of the road, their bark falling away in strips, exposing their light green skins. In their native Australia the bark forms heaps of oily rinds around the bases of the trees. When a fire breaks out, it catches on the discarded bark and sweeps through the forest, scorching but not burning the trees: a short hot blaze being preferable to a cooler but slower one that can inflict more damage. Eucalyptus oil is potent enough to cause trees to explode in a fire. They are growing here because people brought them here, human beings doing more to introduce species separated by millions of years of evolution than any other force on the planet. They have been brought to Spain to be milled into paper pulp, but these look like they were planted here for decoration.

On the outskirts of Melide I see a metal shed with t-shirts hanging in the doorway. A table is open before it and there is the wax stamp man, stamping *Credenciales* with his sealing wax. We wave at one another and shout *"¡Buen Camino!"*

I arrive in Melide, and take a break in a cafe that looks as though it were once a mill by a river. It is in there that I hear the immortal words *"El Presidente Trump"*. It is the news, broadcast onto a big flatscreen television by the door. I turn to watch visions of streamers and balloons rain down on cheering crowds. El Presidente himself smiles and waves. Well, well... Onwards...

"¿Pulpo?" The man shouting at me from his restaurant window is either desperate for customers or inordinately proud of his kitchen. Do I want some *pulpo*?

"Delicious *pulpo*? No?"

Don't I like *pulpo*?

I don't want any *pulpo*. Not even delicious *pulpo*. No. No, I do not. Too many legs, and far too bright to wind up on a plate.

*

I exit Melide by following another pilgrim, a Korean I know to have bad feet from having seen him outside a cafe airing his blistered soles on a tabletop. He hobbles at speed and I follow his lead, though the backstreets and then across the road and past a *cruciero* by a graveyard filled with singing birds.

The road is quiet now and it runs down to Ribadiso where there is a *Xunta*. I carry on, past the *Xunta* and the rustic hostels that surround it. The path climbs, which can be considered cruel and unusual punishment at the end of a day's hiking, and then I am passing one closed country house after another until the closed country houses become open town houses, and I am in Arzúa.

My guidebook has this as an afterthought, focusing on the charm of Ribadiso instead. Arzúa is the Big Town in this vicinity and I book into its newest hostel. I sort out my bed and hand in my clothes to be laundered. Then a voice from the far end of the dorm says hello.

It is Anika. "I'm not having a good day", she grins. Why not? Her Portuguese paramour has just told her he has taken the bus to Portugal. She has also left her evening clothes in her last hostel, meaning that she has only her longjohns to parade around in. This situation won't do so we visit the local Chinese shop where she buys a pair of Aladdin trousers. We then go for dinner.

She has had a bad experience, I tell myself. It's just anger talking. Her previous inability to understand what people do in a church is now outright hostility to them. She tells me that she would not recommend the Camino, and would not have done it had she known what lay in store. I just talk to her, not wanting to, but just talking talking talking. It's the end of the day and I'm just as alone on the Camino as she is.

We go back to the hostel and then I go for a walk. The town is quiet, but its bars and restaurants are full. In this way it reminds me of an Irish country town. I buy a few postcards in the local gift shop, with stamps, and then go to a cafe to write them, drink cider, and eat the honest crisps of the working man. With the postcards in the post-box and nothing much else to do, I am wandering back to the hostel when I see Matt, the reincarnated Templar from Sweden, eating in the restaurant where Anika and I had dinner.

"Sit yourself down!" he says as I pop in to ask how his day went. The barman brings me a *tapa* of *fabada*, the bean stew from Asturias, and we settle into a long chat about The Meaning of Trump. By the time we say our goodbyes, we still haven't figured out What Trump Means.

DAY FORTY

There is puke by the door. Actually, there is only two little particles of puke by the door, but I know it's puke because Anika tells me so, and she knows because she put it there. She was sick during the night and tried to make it to the bathroom before vomiting at the door, right beside my head. The lights came on, a clean-up operation happened, and there were commiserations all round. I didn't hear a thing – that's ear-plugs for you.

It was the food from the restaurant, do doubt, but it is the hat-trick: Jilted by the Portuguese cad, left trouserless in Arzúa, and now food poisoning. Perhaps she's right. Perhaps the Camino is awful. She is barely out of school, and might as well be walking through Asia in terms of the alien nature of this culture. Now she has been jilted, by someone she was trying to meet up with again and again, but who has fled. I wouldn't be surprised if her illness is psychosomatic.

She assures everyone in the room that she is well, but that she will spend the day there. The other pilgrims wish her well, and leave, and I am the last to go. As with so many friends on the Camino, I do not see her again.

*

Breakfast is in the restaurant. A vulgar old man is making the young barmaid laugh with his rough humour. His voice has been wrecked by smoking and he sounds like rusted gears in a clay pipe. I hike my rucksack onto my back and go down the slip-roads. I'm out of Arzúa. I find myself back on forest paths in the early morning haze. The silence is soft and cool, and complete.

The track crosses over low stone bridges across streams, and the eucalyptus that has appeared as one or two lone individuals now occupies plantations, standing with their bark in tatters and their verdigris leaves pale and different against the light trunks. All the same, this remains cattle country. I think about this whilst walking down a boreen (*bóithrín*, 'little road', from *bóthar*, 'road', which in turn is from *bó*, meaning 'cow'; because in ancient Ireland a road was a cattle-path used by cattle-drivers, who were young men, or lads, or boys: *buachaillí*) and think of how different these parts of Europe would be without fields; just woodland from the Galician coast to the Urals. A world of roots and branches, trunks and twigs. I feel at home in the forest. I wonder if it is not fairer to say that my ancestors did not so much come from the forest as remove it from around themselves, so that in our minds we are still there.

I am snapped out of this train of thought by a movement in the embankment. It's a stoat, and it sticks its head up from among the exposed roots and fallen leaves and regards me with its bright, black pearl eyes. Am I watching the stoat, or is the stoat watching me? Which one of us is thinking: What is this?

The stoat vanishes to reappear further up the embankment. Then it slips away for good. These are the small moments that I cherish; they are rare and magical.

The mist is still in the fields, protected from the new sun by the old trees, and through it I hear a hound howling over and over again. There are dead fire salamanders on this part of the track too. They make for a forlorn spectacle.

The Camino surprises like that – random things: a huge stork's nest on an isolated pole, a unicyclist on the *Meseta*, dead salamanders, great black dragonflies, flocks of wheeling vultures; and human surprises like the hermit who lives as a Templar in a hostel with an outdoor toilet, like the unmanned wayside *donativo* stalls, like the crosses worked into the wire fences, like the crosses festooned with beads, like the memorials to the dead scattered with photos, and now this: a long washing-line of laminated flags along the side of a barn and each flag with a quotation about travel. The quotations are in Spanish and English, the trade language of the Camino. I pace the length of the line taking time to read each. They end with thoughts on God and human decency. On the drystone wall opposite there is a pumpkin lantern with an arrow cut into it. The candle has guttered out, but I imagine it would look most welcome on a dark night.

The quotations are food for thought, but one appeals to me above the others. It is attributed to Dagobert D Runes, and Dagobert has this to say: "People travel to faraway places to watch in fascination the kind of people they ignore at home".

*

Ultreia!

It cannot be far now. The next cafe, that is. Despite being so close Santiago, and despite the numbers of pilgrims who begin their Camino in Sarria, there are slim pickings for the hungry traveller. When I do arrive at a cafe I meet a group of Americans, one of whom is Rachel from Astorga. They are in a state of shock because their new president is a game-show host. I commiserate, telling them that Europe had Berlusconi, but that is no comfort. The world outside the Camino seems weird, and the effect these broadcasts about Trump and Clinton have had just serves to reinforce the suspicion that living out there is to have your mind soaking in a tub of nonsense, terror, and distraction. Peter Kropotkin once said that "people are not bad; rather they are driven mad by terrible circumstances". I wonder what forms of madness will seize us if we do not undo the terrible circumstances of our world.

*

A little further on and there is an inn by the highway. It is dangerous to cross, but I make it over to rest a while and try a beer that is made by the owners. It's called 'Pilgrim Beer', and it's good to drink, sitting outside on one of the few plastic patio chairs that doesn't have a puddle of water in it, eating unflavoured crisps, and watching the trickle of pilgrims walking along the path on the opposite side of the road. They look tired, and new to the Camino under heaps of expensive hiking gear. Then I recognise a beret. It's Pedro, who crosses the road and joins me, thanking me for my medical advice on feeding colds as now he has recovered. He has decided to go on to Santiago. He has water-proofed his rucksack with a bin bag so it looks like he is carrying out the rubbish when he has his pack on his back. I leave him there, with his boots off, resting his feet, the only patron in the bar and him not buying anything.

*

I return to the pine-scented Camino, to its silence and its demands on my body and spirit. Every day has involved walking further than I have walked most days of my life and without the flickering sounds and sights that filled life before Saint Jean. Paying Attention to the world around me has shown me how slow it is. I think of how slow the trees grow, of how much time it takes their roots to drive into the soil, and their branches to drive into the air. I see fungi, ears fashioned from wax, marzipan lips, tongues, navels; like fat poured into cold water, and I imagine the slow assembly of these forms.

I pass what looks like a polytechnical college. A student has stepped out for a cigarette and she waves and says "hello", and then I am at a T-junction. I turn right and walk along until I see the path again, and on the other side there is a mother pushing a pram and talking to her baby. We wave at one another, and then I step off the road and onto the path where the scent of the eucalyptus overwhelms me. What must this be like on a summer's day, when the heat of the sun draws the vapours from these trees?

I continue through this fragrant forest until I realise that I have overshot my mark. The deep calm of the forest reassures me that despite having just missed my destination, there will be somewhere for me to rest tonight. O Pedrouzo was the other way at the junction.

I am not the only one who missed it. I use my guidebook to help four pilgrims decide at a fork in the road by an underpass whether to go to a local country hostel, or continue ahead. They are tired. They opt for the local hostel. I continue ahead, but there are only a few villages between here and Santiago. I'm sure I'll find something soon.

There is a shrine by the path: a pair of bronze shoes in an alcove, dedicated to a pilgrim who died at this spot a day away from Santiago. Around the shoes there are photos and medals and there is a cross made from twigs. I wonder if he had died in the company of his friends, or alone, and if alone, who found him. I remember finding a man lying in a park in Manchester one morning as I was going in to lectures. He was in his suit and had his briefcase still in his hand. I called an ambulance from a phone box, but I never found out what happened next

*

Now I walk through the forest, the button cones of the eucalyptus plants popping and skipping from under my boots. I emerge from the forest and it registers that if O Pedrouzo is a staging post for most pilgrims, and this is the off season, I will probably not see another pilgrim for the rest of the day. But then I hear a voice and turn to see Danny walking out of the woods. He and Liam and another pilgrim are going to continue for another while. He keeps his fast pace and is soon ahead of me. Their plan is to walk at their own speeds and meet at an agreed location, then repeat.

Their agreed location this time is a cafe by the highway. There are rooms here, but they are too expensive. Danny tries cutting a deal, but it doesn't work. Sometimes it does, he says; sometimes you can strike a bargain. But not this time. He will wait for the others and then they will go on. I say I'm sure there are plenty of places up ahead and I might see them in a bit.

There are places up ahead, but they are closed. No luck. Time and time again I meet only closed, out of season, or abandoned places. At each stage I think 'next time', but next time is the same as last

160

time. I don't know how far I am now from Santiago, and I'm beginning to think that I could almost keep going until I get there, when I walk down from a tree-lined lane, emerge by a motorway roundabout and see a monolith carved with the single word: SANTIAGO.

Well, well. Be careful what you wish for.

*

I am walking by the perimeter fence of the airport. I walk past candystripe scaffolding and then there are clothes hung on the trees by a blood red stream. This is Lavacolla, the place where pilgrims in the past bathed in order to purify themselves before entering the holy city. Hanging up there with the masses of clothing is an azure and navy chequered flag emblazoned with the legend: Up The Dubs! I wonder where they are now.

*

I meet Danny again as I ponder whether or not to throw in the towel and book into a room in a country club. But when we go into investigate it looks well out of even the most abject defeatist's budget, and we skulk out without having spoken to anyone. I look around the neighbouring village of San Paio. But again, everything is closed. I return to the Camino and I see Danny up ahead. On the long road I see him shrinking into a speck. The daylight is fading.

I begin to follow the sun, but the world turns and it turns me quicker than I can walk, so the sun gets lower and lower and redder and redder, then darkness is with me and I have to fish out an LED lantern I bought in Portomarín. I do not need it to see, my eyes having grown accustomed to the gloom as it grew, but I want motorists to know I'm there. So I walk along, the lantern swinging from one hand, and I wonder if my pilgrim forebears walked through the night with a lantern too. I arrive in small, streetlit towns, and leave them again, and then after a hike up a long path, I pass the headquarters of the Galician radio channel.

Now I see it.

There.

There it is.

Ahead of me, just to the left, there are hundreds of lights. It is the city. It is Santiago de Compostella.

*

There is no change of pace, no sudden rush; there can't be. I have walked almost forty kilometres today and I've done it at a steady pace. But my spirits rise as I walk down the pitch black road, walking in the pool of light from my lantern. A digger is churning up the earth where the pavement is being improved, and I walk on the verge on the opposite side, wary of traffic, and staying as far in as I can go as they approach.

Somewhere on this hill there are supposed to be monuments depicting pilgrims overjoyed at arriving, but all light has failed bar my own and I walk by it, past the out-of-season Municipal, down down down and then I see signs for five star hotels, and for four star hotels, and I want to be in a five star hotel, or a four star hotel, where everything is clean and well-made, and anonymous and uncaring; where nobody knows you or wants to know you, or cares about you or wants to care about you, where it is sleek, fashionable, warm, dry, where my feet don't hurt, and my back doesn't hurt, and my shoulders don't hurt. But the road keeps turning away from them, along suburban access roads, now lit here and there by a yellowed streetlight. And then there are concrete steps, and then a motorway bridge with wooden slats like a rope bridge, with some missing, and with weeds poking through the holes, and I step as though walking on ice, and I am across the bridge, and I walk up to where there is a big abstract monument and where a sign reads:

SANTIAGO DE COMPOSTELLA

I have arrived.

*

Cars turn on the roundabouts. A stream of white lights goes one way. A stream of red lights goes the other. People walk about. None of them have rucksacks or *palos* or wide-brimmed hats. None of them are wearing sea-shells. They are regular city folk. I have seen their kind before and I'm sure they have seen my kind before. I was once one of them, and perhaps they were once on the Camino. Well, I was once on the Camino. Because now, here I am. They stand in groups by the doors of restaurants, or walk arm-in-arm down the street; they chat, and laugh with low-level laughter, social laughter, and none of them look as though there is a care in the world – theirs or anyone else's.

And I feel no sense of elation. I am in a nocturnal landscape of concrete, urban unit restaurants on the edge of town, traffic, and streetlights. I have been to places like this before, but I do not contrast them to the wilds and the old world I have passed through. I only want to stop walking. I walk a little way along the street until I see a sign for a hotel. I book in. I make my way up to my room and shrug off my rucksack. I remove my boots and take a shower, having run the cold water out of the taps. I put on my evening clothes and sit on the end of the bed.

I have arrived.

And still I do not feel any sense of achievement. I feel only clean and hungry. I wander up and down the street and find a pizzeria. I remember the pigs this time, and make it a vegetarian one.

I return and switch on the tablet. June has sent me a picture of her in mid-air as she jumps for joy in front of the cathedral. There is another photo of her and Cristina grinning, with glitter over their faces and in their hair. She arrived earlier, back when the cathedral was lit by the sun. I tell her that I have arrived too, and we agree to meet tomorrow at ten o'clock on the cathedral steps.

*

It has taken me forty days and forty nights to walk from Saint Jean to Santiago. I have done this in the fortieth year of my life. For a Christian pilgrimage the number forty might be a special one: having fled from slavery the Hebrews spent forty years in the desert prior to finding the promised land; Jesus was forty days and forty nights in the wilderness; the flood that had Noah living on an ark lasted for forty days too; Samson was servant to the Philistines for forty years, and Goliath taunted the Hebrews for forty days before David slung that rock at him; there were forty days of Pentecost; and in whatever kind of *sharia* law the Hebrews lived by, you could only flog a man so many times – forty times – before justice was done.

I'm not at the cathedral steps just yet but, give or take, I have walked the eight-hundred kilometres or so from Saint Jean Pied-de-Port, way back there in the French Basque country. I walked it all: tracks, paths, pavements, roads, boreens, *sendas*, footpaths, over streams and rivers and roads, over and under highways and railways, past farmyards and vineyards and scrapyards and backyards, and through parks and forests, through hamlets, villages, towns, and cities, up hill and down dale, to mountain peaks and along valley floors, the treeless plains of the *Meseta*, the forested mountains of León, through cathedrals, through churches, through chapels, through shops, through cafes and bars, through restaurants and past wayside *donativos*, in the shade, under the sun, under the stars, in the rain, in the shine, quickly and then slowly, first as one person, then as someone else.

*

Part Four: The Field of Stars

Morning in Santiago:

The view from my window is of the dimmest of dawns over the quasi-domesticated edge of town. All cities have these areas, half at home in the fields, half at home in town. It's no wonder they are home to feral cats.

I have breakfast in the hotel cafe, where the television is playing a panel show where various smart-arse celebrities I've never seen are having a ball with Donald Trump's colourful escapades. We see El Presidente wrestle, shout, cameo in movies, and are shown pictures of his wife when she was a pin-up. The effect is of a jester capering around with a copy of *Hello*.

For the final time as a pilgrim, I pack my bag, hang the shell around my neck, and take to the road. Pamplona, Burgos, and León; the Camino has taken me through cities before, but it has never finished in one. I walk through the frenetic city, trying to remember it from all those years ago when I visited here from Lugo by bus. Nothing comes to mind, and I begin to slow, to wander, to stroll, to make this moment last. But the cathedral is impatient, and between the roofs of the buildings on each side of the street, I see it. One spire, a thumbs-up, a beckoning finger, a finishing point, a high point: The End.

A slogan etched into the pavement tells me that the idea of Europe was made on the Camino, and I cannot think of one other European city that people will walk to from hundreds, sometimes thousands, of miles away. For centuries Europeans have come here, and they are coming here today, and I am one of them. The street to the Cathedral leaves the busy roads and enters an older part of town. The cathedral is just ahead. I walk towards it and its grandeur and immensity appear from among the high walls and arcades of the old city. I walk down steps, steps, steps and then the broad cathedral square flies away to either side and I must walk across it before I can turn and see the facade of the cathedral.

Santiago Pelegrino, I have arrived. His statue stands up there in his sou'wester and sea-shells, with his crook and gourd, and looks across at his alter ego – *Santiago Matamoros* – rearing on his charger and brandishing his cutlass on the roof of the building behind me. The main door of the cathedral is closed, covered in scaffolding. A builder walks along an upper wall, his wielding visor lifted up. He takes it off and skips down the steps, running a hand through his hair should the visor have ruffled it. A lift climbs the side of the scaffolding, and there is the rasping of a lorry with a robot arm. Blue netting covers the scaffolding, and locals pass it by without looking up.

A man with a pipe approaches me and for a moment I think it is the badger-headed man from Sarria.

"Tyrone", says the man. "Is that it?"

It is it. And then I remember him before he grew the beard, standing outside the cafe in Carrión. He was the man who spoke no Spanish, who had nearly died and was doing the Camino. Brian; So he got here too.

He is waiting for Danny, Liam, "and the rest of them".

It's ten o'clock and cannons boom somewhere out in the city.

In her purple rain jacket, June turns into the square. I see that she still has glitter on her face. We say goodbye to Brian and with my rucksack on my back we go to the *Compostella* office, which is just down around the corner. On the way June tells me that she met tall Jim, the American whom we last saw at Zirikiki thousands of years ago. He had walked to Finisterre and is now on his way to Portugal. She has a picture of him on her phone: He is as brown as a berry. There is no mention of him carrying out his promise of flying to Mars should Trump become president.

I meet Ted Hughes from Triacastela, who has just collected his *Compostella* and picked up a dose of the cold. Despite his English self-depreciating humour, he is smiling, lifting the tube containing his *Compostella* as he talks, as though giving a speech to an audience at an awards ceremony.

I go into the *Compostella* office alone and am given a form asking if I walked the Camino for Religious/Spiritual/Other reasons. I decide I am a Religious and Spiritual person, but not an Other person. The *Compostella* is free but the tube to keep it in is a fiver. Fair enough. I hear there are people who just fold it up and stuff it in their pocket because 'it's not the reason I walked it'. I don't think it's the reason anybody walks the Camino, but it will look nice on the wall up home. For another few quid there is another certificate stating how far I travelled. Fair enough. The clerk is befuddled by my Irish *Credencial*, and his colleague takes over. I get stamped, and my *Compostella* is handed over.

All done.

One the way out, I meet Juliette. She has also just got her *Compostella*. She has walked all this way from Puy. We wish her luck, and she walks off down the street. We are making up our minds what to do when two journalists say hello. They are interviewing pilgrims because this year has seen the largest number of people on the Camino. They ask us "why did you walk the Camino?"

We give our answers. Then we are photographed, beaming. The camera clicks over and over again. We walk back up to the cathedral and down to a cafe on a street corner where we sit down for *churros* and hot chocolate. Beatrice joins us. After Spain she is going to London, but first there are *pinxos* in a restaurant that specializes in seafood. I do not specialize in seafood, so I survive on what are supposed to be side orders. After toasting our success and eating our fill we agree to meet up later for the pilgrim mass in the cathedral.

June and I return to the place where she is staying with Cristina, Alastair and a few others. The place is full of hungover survivors of the night before. Grinning despite their nausea they manage *'hay'*! and a thumbs up before sniffing and sighing as they return to waiting out the effects of the party.

*

The pilgrim mass is packed, the first pilgrim mass I've seen so full and I stand behind pews crammed with hundreds of people. Yet in amongst the people I don't know, there are those I recognise with a sharp stab of happiness.

There is Matt, the Templar; Mandy, who gave me the thumbs up after I read in O Cebreiro; Alastair and Beatrice, and musical Mark, and Cristina; I see both badger-man and his partner from Sarria sitting ahead of me in the pews; and there is Rachel and the Americans from the cafe that I chatted with on what was to be my last day walking before reaching this city; there is Pedro, who made it after all; there is Brian, and Danny, and Liam "and the rest of them".... because I see in spirit those who walked part of the way with me: Lena, and Gene, Jim, and Almo and Milla, Anna from Denmark, and all the Koreans, The Dubs and Eoin who all left at Pamplona, the American mother and daughter in Ponferrada, the Anglican sisters from El Acebo, and the Austrian whom I met there (but that could be him over there by the pillar), and the guy on the unicycle, and the three woman from Ireland who gave me the painkiller just after Roncesvalles, and Anika, Crystal, and Andy with his vow of silence, and the two who had walked from Switzerland, and the one who had walked from Belgium, and the South African who performed surgery on another pilgrim's foot, and the singing old Italians, and Alvar, and Charlotte and Francois, and Bertrand, and all the Japanese, and the pilgrims in Pamplona, and Myrtle, and Sarah with her sore feet, and Sandy, and Lucy, Barnabas with his Irish blood, Wayne with his long-lost brother, Pierre with his guitar, the pilgrims from Orisson, and all the Quebecois, and Dot with her cough, and Jesus, who was the first pilgrim I met in Saint Jean; and the whole of the Camino who gave me their time, and their friendship, and who were there.

And up in the retable is the shrine of *Santiago*, the spirit of this place who has waited and is waiting still for all the pilgrims with all their reasons for coming here, known or unknown, real or imagined, to be freed.

The celebrants light the *botifumero*, the great censer, and they hoist it up so it hangs smouldering in the air. Then, as the choir sings deep and full, they swing the *botifumero* in an arc that gets wider and wider, and higher and higher until it is almost striking the ceiling. It roars as it swings up above our heads and I see the flame inside it blazing to life as it swoops from one side of the cathedral to the other. I see the crowd; all heads tilted back, all eyes trained on this common thing, seeing what pilgrims have seen for centuries, seeing what future pilgrims will see when they stand where we are standing when we are part of the history of this place.

*

Outside the cathedral there are goodbyes and good lucks. Mark takes a photo of himself with June, Beatrice and myself, but it is of our feet standing at compass points and pointing inwards. He later sends us the picture, calling it 'Feet Don't Fail Me Now'. We invite him to the pilgrim meal that is being held in the apartment June and the others have rented. He agrees, but Beatrice is leaving tomorrow, which means that she is leaving now. She walks away past the fountain, and into her future.

In the apartment Matt calls in with his roll-up piano and, as dinner is being prepared, he sings a song that he wrote for June. It's a blues song, and he wails out the lyrics, his fingers stabbing the neoprene keys with Alastair making a mute trumpet sound with his hands. Mark doesn't play any other songs, though. He has been writing material for an album and wants to get back and continue writing. So he goes and, in all the good humour of the song and the meal preparations, it does not occur to me that, as with so many others, I won't see him again. His Grañón song has been playing in my head during my Camino, and I don't get a chance to say goodbye.

The meal is homemade and afterwards we talk long into the night. Some talk longer than others; tiredness works its magic and I go upstairs where I fall into a deep sleep.

*

The owner of the house is coming back today. We tidy up and leave one by one. There are goodbyes. There are farewells. But also 'take cares' and 'good lucks'. June, Cristina and a few of the others are taking the bus to Fisterra. This is Finisterre, the End of the World, and they want to watch the sunset. Alastair is hiking to Lisbon, continuing his eno-Camino through Portugal.

I have hiked enough. The ache that I feel inside my feet throbs and I want to rest.

It's at an end.

Just how do you say goodbye to people at the end of a pilgrimage?

As I cart my rucksack down the staircase I see sepia-tinted photos on the staircase wall. They are of soldiers in a war a long, long time ago. The soldiers are in a bunker, four of them sitting for the camera, and one of them is mugging for it, baring buck teeth and staring. The others are repressing a fit of giggles. I can imagine them, joking about getting their photo taken, making fun of the situation. One of these days all those Camino photos of people laughing around dinner tables are going to be like this: ghosts.

*

I book into a small hotel overlooking the small square at the back of the cathedral. My rucksack is now hand-luggage if I post home Lena's penknife. I look at my *palo*; a dumb wooden pole that has become symbolic of by rise up from the *Cruz de Ferro* to the cathedral gates in Santiago. I don't want to dump it, to forget it on purpose when I go. I'll post it and the knife home, the way I did with my old boots in Logroño.

I slip the penknife and my tablet into my jacket pocket, and then take my *palo* out into narrow streets walled with aquaria full of silver jewellery and souvenirs. I see Crystal again, and I meet Matt who gives me his business card. He is catching the train tomorrow to Barcelona. I meet Charlotte too. Every meeting is a parting, and it is good to see such good people and so sad to let them go.

I go to a place called the Pilgrim's House, a drop-in centre for pilgrims looking for info, accommodation, or one another. Then Andy appears. He uses his phone to tell me that he has taken the bus in to meet people before they go, but he will bus back out again and spend the next two weeks walking in again. He wants to walk into Santiago on his birthday. He got my message, the one about my message. He shows me a photo of the tree in Las Herrerías, and types out "Thanks, Mate". When we say goodbye there are tears in his eyes and I hope that whatever unquiet spirit that had provoked this journey across Spain will soon settle and leave him in peace. I meet Alvar outside the cathedral, grinning, overjoyed at his arrival, carrying his *palo* bedecked with beads and gourds and ribbons. I ask him if he got his chance to walk in the snow, but he didn't. The snow had arrived, but on O Cebreiro and it had even made the news – pilgrims walking through the snow to Triacastela. I meet Bertrand too, whom I'd met just before the *Cruz de Ferro*, who had taken my photo when I had reached my low-point at that high point. He is with his wife, the pair reuniting in Santiago, and when we wish one another all the best we mean it.

Now that the crowds have gone I want to see inside the cathedral. It is a Jubilee Year for the Catholic Church; a year in which sins are forgiven after a pilgrimage to a cathedral into which the pilgrim enters via the Holy Doors. These doors are usually shut tight, and only open on Jubilee years. It is a rare thing to walk through their gates, but I have the good fortune to experience this. Once through the Holy Doors I am inside the cathedral and I walk up the steps behind the retable where the shrine of Saint James is located. Here it is traditional to hug the Saint. The saint is represented as a silver figurine studded with gems. I find myself giving the Saint a hug and thinking '*Gracias, para todos*'.

Is this how sins are forgiven?

What is a sin? What is forgiveness? I have only the faintest idea; so faint that, like a trail of smoke from a blown-out candle, it will vanish altogether if I try to grasp it. Someone could tell me, but I need to arrive at these conclusions myself if I am to understand.

In one part of the cathedral is the chapel of *Nuestra Señora de la Consolación*. The statue representing the mother of God, the creator of the creator, the carer of the carer, mother of the father, is similar to those I have seen before – but she is not an echo of them: they have been echoes of her. I have seen these same images all along the Camino, premonitions of this image in this place. Here, her presence seems more solid for being more final, and the hopes and regrets of the devotees more acute for being revealed to something that feels more present. From beyond the thick cathedral walls, I can hear the sounds of distant *gaïtas*.

I leave the cathedral and visit the pilgrim museum, where they also have an exhibition of Russian Orthodox icons. I like the icons as I don't know who painted them. I like them because they are not realistic. I like them because I'm not supposed to think about them, but about what they are pointing to. And then I'm back in the cathedral square. It is empty in golden hour save for a few isolated souls, sitting in the sun before the cathedral. There is one pilgrim who is crouched in a squat, his hands pressed palm to palm in prayer; he is smiling and tears are running down his cheeks. A pied wagtail flies through the golden square – chit, chat! Chit-chat!

Walking back across the cathedral square I meet Lucy whom I last saw waving from a balcony in Torres del Río. She is not ready to return home, and is not impressed with the city: not because it is Santiago de Compostella, but because it is a city. It is a city, and cities are wired to the world and the world is not the Camino. Perhaps all pilgrims returning from the Camino should stay with their Camino attitude; but it will be difficult to be so open and free with people who are not pilgrims, and perhaps that will lead to reluctance, and even resentment. I understand why Lucy is unhappy about returning to the world, and I have heard tales of people who stayed walking the Camino forever or returned to it to work in hostels, but return to the world we must – if 'return' is the right word. Is the pilgrim who returns the same as the person who set out to 'do the Camino'?

*

Last rites:

I walk up to the *Correos* because I want to post back my knives and my *palo*. But when I get there, I see a sign directing me back to where the *Compostella* office is. There is a service there, promises the sign, which caters for pilgrims. I go, but a woman in a back office tells me that the service is closed for the winter. I return to the *Correos* and begin the laborious procedure of posting the penknife and the *palo*. The clerk smiles a lot and tries to get me the best deal by running through the options available for postage. He offers me a box with which to post my *palo*. It is two boxes taped together. I wrap the *palo* and the jerry-rigged parcel isn't big enough, so I just swathe each bubble-wrapped end in reams of parcel tape. It looks awful and costs sixty Euros to post. The *palo* itself cost six Euros.

The Camino is a luxury.

The penknife is put in a plastic envelope which the man jiggles before me as he mutters *"no sé, no sé"*. I'm not sure what he doesn't know, but it gets posted. Now I have no knife to carry and no *palo*. Neither do I have my shell around my neck – it has been wrapped up and stored with paranoid care in my rucksack. I drop in to a bar and order a drink and tapas, the same little dish of *fabada* as I had in Arzúa. I take stock of all the other things I have gotten rid of during the Camino: t-shirts, my old boots (also posted home), the fedora – left in the shoerack in Atapuerca, the wooden box, and the pencil case, and the hand gel, and the foot smoothing contrivance, and a pair of trousers – worn out and dumped in a clothes store bin, and the phone I forgot in Burgos, and a jacket left behind in Orisson with three blank exercise books and a guidebook, and a pair of flip-flops from *La Casa Mágica* that I left in Grañón, and whatever patience I might have had with myself.

A sparrow flies into the bar, hops across the floor and picks at a fallen chip.

"Behold the fowls of the air: for they sow not, neither do they reap, nor gather into barns; yet your heavenly Father feedeth them. Are ye not much better than they?"

I check my email. Pearl, whom I'd last seen in San Anton Abad, and who promised to find my phone in the Burgos Municipal, is in O Pedrouzo. Where am I? I write back, promising to meet her outside the cathedral tomorrow evening.

There is also an email from June, but it has been forwarded from Lena. It is an invitation to Copenhagen. June is going, leaving from Santiago airport.

"Come and visit!"

*

I return to the hotel and book a seat on the flight.

Then I switch off the tablet, and with the door locked, I let the world go on without me. I allow my mind to drift back over the Camino, remembering the sounds of waking up in hostels, of boots on gravel paths, of birds and insects in the countryside, of the streets of the cities I have passed through;

and there are the remembered smells of food and drink, of the allotment manure heaps and the mountain farms, of hostel boot rooms and mildewed showers, of flowers, the roses and lavender, and the incense of the *botifumero*. I glimpse a stretch of road, of path, of wayside church or the foyer of a hostel, decorated crosses by forests, cobbled bridges, the oceanic *Meseta* and the plunging soaring mountains that led to it and left it behind. I remember my feet soothing in a basin of water, the aches and pains which have left my body as well as those that still remain, the cold of the chapel-dormitory in Grañón, and the heat of the clear high noon.

I fall asleep walking the Camino.

*

The following day I meet still more pilgrims. There are the Anglican sisters from El Acebo who are looking forward to going home, and the Anglican pilgrim from Villafranca who is also looking forward to life beyond the Camino; and there is the Belgian pilgrim, from all those days ago, he who had walked from Antwerp and had needed his boots resoled in France. He is finding it hard to adjust. "It will be the third part of my Camino" he says. "There was going to Saint Jean, and when I had gotten used to that, there were suddenly all these people, and then I got used to that, and now I must return home. It is hard to go back". I ask him if the Camino changed him. "Yes", he says, and shows me his belt. "I had to make extra holes, I lost so much weight". His parents have come to meet him. They brought him his trainers. "I'm enjoying the change" he says smiling at his feet.

*

A souvenir shop is a place to think about those you left behind. It does not matter if the trinket you buy is not classy. All souvenirs represent only one thing: 'You were on my mind'. I buy something for my family, something for my friends, and a ceramic tile: a yellow arrow, which I will fix to the porch of my home, pointing away.

I also buy a gift for Pearl, who has carried my phone all the way here. I meet her, as planned, outside the Cathedral as it is turning plum-red in the dusk. She arrived that day, and will continue by bus to Fisterra, after which she wants to visit London. I ask her if the alarm kept waking her up, but it didn't and the battery ran out anyway. So having thought that I had said my final farewells to my last fellow pilgrim, it is Pearl who is the last of the Camino to whom I say Goodbye.

When I get back to the hostel I plug in the phone and switch it on. There is one message, sent on the day I took the plane to Biarritz. It's from a friend who wished me luck.

Goodnight, Santiago. Goodbye, Camino.

Part Five: The Demon

My worldly goods: eight kilos of clothes and a few bits and pieces. The sack of bric-a-brac I had shouldered over the Pyrenees is now a neat little package with nothing on its outside bar a Tau cross. This is all I have; this is all I am bringing to Copenhagen and I need so very little of it. I leave the hotel in the morning darkness. In the foggy streets there are haloes around the streetlights. In the park, passing the Two Marias, and the streetlights send crepuscular rays through the trees. The flagstones are slippery with dew.

I meet June at the bus stop and we arrive in the airport where the lady at the check-in desk asks if we want to send our rucksacks through as checked luggage rather than carry it as hand luggage "for free". It is nice of her, and we accept. We buy Lena *liquor de hierba* from the duty-free, and continue through security to have breakfast as the sun rises grey and orange from the foggy trees. The Camino skirts this airport, and today, someone else will walk where I walked, out there beyond the irregular serrations of the treeline that looks like a crocodile's jaw.

From the cafeteria window I see a boarding tunnel clamp to a plane with an extension resembling an accordion. It looks like a snake swallowing an egg. On the ground there is pink mist, the sky is now chlorine yellow, and there is a red rash where they meet. A plane taxis through the fog and the tail fin is the prowling signal of a shark in turbid water.

When the plane takes off I remind myself that there is no point hoping, worrying, or praying. There is nothing to do but be tranquil. Things are no longer in your hands. Accept that, and the nausea clears. Now I see the shadow of the plane on the water, like a manta ray heading towards the Cantabrian coast, and then the window goes blank and the plane sails up above the clouds. I look out at icebergs of frozen mist on a sea of milk. The western face of the clouds are glowing glowing glowing as I meet them and when I look back at them they are gloomy, dark and brooding. There is supermarket music on the plane.

Travelling in this way is the opposite of the Camino, and when I think this I realise that in the hour or so I have spent sitting still I have travelled the distance I spent the previous six weeks walking. And in the hour I have spent sitting still, I have flown over the heads of all those pilgrims down there, all of them walking to Santiago, making friends, eating together, walking together, sleeping together, finding themselves- even when what they find makes them sad. And I have flown over those who see something new, or see something in a new light, or someone in a new light, or themselves in a new light. And there will be those who despair because their egos are in rebellion, and there are those who despair because they do not understand what they have done wrong, and there are those who are ashamed because they believe they have disappointed those whom they love, and there are the desperate, the frightened, the worried, and all of them good, good to one another even when it feels like they are not, good for one another, arriving when they are called for, helping by being there.

*

A person on an airborne plane is not flying. Flying is the wrong word for such immobility: sleeping, feeling hungry, eating, wanting the toilet. It's the life of a baby in a pram.

The plane lands and I am in Denmark for the first time. I know I am in a very different country when I am flummoxed by the toilets: The doors have both male and female signs. Which is it? This is no time for games. It doesn't matter. It really doesn't. In free-wheelin' hippy Denmark the Gentleman's contrivance is frequented by the ladies. Or is the Ladies' frequented by the gents? What an age to be alive.

Tanned, rested, and ready I pick up my bag and head for the arrivals hall. It is always a strange experience, exiting the reclaim area to be met by a throng of people behind a barrier. I always feel like a celebrity putting in an appearance at a gala. And then I see them, friends reunited: June and Lena, both smiling. My Camino amigas – my Camigas.

"Welcome to Copenhagen". Lena guides us through the purposeful Danes in their black clothing and as we leave the terminal for the platform I see, of all things, in of all places, a yellow arrow and the words Way Out.

*

Lena lives by a canal on which people live in boats. Her apartment is at the top of a narrow flight of steps that doubles back on itself as it rises. There are doormats before her neighbours' doors with friendly greetings in English or homely pictures on them. Lena tells us that she has lived here for twenty years. I have lived nowhere for twenty years, and wonder if I ever will. I think the longest I have stayed put is eleven years, and that was only because I was a child.

We present Lena with our gifts: June gives her the *liquor de hierba* and a *Credencial* for her daughter, and I give her my Camino guidebook. The guidebook was machine fresh when I bought it. Now it is held together with pink bandage tape, and curls at the corners like a day-old take-away lasagne. Lena cooks for us, and afterwards we go for a walk around the city centre. There are Christmas decorations strung up across the streets and Christmas markets made from wooden sheds form ephemeral alleys of small shops selling food and ornaments. It gets dark early, and soon the coloured lights form a low ceiling above the crowds and the bright shop windows light up people walking past. The city prospers and certain streets remind me of Dublin city; I am being returned to the world and I know that I don't want to go back. Not yet. Not now. We sit up late, talking about the people we met, and people we met after Lena left. She says it has been a strange feeling over the last weeks to pause and think that as she was job-hunting and taking care of the daily chores, we were still walking across Spain.

Late that evening I use my tablet to book my flight home. I hear rain against the window as I go to sleep.

*

In the morning breakfast is tea and scones that Lena makes herself. She makes them every day, preparing the dough last thing at night. We have no plans for the day, but to stroll around town. Our first stop is just off Lena's street. It is The Church of our Saviour, and we climb right up to the top of its spire on a narrow staircase that winds around the outside. People brush past one another with such delicacy because they believe that the slightest touch will knock them over the edge. From the top, the view is of a fen-scape, an atavistic horizon, and the early morning sun is a haw-flesh gash behind the BellaSky hotel. Lena tells me that there was supposed to be a women's-only floor on that hotel, before a man said that such a thing counted as discrimination against men and the plan was dropped. In the distance I see the Øresund Bridge, connecting Denmark to Sweden, and a modern marvel on a par with the Channel Tunnel. The thought of moving between Sweden and Denmark makes me think of Shield-Danes and Geats, and Beowulf, and Grendel.

Inside the church there is a retable of archangels who were released from their marble blocks by sculptors at the turn of the Eighteenth Century. They face an enormous organ, shouldered by elephants in homage to King Christian V's Order of the Elephant; King Christian being the patron of the church. Compared to the churches in Spain, this Danish church feels too open, too well-lit, too much of a well-to-do concert-hall. It is the first ecclesiastical building I have been in since the cathedral in Santiago.

And the little cafe with condensation running down its windows is the first cafe I have been into since the *"fowls of the air"*. There is a framed diagram of a butterfly's life-cycle on the wall of the cafe, and I wonder if the transitional creature in the chrysalis could comprehend its transformation it would ask itself: 'What next?'

June does not say what she will do. Perhaps return to her old job. Perhaps find something else. Lena is also thinking of a new job, and she has to see a counsellor to help her find something to do. I have told those who have asked me about "what next? what after?" that I am not worried about it. And I am still not worried about it. As far as I'm concerned, I'm sitting having coffee in Denmark. Count your blessings.

*

We walk back into the city centre. There are lots of tourists: rich Indians, rich Chinese, small gangs of English yuppies, the occasional Irish accent, the occasional Ulster accent, all huddled around cups of gløgg in the Christmas market. Christmas markets are like Christmas trees and mulled wine; a Germanic version of Christmas pumped into your brain via the advertisement industry. Any other way of celebrating Christmas seems to be 'not really Christmas'. If we don't have a White Christmas we feel cheated of something.

The danger is to go looking for the Christ in the Christmas market, and sneer, and think of this as 'Christ-miss', and resent all this money-grubbing, wine-swilling nonsense for the amusement arcade that it appears to be; but then that would make me... me. It would be anger talking. Anger thinking. And why would I be angry? And since when did I care about Christ in the Christmas market, or anywhere else for that matter?

But this attempt to resist the call of the world is put to the test when we pop into a large, fashionable department store to see how the other half live. The place is filled with expensive crockery, and a number of artists have been allowed to install dioramas depicting their version of Christmas. Opulent dining tables are shown in various states of disarray: one after a wild party; one cut up and reassembled at all angles; and one that is entirely pink. Pink. Everything is pink. Barbie-doll pink. The carpet and wallpaper and lampshade are pink, the chairs and table and glasses and plates are pink. It is a kitchen table as described by Barbara Cartland. And whilst I can see past the tills and price-lists of the Christmas market to see friends enjoying one another's company, I cannot see anything humane in this mirthless, childish, egotistic nonsense. I don't understand how these artists could have reached such conclusions about Christmas.

In the rest of the store people are buying baubles and candles as gifts, and it is good that people are thinking of one another, but it is all a world in which there is nothing grander to which the gaze can be directed than that of another person. I suddenly find myself drifting past racks of snowmen, robins, reindeer, Santa clauses, angels, stars, snowflakes, trees, red socks, candles, and tiny presents with nothing in them, with the detachment of someone casting an eye over a fish counter. At the first

Christmas there were two places you could have been: the inn or the stable. We all know about the stable. No-one remembers anything about the inn, other than that it was packed.

*

Looking at stuff:

A city is a museum without a ceiling, and it is easy to spend all day regarding the buildings as sculptures as demonstrative and literate as what we would typically call a sculpture. But the collections in a museum are a treasure within a treasure: the jewels within the jewellery box. I can spend all day in a museum, and this is no exception.

The following day I am in the National Museum. I don't get to see absolutely everything as it closes before I'm finished. But I do see something special: pilgrims' shells found buried with mediaeval pilgrims who had walked from Copenhagen to Santiago and back. I wonder what stories they had to tell. I feel such a sense of affinity with them – not because of language or the world they lived in, but because of the Camino. They walked the path I walked. Physically, they walked the path I walked. They visited the cathedrals and churches I visited. They saw some of the things I saw: the old city walls, the mountains and rivers, the ancient retables; they crossed the same the Roman bridges. Could they ever have imagined that the shells they wore on their clothes would one day be displayed to pilgrims hundreds of years in the future? No more than I can.

I leave and it is the city is low and glowing under the wide, black sky. Copenhagen seems to be a very dark city. Or perhaps I have simply forgotten how dark cities are. I sit in a cafe, looking out through the window at the perpetual motion of all these unknown lives. People moving through a city is a handful of rice thrown into a shower of rain without hitting a drop.

The darkness makes the Christmas lights brighter. And the lights in the Tivoli Gardens too. After dinner, Lena, June, and I go there to see the sights. Trees blossom with fairy lights, coloured fountains rise and fall to the music of Tchaikovsky, and the carnival rides coruscate like sea-combs and sea-jellies: like polyps, octopuses, and Venus-girdles; the lures, the bait-and-switch, the thrills, the shrieking laughter. June goes on a pendulum swing and Lena and I stand beneath her, sipping *gløgg* laced with brandy as the hammer-blow of the carriage swings down at us time and time again. I can hear June's laughter above the howls of the other passengers. Standing underneath the pendulum is a test of nerves in itself. I hear an American voice laugh to one side: "Back home you'd never be allowed to stand there". There is a net between us and the carriage. It is there to catch falling coins, keys, wallets. People?

A little further on and we enter part of the garden modelled on Chinese pagodas. There is a roller-coaster here called *The Demon*. I have never been on a roller-coaster before. The harness is safe, but I don't feel safe. I know that is part of the thrill, but as soon as the doors open and the train moves forward I want it all to be over. The rail points towards the sky and as soon as we climb it we are flung down the opposite side, first one way, then the other. My innards lurch, my stomach knots, and my testicles feel as though they have vanished inside my pelvis.

I remember sky-diving and the feeling of utter terror that gripped me the moment I had fallen free of the plane. I remember the dread of falling, and the hateful snapping sensation of the parachute opening, and then the overwhelming relief of sailing down towards the green fields of Birr. When I was being driven back to town from the airfield I remember the driver saying that sky-diving "is better than sex", which is true, but that people who have never sky-dived cannot understand that. I can understand the appeal of sky-diving.

I cannot understand the appeal of roller-coasters. *The Demon* feigns a second of respite before it plunges us down again and then we are lifted up up up and around, upside-down around and we are falling again only to be slung upwards into a sickening horizontal spiral that qualifies as the worst experience of my life, and then it throws us one way and another and then it's over... I hope. I see the flat line of track ahead of us and hope hope hope that this is it, that this isn't a trick, that this isn't some attempt to lure us into a false sense of security before catapulting us forward again.

The train stops. I feel like a seal that has just been attacked by a shark. We descend the steps. Lena is laughing at the spectacle. "Awful" I keep mumbling, keep laughing. "Awful, awful, awful" and then I buy the souvenir photo in which I look like I'm ducking a thump and June could be laughing or crying. Well, now I've been on a roller-coaster. I won't do that again, until I see another one and then I'm on a roller-coaster again.

We walk back to the apartment by way of Christiania, the commune that became infamous for its open drug-dealing. There was even a drug-dealer's shack in the museum as part of a history of the city. I have a great fondness for self-standing folk, but there is a downside to doing your own thing; "Christiania attracts a certain type of person", says Lena, "people who just can't fit in elsewhere. Some of their kids have dreadful childhoods".

*

The next day we meet with Anna, whom I'd last seen in that cafe the day I set out from Castrojerez. For someone I had only spoken to briefly, we are now meeting up for the *gløgg* festival that is happening in the town centre. We meet her where the festival organizers have put up white marquees, one for each group who have brought their own distinctive *gløgg* to the festival. Anna explains that this festival is only a few years old and serves as a promotional competition for local cafes and bars.

The festival opens with the post office band playing Christmas carols, many of which are the international standards, but there are still a few Danish songs in there much to her satisfaction. It is true that just as with trees and Santa, the carols are generic too, and as good as they are, it's easy to get the feeling that these carols are being played because they are supposed to be played rather than because anyone wants to play them or listen to them. When they stop there is a polite smattering of applause before a couple of men take to the stage and sit down. These are the judges.

Nobody cares what the rules are. A crowd has gathered because there are free samples from each group and, as Anna maintains, "Danes love free stuff". Indeed they do. As soon as the judges have finished reading out the rules, the marquees open and mobs of people gather around each one. The *gløgg* is kept warm in electric cauldrons and ladled into the type of plastic glasses medicine is measured into. As the lids come off the cauldrons the effect is of being in a refugee camp full of rich people who need mulled wine to survive. They mob the marquees, but we are part of it all and come away from each cauldron with our precious measures of fancy *gløgg*.

Some contain almonds, some oranges; some contain both, some contain both with raisins for good measure. We have no idea what the judges make of any of this, and I get the impression that nobody else does either. The bins fill with empty glasses as the cauldrons run dry and people drift away. Anna leads us through a shopping mall, explaining how English has become so prevalent that old Danes feel excluded when they go into a restaurant and cannot read the menu. She takes us through the streets, explaining her plan to give up her life here and go to work on a farm to learn how to make cheese. It's a skill she wishes to use in a new life, living closer to nature, and getting away from the rat race. It's a noble ambition and we tell her about the organic farms on the western islands of Ireland where people volunteer to be close to the earth.

Our walk takes us to a series of half-built cabins in a small square. They are made from recovered wood, and exist to be an example of recycling in action. And that is where we say goodbye to Anna. I call Lena to tell her we are on our way back. Lena is in the library, filling out forms for her job-seeking counsellor. We have a spare key and let ourselves in. I make a pot of tea and we sit in the front room, reading. When Lena returns we have dinner and then decide to spend the last night together watching a movie. The first choice is a comedy with no jokes in it and which we switch off. We settle on an action film about a gang who over-run the White House and hold Barak Obama hostage. Obama takes to running around in funky trainers, gunning down his assailants. It's gibberish, and the only entertainment it offers involves using the subtitles to pick up a few words of Danish.

Words such as: *LØB!*

*

Well, maybe not so much a RUN! as a WALK! from Lena's apartment to the cafe a few doors down for breakfast. I have my whole world on my shoulders again. We have coffee under vintage posters from *fin de siècle* newspapers. On one of them there is a photo of lush Italian poet Gabriele D'Annunzio. Gabriele was larger than life, but was a freak in many ways, and may have paved the way for Fascism. I used to think that to live life one had to be larger than life; that one had to do it all: write, compose, discover, uncover, love, lose, win, fight, lead, live through a war, perform 'Boy's Own' acts of daring do, and generally blaze a trail.

"For what shall it profit a man, if he shall gain the whole world, and lose his own soul?"

I've no idea if Gabriele lost his own soul, or led others to losing theirs. Perhaps he lost his mind from time to time, but then so did the world he lived in. And the world I live in seems to be losing its mind, maybe even losing its soul. Who would want to be the exemplar of such a place? Who would want to be the *Man of the Moment* when the moment is such an embarrassment?

I am glad that I am having breakfast with Lena and June. I'm glad I'm in Copenhagen this morning. And I'm glad to be going home. When I say goodbye to them both it is the way I'd say goodbye to friends I will be seeing again. Maybe, maybe...

... but I'm walking down the street by the canal to the tram. And now I am on the tram, and now the airport, and now on the plane. All the Danes are in black. I stand out like a gaudy popinjay in my grey hiking trousers and fleece. Seat-belts are buckled. Trays are stowed in the upright position. The safety demo is considered in polite silence, and then I look out the side window and wait for lift-off.

*

Céad míle fáilte!

The arrival doors open on Ireland. I left from this very airport, sitting at the departure gate for Biarritz. Now, I'm back again. I take the bus from outside the airport all the way up through Meath, Louth, and Monaghan, to Tyrone. Three and a half hours with the heating on full blast and seats so close that the journey is conducted in the foetal position. I step off at the bus depot in Strabane. A few empty cars are still in the park'n'ride and the cargo container used by a Romanian car wash business hulks in the darkness. The red lights of the bus cross the bridge in the distance to the faintest sound of its engine.

Now, I am back again. Or am I? The place is the same at any rate, and my room here is floor to ceiling with books. There are books on every subject but one; and where there is no room for them on the shelves that are stacked three books deep with more lying flat on top of them, there are cupboards of books, drawers of books, there are books in boxes under the bed. They are just so much out-of-date medicine.

*

The Way

"All truly great thoughts are conceived while walking."

— Friedrich Nietzsche, *Twilight of the Idols*

Are they, Friedrich? Are they really?

It was around the turn of the New Year that I got a call from Andy. He had completed his silent pilgrimage and was home again in Canada. It was a strange experience, speaking to him when he was thousands of miles away after having had all those 'silent conversations' with him when we were sitting at the same table.

"How did people react when you got back?" I knew from his blog that he had found it frustrating to leave a world where everyone occupied the same rarefied atmosphere to return to the world where people did not appreciate what he had been through. I understood. I felt as though I had returned from a trip through a black hole. But when I got back, those whom I met acted as though I had just been to the end of the street. To them, it seemed, the Camino was just a holiday in Spain; it was no different from a couple of weeks in Alicante, or a spell on the beach on the Costa del Sol. I had bunked off work to go and have fun in Spain. Haven't we all? Big deal.

But it was a Big Deal, and Andy and I knew it. All pilgrims know it. Time and time again I heard the refrain 'the Camino changes you'. And the Camino did change me, but not in ways I could ever have anticipated. Unlike the gym on Macken street, or the bookshops of Dublin, this was an experience of self-improvement that was not in my hands. There was nobody to talk to about this. Were it not for Skype and social media, I would not even be able to keep touch with some of my fellow pilgrims (The Internet: it's an ill wind...).

And that was the big question that occupied most of our call: "Has the Camino changed you?"

"It has", I said, "but I can't say how. I just know that the person I was before going on the Camino is a different person to the one I am today". How, though? How?

How? It's not finished. I can't say. This is not a case of 'before and after', like in some gammy fitness plan commercial:

'Have fun and lose problems by walking yourself to a new you! In just thirty days YOU could have a NEW soul! Sign up today for the patent Camino experience!'

Followed by testimony by people who 'can't believe the difference' or who 'feel like a new person'.

No. It is more like: Before the Earthquake struck, compared to During the Earthquake. The Camino isn't over.

*

According to the pilgrim office in Santiago, there were 278,224 pilgrims in 2016. That made it the most popular year for the Camino in living memory. Contrast this with the fact that in 1990 there were 4918 pilgrims in total and you get the idea: The Camino de Santiago is attracting more and more people.

Of that rough quarter of a million people arriving in Santiago, the most popular starting point was Sarria with 71,861 pilgrims. Saint Jean, where I began my Camino, was the starting point for about half that figure at 33,720 pilgrims. Of the total number of pilgrims arriving in Santiago in 2016, the Irish accounted for 6542 of them.

There were 5841 pilgrims who left Saint Jean in October 2016 and there were 6401 Compostellas awarded in Santiago in November of that same year. Lost in amongst those statistics is my own story. I was one of that 5841 and one of that 6401. I was one of the Irish 6542, and one of those 278,224 who made the Jubilee year of 2016 the most populous yet.

Every other pilgrim has their own tale to tell. Some will have told it, some never will. Some are trying to make sense of it. For others it is all as clear as fresh air. And perhaps there are pilgrims who just enjoyed the walk and thought no more about it. And then there are pilgrims who, like me, have stepped off the Camino having had a mind-altering experience.

*

Well, well. What "truly great thoughts" has the Camino provided me with?

All pilgrims who walk the Camino come a long way. In space they walk the length of northern Spain if they walk from Saint Jean to Santiago. Some come further. At the very least, it is still an impressive 100Km from Sarria. Physically, they put their bodies under tonic stress for weeks on end. They have to cope with weather from burning sunshine, to icy rain, from hiking through clouds, to the dusty *Meseta*. But the Camino is a pilgrimage, whether we want it to be or not, and so they also come on a spiritual journey as well as a religious one.

Prior to the Camino I would never have said such a thing. Prior to the Camino I knew for a fact that religion was the preserve of bigots and fanatics, and I still know why it is. Prior to the Camino I knew that spirituality was the preserve of quacks, charlatans, and vain solipsists. This is still the case.

Prior to the Camino I was an Atheist. Everything I felt then, I still agree with. All the things I rejected as an Atheist I still reject, because as an Atheist I rejected the unsatisfying God for Children that I'd had when I was a child. To grow up is to out-grow all that framed our life as children. The God for Children that I found to be frankly incredible remains incredible. There is no reason to go back to such childish things. But Atheism represents an adolescent mentality; it is the attitude of a teenager who knows that 'kids are dumb', but has no concept of what it takes to be an adult.

By the time I reached Santiago, I still thought what I thought when I was an Atheist – but I was no longer an Atheist. Everything that an Atheist believes I agree with, but I find it unsatisfying. I think Atheism is neotonous, puerile even. And just as the Atheist is not satisfied with the God for Children, I am not satisfied with the Atheism for Adolescents.

Atheists don't go far enough.

If the God for Children is a craftsman who makes objects, then the Camino hinted at a creator who creates us just as the sea creates waves. We rise and we fall, exist and then cease to exist, we come into being and leave it, always part of this greater, grander thing. The same is true for everything. God is closer to me than I am.

If the God for Children is a god to beg from, then the Camino hinted at a God that is to be listened to, is to be sensed; it is a God that is on display, an audible God, and all this God requires is open eyes, open ears.

*

On New Year's Eve, I go to the Cuilcaigh Way in Fermanagh. It is a meandering pier that runs across a vast blanket bog towards the eponymous mountain. It is a day of new beginnings. On each side of the pier the bogland is carpeted with sphagnum moss. It surrounds me. That is apt for a new start; sphagnum was once used as swaddling for newborn children. It was their first experience of the outside world and, as such, it was their comfort and joy.

This new year will be my fortieth. Prior to the Camino I would think back to when I was starting out in life and think: That was the young me. This is the old me.

Today I think: That was the old me. This is the new me.

On New Year's Eve the peak of the mountain is buried in thick, low-lying cloud. The pier runs to the mountain and then climbs it in a long flight of wooden steps that looks like a distant waterfall. The steps are nick-named 'The Stairway to Heaven'. To the side of the pier there is a signpost, a stout pole with a single yellow arrow pointing forwards.

Printed in Poland
by Amazon Fulfillment
Poland Sp. z o.o., Wrocław